Did Jesus Really Say He Was God?

MAKING SENSE OF HIS HISTORICAL CLAIMS

Mikel Del Rosario

FOREWORD BY DARRELL L. BOCK

ivp
Academic
An imprint of InterVarsity Press
Downers Grove, Illinois

InterVarsity Press
P.O. Box 1400 | Downers Grove, IL 60515-1426
ivpress.com | email@ivpress.com

InterVarsity Press® is the publishing division of InterVarsity Christian Fellowship/USA®. For more information, visit intervarsity.org.

Scripture quotations, unless otherwise noted, are from The Holy Bible, English Standard Version. ESV© Text Edition: 2016. Copyright © 2001 by Crossway Bibles, a publishing ministry of Good News Publishers. Used by permission. All rights reserved.

The publisher cannot verify the accuracy or functionality of website URLs used in this book beyond the date of publication.

Cover design: Faceout Studio, Tim Green
Interior design: Daniel van Loon
Author photo on back cover: © 2024 Mark Wilcox Photo Film, all rights reserved.

ISBN 978-1-5140-1101-0 (print) | ISBN 978-1-5140-1102-7 (digital)

Printed in the United States of America ∞

Library of Congress Cataloging-in-Publication Data
Names: Del Rosario, Mikel author
Title: Did Jesus really say he was God? : making sense of his historical
  claims / Mikel Del Rosario.
Description: Downers Grove, IL : IVO Academic, [2025] | Includes
  bibliographical references and index.
Identifiers: LCCN 2025012298 (print) | LCCN 2025012299 (ebook) | ISBN
  9781514011010 paperback | ISBN 9781514011027 ebook
Subjects: LCSH: Jesus Christ–Knowledge of his own divinity | Jesus
  Christ–Divinity | Jesus Christ–Historicity
Classification: LCC BT216.5 .D45 2025 (print) | LCC BT216.5 (ebook) | DDC
  232/.8–dc23/eng/20250529
LC record available at https://lccn.loc.gov/2025012298
LC ebook record available at https://lccn.loc.gov/2025012299

31   30   29   28   27   26   25 | 13   12   11   10   9   8   7   6   5   4   3   2   1

"'Who is Jesus?' is a good question. But 'Who did Jesus say he was?' is even better. In this book, Mikel Del Rosario probes that very question with historical acumen and intellectual verve. He explores the biggest question of them all: Did the man Jesus of Nazareth claim to be a divine person? Not just a prophet, king, or a miracle-worker, but the personal expression of the God of Israel? Mikel gives an answer that is well-reasoned, convincing, and—some may even find—startling. An amazing exploration of a fascinating subject."

Michael F. Bird, deputy principal at Ridley College in Melbourne, Australia

"Claiming to be a prophet speaking on behalf of God is an audacious claim. But such pales in comparison to claiming to be God! Although Jesus is not reported to have ever said 'I am God,' the Gospels portray him as claiming things about himself that are virtual equivalents. But did he actually say these things? This is one of the most important questions one can ask. In this volume, Mikel Del Rosario answers yes, combining solid historical scholarship with an accessible presentation. This excellent investigation will equip you with key talking points for discussing Jesus' divinity with others."

Michael Licona, professor of New Testament Studies at Houston Christian University

"This is a unique, timely, and important book. Mikel Del Rosario defends the vital doctrine of the deity of Jesus but does so in a remarkably systematic and careful way. He lays out his historical methodology, applies it to two key texts in the Gospel of Mark, and then responds to leading critics. This is not only a wonderful defense of the deity of Jesus but a model for how to do historical Jesus scholarship."

Sean McDowell, professor of apologetics at the Talbot School of Theology, author of *The Fate of the Apostles*, and YouTuber

"Mikel Del Rosario's *Did Jesus Really Say He Was God?* uses traditional, widely accepted, academic historical research methodology to make a solid argument that the Jesus of Nazareth who lived in the first century CE claimed to be God. This work needs to be standard reading for undergraduate and graduate students confronted by classroom proposals to the contrary. The faithful believer will be strengthened to face counterarguments, and the skeptic will be challenged to consider weaknesses in positions that deny Jesus' claim to deity. I am very encouraged by this work."

Eric C. Redmond, professor of Bible at Moody Theological Seminary

"This is a multifaceted book that concisely accomplishes several tasks. Not only does it inform readers, but it does so in an entertaining way that also equips. Readers are introduced to historical methods as well as different positions taken by scholars regarding the question 'Who is Jesus?' Readers will learn some common objections to the traditional portrait of Jesus (and some lesser-known ones) and the historical pitfalls or challenges that confront such portraits. Throughout the book, Mikel Del Rosario works to provide the reader with the information in such a way that allows them to be better prepared and more confident to discuss what the New Testament says about Jesus."

Ben Shaw, president of CORE Apologetics, adjunct professor at Liberty University, and author of *Trustworthy*

TO MY WIFE, CHRISTINE:

With heartfelt gratitude for your loving support throughout

my studies and the creation of this book.

Contents

PART ONE *1*

PERSON OF INTEREST
Investigating Jesus as a Figure in Ancient History

PART TWO 45

THE FIRST BLASPHEMY ACCUSATION SCENE
How Jesus Claimed to Have Divine Authority to Forgive Sins
The Healing of the Paralytic (Mark 2:1-12)

PART THREE 95

THE SECOND BLASPHEMY ACCUSATION SCENE
How Jesus Claimed to Have Divine Authority to Judge Sins
Jesus' Jewish Examination (Mark 14:53-65)

BATTLE OF THE VIEWS
*Testing Key Explanations of Jesus' Claims in the
Blasphemy Accusation Scenes*

Foreword

DARRELL L. BOCK

One of the iconic detective shows of TV history is the *Dragnet* series. It ran from 1967 to 1970, and Jack Webb played the show's most famous policemen, Joe Friday. The show was known for its interviews of witnesses, and Sergeant Friday's consistent line was, "Just the facts, ma'am. Just the facts." In an age dominated by skepticism about the Bible and its history surrounding Jesus, *Did Jesus Really Say He Was God?* examines what certainly is an important question. For if the answer is yes and the resurrection really took place to vindicate such claims, then the emergence of Christian faith becomes a framing event for all of history, not to be ignored nor missed.

This book takes a close look at two key events in Jesus' life and asks whether they reflect real historical activity. To get there, Mikel Del Rosario examines how history works, the ways scholars discuss assessing such events, and how we can consider the credibility of such claims. Then he works through an array of theories, some skeptical and others not, that seek to explain these two strategic accounts in Jesus' life, and which approach has the most going for it. The study is rich and deep in detail, an assessment driving toward a "just the facts" approach to the question while acknowledging that history works with judgment and probability, not certainty.

This study is fair about the questions skeptics ask and works through the historical and cultural context to answer the issues they raise. It models how to engage with the study of ancient events and how to respond to honest questions some raise about these events with careful attention to detail. It contends for what is often the case in Matthew, Mark, and Luke, namely, an awareness of implicit claims to deity by the things Jesus claimed to be able to do or by things he said God would do for him to show his divine authority and position. It is a rich study that repays careful study. It shows how to proceed when people raise questions about how the text and history work. Even as there are judgments made about how the details work, we do not proceed blindly but can assess the options people raise with a tone and approach that examines what we have, what we know, and how to discern the alternatives people raise.

The book contends we must consider a Jesus who claimed to have a central place in the program of God. Making him one religious great among many is not enough. Jesus' claims to divine authority make him unique. So there is much at stake in the issues this book raises, and it points the way to an answer that is about more than facts. It is about who stands at the heart of Christian faith and why the unique role Jesus has should matter to anyone and everyone.

Acknowledgments

First, I extend my heartfelt thanks to my mentor, Dr. Darrell L. Bock, whose guidance as my dissertation supervisor and inspiration during our historical Jesus class contributed to this project. His invaluable insights (often shared over lunches at the original Dickie's Barbecue Pit in Dallas), example of courageous, compassionate leadership, and gracious foreword for this book are gifts I deeply treasure.

I also wish to thank Rachel Hastings, my editor, whose belief in this project gave me the confidence to bring this book to completion. Her encouragement has made a lasting impact.

To my *titos*, Attys Ruben and Johnny Del Rosario: thank you for your generous support during my studies at Dallas Theological Seminary—a pivotal period when my passion for the study of the historical Jesus truly began to take shape.

Finally, to my mother, Dr. Marlyn Del Rosario, the first PhD I ever met: thank you for instilling in me a commitment to excellence and sparking my curiosity about earning a doctorate. And to my father, Dr. Bob Del Rosario, in loving memory—your ministry laid the foundation for my spiritual journey. Thank you for preaching the message that drew me to Jesus.

More Than a Man?

Did Jesus really say he was God? I'll never forget the day a middle-aged woman cornered me after church one Sunday afternoon in California. I was surprised when she began to raise questions challenging the deity of Christ. I had my Bible out on a table as we began to talk. Suddenly, she grabbed my Bible, held it up with both hands like a visual aid, and confidently declared, "According to this, Jesus never claimed to be God!" I was stunned. Even though she went to church regularly, her words echoed popular challenges to the historic Christian view of Jesus as divine. Still, there was another question lurking behind the Bible grabber's challenge. She also seemed to be asking, "Why should anyone believe that Jesus is God if he never even said he was God?" People who raise these kinds of questions may read the Bible but see the Jesus of history as totally different from the Christ of faith preached by the church. This woman's suspicion was that the church must have made up the deity of Jesus—totally apart from his self-claims. For her, the things that Jesus actually said about himself had nothing to do with being divine.

Things were dying down at the gathering after church when she got up to leave. I walked away less than satisfied with where we left our conversation. But over the next few days, the vivid scene of her dramatic declaration played over and over again in my mind. There she was in my memory, holding my Bible. I can still hear her voice and the way she said it. "According to this, Jesus never claimed to be God!"

The State of Theology

Her views aren't rare. Doubts raised by skeptical approaches to the Bible are affecting more and more people—even those who regularly go to church. A Ligonier Ministries and LifeWay Research study called The State of Theology indicated that 43 percent of evangelical adults in America agreed with the statement, "Jesus was a great teacher, but he was not God."[1] Let that sink in. Think about the people you see sitting around you at a Sunday church service. Could any of them really think this way? This represents an increase from 30 percent in 2020 and 2018.[2] According to the same study, the statistic grows to 53 percent of churchgoers if we include people who do not identify as evangelicals.[3]

This tells us at least two things. First, those of us who hold to the historic Christian view of Jesus' deity may soon find ourselves faced with challenges from people like the woman who grabbed my Bible—not just in the public square but even inside the walls of our own churches. Second, many people in the church today have their doubts about Jesus' divine identity. Some outright reject it. Others may not be coming from a skeptical place but still wonder how well the things the church teaches about Jesus really line up with what Jesus himself said. Perhaps they've heard some tough challenges or intriguing questions raised and now they're wondering, "Did the historical Jesus claim to be divine?"

Twenty-first-century scholarship in New Testament studies has sparked renewed conversations, books, and public-square debates about Jesus' self-claims—including the kind of authority he claimed to possess. For example, Houston Christian University professor Michael Licona debated Yale professor Dale Martin on the question, "Did Jesus believe he was divine?" in 2012. A couple of years later, two contrasting books on this divisive topic were simultaneously released. One was called *How Jesus Became God: The Exaltation of a Jewish Preacher from Galilee*. It was written by Bart Ehrman, who teaches in the Department of Religious

---

[1] The State of Theology, "Statement 7," accessed November 3, 2022, https://thestateoftheology.com /data-explorer/.

[2] State of Theology, "Statement 7."

[3] The State of Theology, "Data Explorer," accessed July 31, 2024, https://thestateoftheology.com /data-explorer/.

Studies at the University of North Carolina at Chapel Hill. In this *New York Times* bestseller, he argues that the historical Jesus never claimed to be God. A critical response to Ehrman's book was simultaneously released: *How God Became Jesus: The Real Origins of Belief in Jesus' Divine Nature.* This was penned by five experts, including Australian Anglican scholar Michael Bird at Ridley College. Two years later, Ehrman debated Bird at a public event in New Orleans called "How Jesus Became God." In 2022, a transcription of this debate was also released as a book, *When Did Jesus Become God? A Christological Debate.* The next year, popular atheist YouTuber Alex O'Connor stated, "The question of whether Jesus claimed to be God, I find to be one of the most interesting in biblical scholarship," during an interview with Ehrman.[4] These examples show that the meaning of Jesus' self-claims continue to be hotly debated and discussed—in the public square, in the academy, on YouTube, and even in churches. People who represent a range of backgrounds and religious commitments are deeply interested in Jesus and want to get to the bottom of their historical questions about him.

SKEPTICAL SCHOLARSHIP

A Christian friend once reached out to me with doubts about the way the Gospels present Jesus. He had just discovered a couple of books by Ehrman (an influential agnostic atheist New Testament scholar) and other critics who treat the Bible with suspicion.[5] These authors tend to argue by pitting the Gospels against each other. Such an approach causes many readers to wonder whether John's Gospel is really the only account that presents Jesus not only as a good teacher but also as God. My friend heard challenges to the consistency of the Gospels, such as, "In John, Jesus is God. But in Mark, he's not God." The implication is that the sayings in John's Gospel do not accurately represent the historical Jesus— they were made up by the church.

---

[4]Alex O'Connor, "Did Jesus Even Claim to Be God? Bart Ehrman Says No . . . ," June 19, 2023, YouTube, 1:31:12, www.youtube.com/watch?v=2STiabRV8TE.
[5]Ehrman identifies as an "agnostic atheist." Bart Ehrman, "On Being an Agnostic Atheist," *The Bart Ehrman Blog*, May 23, 2021, https://ehrmanblog.org/on-being-an-agnostic-or-atheist.

The woman who grabbed my Bible raised a more nuanced form of this challenge after we discussed Jesus' claims in the Gospel of John: "If Jesus really said, 'Before Abraham was, I am' [Jn 8:58] and 'I and the Father are one' [Jn 10:30], why don't we see any hint of a divine claim anywhere in the earlier Gospels?" In the scenes tied to both of these sayings from John's Gospel, Jesus' hearers are so offended that they pick up stones in order to kill him. Why? Because they believe he has committed blasphemy. Here is how Ehrman raises questions about the historicity of Jesus' divine claims in a popular introduction to the New Testament used in college classrooms:

> In the Synoptic Gospels of Matthew, Mark, and Luke, Jesus never says he is God. . . . For John, Jesus is obviously God and he says he is (not God the Father but is he equal with God?). Why do you suppose these sayings are not in the earlier Gospels? If Matthew, Mark, and Luke knew that Jesus had said such things, wouldn't they want to tell their readers? It's worth thinking about.[6]

People who discover skeptical scholarship often wonder, "Is John really giving us a totally different picture of what Jesus claimed about himself?" When a critical scholar such as Ehrman writes, "Almost certainly, [Jesus'] divine self-claims in John are not historical" and "Jesus did not declare himself to be God," many readers can get the false impression that these confident declarations represent a virtual consensus among historians.[7] For some, this can contribute to a crisis of faith. A Christian man posted on Reddit:

> Unfortunately, today I have discovered Bart Ehrman. According to his scholarship, Jesus never claims to be God outside the Gospel of John and he doesn't take John as historical because it came later on. This is destroying my faith, and unfortunately, it appears that nearly ALL scholars agree with him! How can this be? There has to be a defense against this. No matter what, I will not give up my faith but man this is making me doubt big time.[8]

---

[6]Bart D. Ehrman, *The New Testament: A Historical Introduction to the Early Christian Writings*, 7th ed. (New York: Oxford University Press, 2020), 181.

[7]Bart D. Ehrman, *How Jesus Became God: The Exaltation of a Jewish Preacher from Galilee* (New York: HarperOne, 2015), 128.

[8]CorbinTheChristian, "According to Bart Ehrman, Jesus Never Claimed to Be God?," Reddit, *R/Christianity*, September 7, 2023, www.reddit.com/r/Christianity/comments/16cprgr/according_to_bart_ehrman_jesus_never_claimed_to/.

These ideas can cause people to doubt how much John's Gospel tells us about what Jesus actually said. Since it was the last Gospel written, skeptics say that this later portrait is merely a theologically motivated development rather than an accurate reflection of Jesus himself. As a result, much of the focus in academic discussions of Jesus centers on the Synoptic Gospels (Matthew, Mark, and Luke). Mark is of special interest because most scholars believe that it was the very first Gospel written. Even scholars who are rather skeptical of the Gospels believe that the least amount of embellishment is likely present in Mark.

WHY I WROTE THIS BOOK

While speaking at a variety of Christian apologetics events, it struck me that many conference programs followed a classical apologetics model that moved quickly from discussing arguments for God's existence to defending the historicity of Jesus' resurrection. This represents a significant gap that can leave participants ill-equipped to explore the self-claims of Jesus. Recovering the historicity of Jesus' divine claim is crucial to appreciating the significance of the resurrection. Indeed, the divine claims of Jesus are what fill the resurrection with theological meaning. The apostle Peter's speech on the day of Pentecost was the very first apologetic sermon in church history. He argued for Jesus as Lord and Messiah and emphasized the resurrection as God's vindication of Jesus' claims. Luke writes that about three thousand people came to faith that day (Acts 2:41). So, understanding a historical approach to the claims of Jesus is important for Christians who study evangelism or apologetics, or find themselves in spiritual conversations with people who see Jesus differently. This includes not only atheists and agnostics but Muslims, Jehovah's Witnesses, and others who ask us, "Did Jesus really say he was God?"

Although the question occupied my thoughts on an academic level, it also stuck with me on a personal level because of my encounter with the woman I met after church. I carried her memorable challenge in my mind for a decade as I earned my master of theology and PhD in biblical studies at Dallas Theological Seminary. During my decade in Dallas, I thought about how a historical approach to Jesus' claims could help us discuss the idea of his deity with anyone, regardless of their religious background or lack thereof. Unbeknownst to the Bible grabber, her vivid challenge inadvertently influenced various research projects that culminated in my doctoral dissertation—a historiographical approach to investigating Jesus' claim to possess divine authority.

Still, I didn't want to produce an academic study merely for the sake of fulfilling the requirements for my doctoral program. From the beginning, I envisioned publishing an approachable work that not only engaged the scholarly debate at an academic level but could also help a more general audience understand the historicity of Jesus' divine claims. This is the book you are now holding in your hands (or reading on an electronic device). Along the way, I discovered that I may be the first American-born Filipino scholar to publish a study investigating the historical Jesus.[9] If so, expanding diversity within scholarly conversations in this area, and New Testament studies in general, is another part of my contribution to a field with a dearth of Filipino voices represented in the literature.

I wrote this book as a resource to help Christians find historical answers to their questions about Jesus' divine claim. I also wrote it to help you supply the rest of the story to those who have written off the church's view of Jesus' divine claim as a misguided notion with no basis in reality. I've found that studying Jesus as a figure in ancient history is not only fascinating but makes a difference for careful, well-balanced Christian apologetics. Why? Because the church has always preached that God acted in history through the person of Jesus Christ. By the time you finish reading this book, you will be better equipped to discuss the divine claim of Jesus with anyone who is interested in the answers of history. I pray that God would use your conversations about Jesus to help

---

[9]I don't know of anyone else. I may also be one of only two Filipino Americans contributing to historical Jesus scholarship. Another Filipino American is Jordan Ryan, a half-Filipino, Canadian-born assistant professor of New Testament at Wheaton College in Illinois. He is the only Filipino American scholar of whom I am aware who has published work on the historical Jesus. See Jordan Ryan, "No Model Minority, Part I: Invisible Asian Americans in the Midst of Apocalypse (RECLAIM)," Asian American Christian Collaborative, January 5, 2021, https://web.archive.org/web/20210106130123/https://www.asianamericanchristiancollaborative.com/article/no-model-minority-invisible-asian-americans-apocalypse.

more people develop an openness to the historic Christian teaching that Jesus is divine.

A Virtual Consensus

Where can we begin conversations with people who see Christianity differently? If you want to talk about something that virtually every critical scholar can agree on, something that can serve as a helpful starting place for a study of Jesus' claims, consider this: a Cambridge New Testament professor named Andrew Chester noted a substantial consensus among critical scholars that Jesus was believed to be divine early and in a Jewish context.

> What has emerged from recent discussion, then, is a very strong emphasis on the way that Christ is portrayed, in several strands of the New Testament, as divine, within a Jewish context and in quintessentially Jewish terms. The clear (though not unanimous) scholarly consensus is that, despite all the problems it creates for our understanding of early Christianity, a Christology that portrays Christ as divine emerges very early, in distinctively Jewish terminology and within a Jewish context.[10]

So, the current scholarly conversation suggests a place to begin a historical investigation of Jesus' claims in light of early Christian views about his deity. Even Ehrman holds that "not long after [Jesus'] death, his followers were claiming that he was a divine being."[11] But here's the million-dollar question: How much continuity is present between this early belief and Jesus' own claims? The answer will fall somewhere on a spectrum: On one end, the belief is continuous with Jesus' remembered words and deeds. On the other end, it is discontinuous with Jesus' words and deeds (i.e., it is a product of the church). Skeptics see the deity of Jesus as a later theological development that says more about the church's reflection and contemplation of Jesus than anything Jesus actually said. But what about this? Did the historical Jesus really say or do anything

---

[10]Andrew Chester, "High Christology: Whence, When and Why," *Early Christianity* 2, no. 1 (2011): 38.

[11]Ehrman, *How Jesus Became God*, 1.

that might have been interpreted as a divine claim? How much continuity is demonstrable from a historical perspective?

As I studied key events in Jesus' life along with recent theories about his self-identity, I began to realize something very important that many recent studies have missed: recognizing highly evidenced data reflected in the Synoptics and putting those pieces together supports the historicity of Jesus' divine claim. For me, discovering these pieces and connecting them together was like joining key pieces of a jigsaw puzzle and seeing the claims of the historical Jesus more fully. Along the way, I discovered the pivotal importance of what I like to call the "blasphemy accusation scenes." I'm talking about two key Synoptic narratives: the healing of the paralytic (Mt 9:1-8; Mk 2:1-12; Lk 5:17-26) and Jesus' Jewish examination (Mt 26:57-68; Mk 14:53-65; Lk 22:66-71). These two events became ground zero for my study.

To my knowledge, no published study has ever analyzed key twenty-first-century theories about the kind of authority Jesus claimed to possess in light of highly evidenced data present in both of these events in Jesus' life. That's exactly what I decided to do with the historical data arising from both blasphemy accusations. While all three Synoptic Gospels include an account of these two events, I wanted to focus on the stories as they appear in Mark's Gospel for two reasons. First, these two Markan texts are the earliest accounts of each of these key scenes (again, most scholars view Mark's Gospel as the first Gospel written, with Matthew and Luke making use of his work). Second, the historical data arising from even just two scenes can help Christians formulate an informed response to the challenge that Jesus never claimed to be divine.

THE BIG IDEA

While most books about Jesus' claims focus on the perspectives of Jesus' earliest followers, I wanted to focus on the perspective of Jesus' enemies. How did they understand Jesus' claims? For me, this unlocked a fascinating angle from which to approach my study. Here is the central idea of my book: *There is continuity between Jesus' claims and the early*

Christian belief in him as a divine figure because at least some of Jesus'
words and deeds were likely interpreted by his Jewish adversaries as claims
to possess divine authority.[12]

I have a plan to recover the historicity of Jesus' divine claim, and I
want to take you along with me on this exciting journey. Here's what you
can expect as we dive into our investigative historical study. On the basis
of highly evidenced data arising from analyzing the healing of the paralytic in Mark 2:1-12 and Jesus' Jewish examination in Mark 14:53-65, I will
advance two lines of argumentation:

1. Jesus was accurately remembered as a unique miracle worker who
   claimed to possess authority on earth to forgive sin.
2. Jesus was accurately remembered as claiming to be the eschatological Son of Man who possessed authority in heaven to
   judge sin.

Building a historical case for both points will help us demonstrate
two things:

1. The sayings of the historical Jesus include claims to possess divine
   authority.
2. There is continuity between Jesus' own claims and the early belief
   in him as a divine figure.

Along the way, we'll dive into the fascinating world of Greco-Roman and
Jewish backgrounds to show that the two lines of evidence can work
together to support the historicity of Jesus' divine claim better than the
idea that he claimed to possess a merely human kind of authority.

From the very beginning, the historic Christian church taught that
Jesus was a real human being who spoke and acted in history. However,
many critics who read the Bible approach the text from a more skeptical
place. In order to better engage with scholars and interested laypeople
from a variety of religious backgrounds, this study will follow in the
footsteps of the Third Quest for the Historical Jesus while demonstrating that both lines of evidence can stand up to scrutiny. That means

---

[12]Besides Jesus' opponents, this interpretation was also appreciated by his followers.

we won't appeal to the inspiration or inerrancy of the Bible as we analyze the data and build our case. Instead, we'll be playing by the rules historians use and pay close attention to Jesus' first-century Jewish culture.[13] If Jesus really claimed to be divine in a setting like that, how did he do it?

A HISTORIOGRAPHICAL APPROACH

Our study of Jesus as a figure in ancient history will take a historiographical approach to the question of whether he made any divine claims. We will investigate arguments and hypotheses, examine sources, identify highly evidenced data from authentic sayings and events in the life of the historical Jesus, and synthesize the data.

Two major questions guide our study:

1. What key events and sayings of the historical Jesus can best be demonstrated as being at least probably historical?[14]
2. In light of Jesus' cultural context, what is the most likely significance of the sayings tied to each key event?

Every historical study has its limits, and this one is no different. It would take several lifetimes to pore over the innumerable scholarly works on Jesus' claims. So, we will restrict our investigation to two key scenes, asking, "What do these tell us about Jesus' claim to possess divine authority?" We will also restrict our analysis of major hypotheses about Jesus to key, representative views published in the twenty-first century.

Part of preparing to engage with those who see Christianity differently means trying to put yourself in someone else's shoes—especially someone who doesn't see the Bible as an authority. To this end, I approach the study of Jesus of Nazareth as a historian with the hope that this book will help inform future studies of the historical Jesus outside

---

[13]Even many who reject the standard criteria of authenticity in historical Jesus studies accept this kind of work. E.g., Jonathan Bernier makes a distinction between using the criteria and incorporating insights that may have led to the formulation of specific criteria. See Bernier, *The Quest for the Historical Jesus After the Demise of Authenticity: Toward a Critical Realist Philosophy of History in Jesus Studies*, Library of New Testament Studies 540 (New York: T&T Clark, 2016), 75n5. Later, I will discuss challenges to the criteria as presented by Bernier and others.

[14]Earning a rating of at least "more probable than not."

biblically conservative spaces. To this end, we will focus our investigation on key sayings and events on which most critical scholars can agree. Again, we will not require an assumption of the inspiration or inerrancy of Scripture. Rather, our study will proceed according to standard historical methods and criteria employed outside biblical studies. We'll use the same kinds of tools that historians who study figures such as Alexander the Great and Caesar Augustus use to study Jesus of Nazareth as a figure in ancient history. I've found this approach creates enough common ground for people from a variety of backgrounds to come to the table and join the conversation.

Outline of This Study

Here's the big picture of our journey to Jesus' claims about himself. First, we will identify what historians consider when studying Jesus of Nazareth and how they attempt to discover what happened in the past. Then, we will assess historical data from two key events in the life of the historical Jesus that I call the Markan blasphemy accusations scenes. Finally, we will test each of the theories about Jesus' self-claim and adjudicate between them. Which theory makes the most sense of the data? Let me give you an overview of each major part of this book.

In part one, we will see how historians discover past events and consider rules of evidence when studying Jesus as a figure in ancient history. Despite challenges to the traditional criteria of authenticity, I will argue that historical data can lead to knowledge about Jesus and that texts based on the memories of those who had experiences of Jesus can help us construct an adequate representation of sayings and events in Jesus' life. The core of the book is composed of three key sections: critical analysis of Mark 2:1-12 (part two), critical analysis of Mark 14:53-65 (part three), and a synthesis of highly evidenced data by which competing hypotheses are analyzed (part four).

In part two, we will engage with our first blasphemy accusation scene to discover the kind of authority Jesus claimed to have in the healing of the paralytic, using his reputation as a miracle worker and exorcist as a foundational fact. How probable is it that the historical Jesus was accurately remembered as a unique miracle worker who claimed to forgive sins? I will also engage with theories challenging the historicity of the scene and the idea that Jesus claimed to do something that only God had the right to do.

In part three, we will engage with our second blasphemy accusation scene to discover the kind of authority Jesus claimed to have at his Jewish examination, using his arrest and interrogation by Jewish authorities as a historical starting place. How probable is it that the historical Jesus was accurately remembered as one who claimed to be the apocalyptic Son of Man who judges sin? I will assess challenges to the authenticity of the core scene and the exchange between Jesus and the high priest.

In part four, I will analyze two major hypotheses concerning the type of authority that Jesus claimed to possess by using five criteria for weighing hypotheses about the sayings of a person or the cause of a past event. Did Jesus claim to possess only a kind of human authority? Or does the evidence show that he claimed to possess a kind of divine authority? Combining highly evidenced data from both scenes will allow us to present a historically defensible case for Jesus' divine claim.

WHAT YOU WILL LEARN

In the many pages that follow, we will embark on a quest to uncover highly evidenced data for the divine claim of Jesus. We'll investigate ancient manuscripts and miracle-working accounts, explore Jewish concepts of blasphemy and divine authority, and carefully analyze recent reconstructions of a merely human Jesus. Along the way, you will be equipped with the tools of a scholar who specializes in a discipline called historical Jesus studies. You'll learn how to explain the truth and significance of Jesus' divine claim—even in conversations with people who doubt the historical reliability of the Bible. I've personally seen how sharing the historical facts in this book can help nonbelievers appreciate a credible investigation of the claims of the historical Jesus and the data that must be accounted for by any theory of Jesus' claims and self-understanding. It's my hope that this book becomes a key that will help you unlock the ability to talk to anyone about Jesus as a historical figure. I've found that doing this can open the door to sharing reasons to believe that Jesus is more than a man—he's God Almighty.

PART ONE

Person of Interest

INVESTIGATING JESUS AS A FIGURE IN ANCIENT HISTORY

Long before Christianity was legalized and long before the deity of Christ was discussed at the Council of Nicaea, an artist meticulously arranged small pieces of glass and colored stone to decorate the floor of a small worship hall with a beautiful mosaic. It included a remarkable dedication mentioning the contribution of a woman named Akeptous to the prayer space: "The God-loving Akeptous has offered the table to God Jesus Christ as a memorial." Dating to around AD 230, the Megiddo

mosaic is striking physical evidence of Jesus being called God.[1] The table mentioned was likely used to worship Jesus during the eucharistic ritual in what is now the earliest Christian prayer space to have been discovered in Israel.[2]

On September 15, 2024, the Museum of the Bible in Washington, DC, unveiled this groundbreaking artifact to the world.[3] Conversations surrounding this archaeological find bring us back to the million-dollar question: How much continuity is present between the early belief in Jesus as a divine figure and the things Jesus said about himself? Before we investigate his historical claims, we need to get oriented to the world of professional historians. That's what part one of this book is all about.

In many role-playing video games, players often begin with a tutorial level or staging area that introduces the world of the game as well as basic moves and rules before embarking on an important quest. Consider the next two chapters as two parts of the staging area for our historical investigation of Jesus' words and deeds.

- Chapter one introduces you to the world of professional historians. How do they seek to discover what happened in the past?
- Chapter two shows you the basic moves and the rules for our quest—how can we operate in the world of historical Jesus studies using the rules of evidence that apply to a critical investigation of any figure in ancient history?

You are about to engage with the top philosophical and methodological considerations that face historians as they seek to uncover what happened in the past. The staging area is ready. Let's get started.

---

[1] Vassilios Tzaferis, "Inscribed 'To God Jesus Christ,'" Biblical Archaeology Society Library, accessed December 16, 2024, https://library.biblicalarchaeology.org/article/inscribed-to-god-jesus-christ/.

[2] "The Megiddo Mosaic," Biblical Archaeology Society, November 13, 2024, www.biblicalarchaeology.org/exhibits-events/the-megiddo-mosaic/.

[3] "The Megiddo Mosaic: A Community Coming Together to the Table," Museum of the Bible, September 26, 2024, www.museumofthebible.org/magazine/exhibitions/the-megiddo-mosaic-a-community-coming-together-to-the-table.

Let's Make History

HOW HISTORIANS DISCOVER PAST EVENTS

Imagine finding yourself in an elegant castle-style home that features a two-story turret library. As you begin to climb the spiral staircase, you recognize the sweet, enchanting scent of well-worn books. You emerge high atop the library and admire the high ceiling and rolling ladders. Dark built-in bookshelves hold decades of academic journals and books on the philosophy of history and literary theory. Peering over the balcony to the lower level, you look down at the open workspace and see an antique oak desk with a magnifying glass and a 1920s-style brass banker's lamp illuminating a variety of tomes, including a large open codex—an ancient book. Fragments of old parchment manuscripts are framed on the walls of the lower level. Dark academia meets Harry Potter meets Indiana Jones. Your eye is drawn to some gentle track lighting, which softly illuminates an intriguing collection of red, pink, gray, and black beads displayed on the lower level, right next to the bottom of the spiral staircase where you began your ascent.

Welcome to our staging area. We will use this mental construct as a metaphor for the world of professional scholars who study Jesus as a figure in ancient history. First, think of the theoretical space as the upper level of the library. This is where we consider questions such as, "Can we know things about the past?" and "To what extent can we know those things?" These epistemological concerns are related to the philosophy of history—the way historians can obtain knowledge about the past. Second, think of the methodological space as the lower level of the library. Here, we encounter questions such as, "How do historians work to accurately reconstruct past events?" and "Can we investigate Jesus' words and deeds using the same tools that historians employ to study any other figure in ancient history?" Answering these questions will help us learn to employ standard rules of evidence in our own investigation.

We will need to play by these rules as we embark on a quest to recover the historicity of Jesus' divine claim. Why? In order to find common ground with those who do not privilege the Bible as an authoritative source. Thinking about the upper and lower levels of our library can help us visualize and distinguish two levels of scholarly discussion in the world of historical Jesus research: theoretical and methodological considerations for investigating the evidence surrounding any figure in history.

Your orientation to the world of professional historians begins on the upper level. This is where we will survey the following seven theoretical considerations that relate to investigating the past:[1]

1. understanding historiography
2. the question of hermeneutics
3. the concept of horizon
4. the limits of historical knowledge
5. the challenge of postmodernism
6. the nature of truth
7. the nature of historical facts

These are important because of two kinds of objections we encounter to investigating Jesus as a figure in ancient history. First, some people say that the limitations of historical inquiry prevent us from discovering anything about the past. Is our historical project really doomed to failure from the very beginning? Second, others may automatically reject any

---

[1]This list of considerations is adapted from Michael R. Licona, *The Resurrection of Jesus: A New Historiographical Approach* (Downers Grove, IL: IVP Academic, 2010).

book written by a Christian scholar—especially if its conclusions support the historic church's view of Jesus as a divine figure. Why? Many skeptics doubt that a Christian scholar can conduct a sound investigation of the historical Jesus due to their personal bias. However, let me explain why neither of these concerns prohibits the kind of detective work that allows us to discover real, historical facts about the words and deeds of certain people who lived in ancient times—even Jesus.

What Happened Here? Defining History

Before we survey the seven theoretical considerations, we need to define a key term: *history*. What is history? What we commonly call history is actually someone's reconstruction of the past. That's because historians distinguish a past event itself from a written report that describes that past event. For example, think of the dramatic surge in remote work and online education during the lockdowns associated with the Covid-19 pandemic. The widespread practice of telecommuting and remote instruction that began in 2020 represents a unique historical shift that is distinct from the ways that various news outlets reported on it. So, writing a history of something means writing an explanation of a past event.[2]

Robert L. Webb is a historian who founded the *Journal for the Study of the Historical Jesus*, a respected periodical for academic discussions of Jesus within his first-century Jewish context. He perhaps gives the best definition of history: it is "a narrative account that we historians write to express an understanding of past events based on our interpretation of the traces which have survived from those past events."[3] This was the approach of the Institute of Biblical Research Jesus Group's decadelong collaborative project, published in 2010 as *Key Events in the Life of the Historical Jesus*. It is a significant critical investigation of twelve highly evidenced events in Jesus' life that employed rules of evidence we will

[2]G. Kitson Clark, *The Critical Historian: Guide for Research Students Working on Historical Subjects*, History and Historiography (New York: Garland, 1985), 1.
[3]Darrell L. Bock and Robert L. Webb, eds., *Key Events in the Life of the Historical Jesus: A Collaborative Exploration of Context and Coherence* (Grand Rapids, MI: Eerdmans, 2010), 16.

discuss in the next chapter—rules that were not invented by the church but grew out of critical scholarship's quests for the historical Jesus. We will adopt Webb's definition of history for our investigation of Jesus' claims.

LET'S MAKE HISTORY: UNDERSTANDING HISTORIOGRAPHY

Philosophers of history ask, "To what extent can we actually know things about the past?" and "How can we really know what someone said or did?" Epistemological questions such as these are part of the theoretical side of historical research called historiography. Historiography relates to the means by which historians can know things about past events and to what extent they can know them. If you look up "historiography" in *New Dictionary of the History of Ideas*, you'll find it defined as "intentional attempts to recover knowledge of and represent in writing true descriptions or narratives of past events."[4]

Some insist that it's impossible to accurately represent a past event. But adopting this view would mean throwing out virtually everything we know about the past. Most historians reject such radical skepticism and work with the understanding that we can reach at least an adequately accurate account of the past. Like an archaeologist on a dig, we can do the historical spade work to uncover highly evidenced data relevant to our question about Jesus' divine claim. As we dig deeper into ancient texts, we will seek what British scholar James D. G. Dunn famously described as the only realistic objective of any quest for the historical Jesus—discovering Jesus as he was remembered.[5] So, the purpose of historical Jesus investigations in general is to explain Jesus' words and works as preserved in the memories of ancient people who wrote about him. To do this, we will have to get our hands dirty sifting through the data. This kind of work can be technical and nuanced. At times, it may seem like we are employing the precision of a toothbrush to dust off the debris so we can arrive at historical bedrock. Despite the challenges, we can

---

[4]Daniel Woolf, "Historiography," in *New Dictionary of the History of Ideas*, ed. Maryanne Cline Horowitz (New York: Thomson Gale, 2004), 1:xxxv.

[5]James D. G. Dunn, *Jesus Remembered*, Christianity in the Making 1 (Grand Rapids, MI: Eerdmans, 2003), 882.

work to put together an adequately accurate representation of at least some of Jesus' words and deeds.

What Do You Mean by That?
The Question of Hermeneutics

Historical Jesus researchers include Jews, Christians, agnostics, atheists, and others who represent a range of religious views. When these scholars disagree on something Jesus said or what he meant by what he said, the disagreement often comes down to the way they interpret historical data that can be gleaned from the Bible or other ancient sources.

Can we adequately determine what a person meant to communicate? This is the question of hermeneutics—the study of interpretation. Since we as twenty-first-century readers are so separated from the time and place of biblical authors or the events they describe, some say it is impossible for us to understand what an author was trying to communicate.[6] Again, most historians reject such radical skepticism. The mere fact that someone decided to write a literary work tells us that the author intended to communicate something to people who would later read the work. In the same way, speakers also speak in order to communicate with hearers. What applies to understanding authors also applies to understanding reports about what a speaker said.

True, we cannot hop into a DMC DeLorean equipped with a working flux capacitor to go back in time to interview someone who wrote in the past. While this retrofitted time-traveling vehicle from the classic *Back to the Future* movies remains the stuff of science fiction, an author's intention or voice is still accessible enough that we can move toward an adequate interpretation of what someone meant to communicate.

For example, if you read Mark Akenside's eighteenth-century poem "The Pleasures of the Imagination," you might be initially confused by a line that says that the great creator "rais'd his plastic arm."[7] To modern

---

[6]Robert H. Stein, *A Basic Guide to Interpreting the Bible: Playing by the Rules*, 2nd ed. (Grand Rapids, MI: Baker Academic, 2011), 25.

[7]Mark Akenside, *The Pleasures of Imagination: A New Edition* (London: Old Bailey, 1806). See line 313 on page 61. https://ia803207.us.archive.org/27/items/pleasuresofimagi00aken/pleasures ofimagi00aken.pdf.

readers, this could sound like the creator had a prosthetic arm made of plastic. However, when we discover that the word *plastic* used to carry a "formative" or "creative" sense in the author's day, we take one step closer to the world of the author and his intended message.[8] This shows that an author's meaning is not hopelessly inaccessible to today's readers, as a famous educational theorist, E. D. Hirsch, once observed: "It is far more likely that an author and an interpreter can entertain identical meanings than they cannot. . . . The inaccessibility of verbal meaning is a doctrine that experience suggests to be falsity. . . . The skeptical doctrine of inaccessibility is highly improbable."[9] Indeed, the nature of human communication ensures that at least some of an author's meaning is accessible to the reader who works to understand a text. When we recognize an author's cultural and situational context (as well as our own), we can better position ourselves to accurately understand what a figure in ancient history said and what the figure likely meant by it.

WELCOME TO MY WORLD: THE CONCEPT OF HORIZON

It's been said that when scholars go on a quest for the historical Jesus, they peer into a dark, deep well of data and tend to see a reflection of a Jesus who looks very similar to themselves.[10] This is because everyone has a bias. Every historian writes from the perspective of their own worldview and ideology. Scholars call this your *horizon*. But this doesn't mean that researchers never change their minds. It's very possible to transcend your horizon and even be persuaded by opposing theories—even in religious matters.[11] For example, Ehrman was a former pastor of

---

[8]For example, consider the term *plastic surgery*, used to indicate reconstructive surgery. The first known use of *plastic* with this kind of creative sense likely occurred in 1624. See "Plastic," *Merriam Webster Dictionary*, accessed October 22, 2018, www.merriam-webster.com/dictionary/plastic.

[9]E. D. Hirsch, *Validity in Interpretation* (New Haven, CT: Yale University Press, 1967), 18.

[10]Although this image is associated with Albert Schweitzer, it perhaps originated with George Tyrrell: "The Christ that Harnack sees, looking back through nineteen centuries of Catholic darkness, is only the reflection of a Liberal Protestant face, seen at the bottom of a deep well." Tyrrell, *Christianity at the Cross-Roads* (New York: Longmans, Green, 1913), 44.

[11]Licona notes some of the same examples in *Resurrection of Jesus*, 51.

Princeton Baptist Church but became an agnostic atheist.[12] Although C. S. Lewis (the author of *Mere Christianity* and the Chronicles of Narnia) was baptized in the Church of Ireland, he left his faith for atheism as a teenager but later returned to the Anglican tradition.[13] Historian Jaroslav Pelikan converted from Lutheranism to Eastern Orthodoxy.[14] Historical Jesus scholar Geza Vermes was a Hungarian Jew who escaped the Holocaust and became a Catholic priest but eventually left the church for a Jewish synagogue.[15] Philosopher of religion Anthony Flew gave up his atheism and embraced belief in God, in part because he was persuaded that DNA investigations revealed evidence for an intelligent designer.[16] Yes, everyone has a perspective and a bias. But people can change their minds. They may shed previous beliefs and adopt new ones. They may even reject or revise their once deeply held religious beliefs and adopt different ones.

Still, some critics view Christian faith as a showstopping liability when it comes to doing historical work. Gerd Theissen and Dagmar Winter wrote *The Quest for the Plausible Jesus* and go so far as to say that "Christian faith . . . is guaranteed to corrupt objective scholarly work."[17] But this bold insistence seems too fatalistic. If Jewish scholars can conduct sound investigations of the historical evidence surrounding the Hebrew Scriptures, the Dead Sea Scrolls, and the Holocaust, why can't Christian scholars conduct sound investigations of the historical Jesus? Perhaps they mean that one cannot be absolutely objective—totally devoid of presuppositions of any kind. But why single out Christian scholars? Again, everyone has a perspective. Although views of faith,

---

[12]"Author Traces Christianity's Path from 'Forbidden Religion' to a 'Triumph,'" *Fresh Air*, National Public Radio, March 20, 2018, www.npr.org/2018/03/20/595161200/author-traces-christianitys -path-from-forbidden-religion-to-a-triumph.

[13]C. S. Lewis, *Surprised by Joy: The Shape of My Early Life* (San Francisco: HarperOne, 2017).

[14]Robert L. Wilken, "Jaroslav Pelikan and the Road to Orthodoxy," *Concordia Theological Quarterly* 74, nos. 1-2 (January 2010): 92-103.

[15]"Geza Vermes," *The Economist*, May 18, 2013, www.economist.com/obituary/2013/05/18/geza -vermes.

[16]Antony Flew and Roy Abraham Varghese, *There Is a God: How the World's Most Notorious Atheist Changed His Mind* (New York: HarperOne, 2008).

[17]Gerd Theissen and Dagmar Winter, *The Quest for the Plausible Jesus: The Question of Criteria* (Louisville, KY: Westminster John Knox, 2002), 252.

religion, and spirituality are part of what all of us bring to the table as researchers, it does not follow that Christian faith must prevent us from uncovering highly evidenced data about Jesus—in the same way that our peers in the scholarly community can. This is especially true when we observe the common checks and balances used in critical studies of other figures in history.

So, we can work to recognize and reduce our biases when it comes to interpreting data about Jesus. A great way to do this is to hold ourselves to high standards. We can insist that our own views of Jesus must account for historical bedrock. By this I mean strongly evidenced data, supported by multiple arguments, that most historians recognize as facts.[18] This is not a mere appeal to authority. Rather, it is the recognition that when scholars across a range of commitments agree on bedrock facts, there is likely enough data to take the event or saying seriously. In other words, there are probably some very good reasons why scholars from opposite sides of the aisle and across a spectrum of belief can agree on something. That should turn our attention to evaluating the data that so many from disparate views find persuasive. Despite challenges, it is possible for us to sufficiently transcend our own horizons enough to do sound historical work.

What Do You Know? The Limits of Historical Knowledge

How sure can we be that a past event occurred? Historians work to determine the degree of certainty we can have in a hypothesis such as "Jesus claimed to possess divine authority" or "Jesus did not claim to possess divine authority." This represents the way most historians approach their investigations.[19] In Michael Licona's study of the historical Jesus, he explains the concept of "adequate certainty":

> When historians say that "*x occurred*" in the past, they are actually claiming the following: *Given the available data, the best explanation*

---

[18]Licona, *Resurrection of Jesus*, 55-58.
[19]Licona, *Resurrection of Jesus*, 89.

indicates that we are warranted in having a reasonable degree of certainty
that x occurred and that it appears more certain at the moment than com-
peting hypotheses. Accordingly, we have a rational basis for believing it.
However, our conclusion is subject to revision or abandonment, since new
data may surface in the future showing things happened differently than
previously proposed.[20]

The data we find in ancient manuscripts can help us arrive at provisional answers to historical questions. Why? Because future data may come to light that invite us to reassess a hypothesis. So, historical answers fall somewhere on a spectrum of certainty.

However, this does not mean that investigations are futile because we cannot have 100 percent certainty about the past. We don't have to be omniscient to have a reasonable or justified belief and come to historical knowledge. To be fair, we just need to be humble when we come to our conclusions. Despite the limits of historical knowledge, we can have adequate certainty (a high degree of confidence) in the hypothesis that a past event happened (e.g., that Jesus was crucified) when that hypothesis is the best explanation of the available data. This represents what scholars call "critical realism." Here, the word *critical* refers to making judgments, and *realism* refers to making judgments about reality. This is how the overwhelming majority of practicing historians approach investigations of surviving traces of past events in the real world.[21]

LET'S BE REAL: THE CHALLENGE OF POSTMODERNISM

John Dominic Crossan is a historian who rejects supernatural explanations for Jesus' reported miracles and many of the words and deeds attributed to Jesus in the Gospels. In his book *The Historical Jesus: The Life of a Mediterranean Jewish Peasant*, he calls the "stunning diversity" of

---

[20]Licona, *Resurrection of Jesus*, 69, emphasis original.

[21]Licona, *Resurrection of Jesus*, 89. While Bernier recognizes the variety of critical realisms, he notes that Wright's, Dunn's, and Meyer's critical realism is the kind of "critical realism already present to a certain extent in New Testament scholarship . . . pioneered by and associated with Bernard Lonergan." It is this he believes must be developed in historical Jesus studies. See Jonathan Bernier, *The Quest for the Historical Jesus After the Demise of Authenticity: Toward a Critical Realist Philosophy of History in Jesus Studies*, Library of New Testament Studies 540 (New York: T&T Clark, 2016), 5-6.

scholarly conclusions about Jesus "an academic embarrassment."[22] Indeed, it can be frustrating to discover various researchers who peer into the same well of data and yet end up with vastly different ideas about what Jesus thought about himself (scholars call this his "self-identity"). Because of this, some wonder whether ancient texts can tell us anything at all.

In the mid-twentieth century, a French philosopher named Jacques Derrida challenged traditional views of language and meaning. In *The Postmodern Bible*, he and other poststructuralists assert that readers must endlessly create and re-create the meaning of the text themselves, because the author's words do not have a fixed meaning.[23] This approach to the Bible is based on an underlying philosophical assumption that all interpretations are equally valid because there are no such things as objective historical events. On this view, all historical reporting is powerless to inform the reader about the details of real past events.[24]

Postmodern scholars say that it seems too limiting to restrict the text to any one "correct" interpretation. On this view, the words *red ball* do not unequivocally indicate a specific, unchanging referent (such as an actual spherical object with the property of redness). At first, this does not seem too problematic. After all, *red ball* may refer to a setting sun or the planet Mars rather than a piece of playground equipment used in a game of kickball. However, the observation that a metaphor can refer to one thing and not another thing is not proof that a word can mean just anything at all! In reality, an author may intend to use a metaphor precisely to refer to one thing and not another. Referents are not as fluid as some suppose. In fact, the limitations of postmodernism seem to render the approach less helpful in historical investigations.

It is the postmodern view that is too limiting. Why insist that the text cannot have a definite meaning at all? Just think about why postmodern authors write books (seemingly to educate their readers and persuade them to adopt their views). Presumably, these authors want to be understood.

---

[22]John Dominic Crossan, *The Historical Jesus: The Life of a Mediterranean Jewish Peasant* (San Francisco: HarperSanFrancisco, 1991), xxviii.

[23]Bible & Culture Collective, *The Postmodern Bible* (New Haven, CT: Yale University Press, 1997), 124, 130-31.

[24]On this view, its power is to elude the reader and continually overturn one's interpretation.

You can imagine how they might object if someone were to deconstruct their texts and reinterpret their work in a way that misrepresented their intentions or their views. However, this is similar to many postmodern approaches to texts about Jesus. How well can seeing the biblical text as totally independent from the author's intended meaning advance historical studies? Trying to live out the postmodern approach in the world of historical research would create methodological chaos for researchers.

While no one can be absolutely objective or mechanically neutral in historical studies, literary deconstruction seems unhelpful when applied to documents such as police reports, hospital records, academic transcripts—or ancient narratives that purport to describe actual events. We should allow the genre of a text (e.g., poetry, biography) to determine how it should be read rather than blindly proceeding with a one-size-fits-all kind of reading.

In order to do any productive historical work, we must approach the text believing there is an objective reality independent of human knowledge and language. Indeed, books on the historical Jesus make a kind of truth claim about the nature of reality. In *Historiography and Hermeneutics in Jesus Studies*, Donald L. Denton rightly observes that "the world of historical Jesus studies would have little sympathy with any form of anti-realism in historiography."[25] In fact, Licona notes, "Replies by realist historians to postmodernists have convinced the majority of practicing historians and philosophers of history that realism, rather than postmodernism, is correct and practical. . . . Postmodernism has lost the battle of ideologies among professional historians."[26] Indeed, the postmodern approach doesn't seem useful to our investigation of Jesus' words and deeds.

WHAT IS TRUTH? THE NATURE OF TRUTH

According to John 18:38, the Roman procurator Pontus Pilate asked Jesus, "What is truth?" The correspondence theory of truth is the most helpful

---

[25]D. L. Denton Jr., *Historiography and Hermeneutics in Jesus Studies: An Examination of the Work of John Dominic Crossan and Ben F. Meyer* (London: T&T Clark, 2004), 170.
[26]Licona, *Resurrection of Jesus*, 86.

and the most widely accepted view among historians, including those who study Jesus.[27] The correspondence theory refers to the idea that when a proposition corresponds to the actual state of the world, we can say that proposition is true. For example, the proposition "It is raining outside" is true if and only if it is raining outside. Similarly, the proposition "Jesus of Nazareth was crucified in the first century AD" is true if and only if Jesus of Nazareth was really crucified in the first century AD.

Still, some say that historical truths are just the stories told by those with privilege: "History is always written by the winners."[28] But those who reject metanarratives (overarching, grand stories that explain reality) promote a competing metanarrative. Even though history as a discipline cannot yield 100 percent certainty about the past, we can have at least a reasonable level of certainty about the truth of propositions about the past. Based on a justified belief, research can produce an adequate (even if not completely exhaustive) narrative account that positively corresponds to the past event described. The most reasonable view is that truth exists independent of language and the interpretations of researchers. Correspondence theory best conforms to our everyday experience of the world. To do good historical work, we must proceed with the idea that truth is something we discover, not something we invent.

Is That a Fact? The Nature of Historical Facts

Richard Evans, a leading British historian of nineteenth- and twentieth-century Germany at Cambridge University, saw a historical fact as a past event that researchers seek to discover through verification.[29] This definition is used in historical Jesus studies as well. For example, Licona uses it in *The Resurrection of Jesus: A New Historiographical Approach*.[30] We will adopt this view for our study.

---

[27] Scot McKnight, *Jesus and His Death: Historiography, the Historical Jesus, and Atonement Theory* (Waco, TX: Baylor University Press, 2005), 14-15.

[28] This phrase was popularized by Dan Brown, e.g., *The Da Vinci Code* (New York: Vintage, 2003), 256.

[29] Richard J. Evans, *In Defense of History* (New York: Norton, 1999), 66.

[30] Licona, *Resurrection of Jesus*, 94.

One of our first tasks will be to discover historical bedrock and the evidence that supports it. This will allow us to begin our investigation with common ground accepted by critical scholars who are not sympathetic to our cause.[31] The beauty of building our case on what some might call "minimal facts"—highly evidenced data the majority of critics acknowledge as facts—is that it can allow us to come to the table with people from a variety of religious backgrounds (as well as those who do not identify with a faith tradition) and have a reasoned conversation about some of the things that Jesus did and things he said about himself.[32] It can also demonstrate how certain details in the Bible can be corroborated and qualify as historical facts—even when working in scholarly contexts that do not privilege the biblical text beyond any other source from antiquity.

For the most radical skeptics, however, almost everything is up for debate. This limits a scholarly consensus on what constitutes a historical fact. The reality is that everyone has biases, agendas, and horizons. For example, some people claim that Jesus never even existed. This idea represents a small group of conspiracy theorists who advocate for the Jesus-myth theory online and in fringe publications. Virtually every respected historian believes that Jesus existed—not because of a religious commitment but due to the overwhelming weight of data supporting the reality of Jesus' life and death.

Influential critic Rudolph Bultmann questioned supernatural elements of the Bible but still wrote, "The doubt to whether Jesus really existed is unfounded and not worth refutation."[33] More recently, Crossan acknowledged that "Jesus' death by crucifixion under Pontius Pilate is as sure as anything historical can ever be."[34] Ehrman, an agnostic atheist, recognizes that "there was a Jesus of history" and that "it is a historical fact that some of Jesus' followers came to believe that he had been raised from the

---

[31]Licona, *Resurrection of Jesus*, 55.
[32]Gary Habermas popularized the term *minimal facts* in his work with Michael Licona, *The Case for the Resurrection of Jesus* (Grand Rapids, MI: Kregel, 2004).
[33]"The doubt to whether Jesus really existed is unfounded and not worth refutation." Rudolf Bultmann, *Jesus and the Word*, trans. L. P. Smith and E. H. Lantero (London: Collins, 1958), 13.
[34]John Dominic Crossan, *Jesus: A Revolutionary Biography* (New York: HarperOne, 2009), 145.

dead soon after his execution." These "minimal facts" are part of the historical bedrock about Jesus.[35] Indeed, online discussions with self-proclaimed mythicists do not represent scholarly conversations about Jesus happening in academic journals. In fact, the editorial board for the *Journal for the Study of the Historical Jesus* represents a diverse group of scholars, including atheists, agnostics, Jews, and Christians from a range of theological persuasions. All of them agree that Jesus existed. For example, Ehrman posted this on the HuffPost Contributor platform:

> One may well choose to resonate with the concerns of our modern and post-modern cultural despisers of established religion (or not). But surely the best way to promote any such agenda is not to deny what virtually every sane historian on the planet—Christian, Jewish, Muslim, pagan, agnostic, atheist, what have you—has come to conclude based on a range of compelling historical evidence. Whether we like it or not, Jesus certainly existed.[36]

While discovering minimal facts can be helpful, the reality of historical facts themselves is not dependent on consensus or a majority view. When we find highly evidenced data that is widely acknowledged by scholars, we must remind ourselves to avoid *argumentum ad verecundiam* (appeal to authority), *argumentum ad numerum* (appeal to the majority), or similar logical fallacies. All that a consensus or majority view tells us is what a group of historians—whether on the theological left, right, or center—regards as authentic. For example, although there is strong agreement among virtually all critical scholars on the existence of Jesus, a consensus on the historicity of Jesus' claim to possess divine authority may not seem likely outside conservative biblical scholarship. Not everyone will believe that Jesus made divine claims regardless of the strength of the evidence because persuasion will always be person-relative. But the recognition that not everyone will be persuaded by our findings should not prohibit us from potentially concluding that our hypothesis that Jesus

---

[35]Gary R. Habermas, "Resurrection Research from 1975 to the Present: What Are Critical Scholars Saying?," *Journal for the Study of the Historical Jesus* 3, no. 2 (June 2005): 135-53.

[36]Bart D. Ehrman, "Did Jesus Exist?," *HuffPost*, March 20, 2012, www.huffpost.com/entry/did -jesus-exist_b_1349544.

made divine claims is strongly supported by the data and is a true fact of history.

So, how can recognizing a consensus or majority view be helpful? For some who may be hesitant to begin a conversation about Jesus assuming the truth of the Bible, this could serve as an invitation to read the Gospels and consider the claims of Jesus. When researchers discover agreement across a spectrum of historians holding various theological and philosophical positions, it's like getting an audible ding that alerts you to a text message on your phone. The message is, "Pay attention to the evidence that led to this majority view! These facts may help us come to a better understanding of the historical Jesus."

CONCLUSION

What is history? History is a narrative account written to explain past events based on what a historian believes is the best interpretation of the surviving traces of those events. The surviving traces of Jesus' words and deeds include highly evidenced data gleaned from ancient texts. Contrary to those who remain hyperskeptical, our historical project is not doomed to failure. The limitations of historical inquiry do not prevent us from obtaining knowledge about the past—even as Christian scholars.

The following key points from our discussion of the seven theoretical considerations are foundational to our study:

1. We can create an adequately accurate representation of at least some of Jesus' words and deeds.
2. Understanding Jesus' cultural context can help us more accurately understand what he said and what he likely meant by it.
3. It is possible to sufficiently transcend our own horizons enough to conduct a sound historical investigation of Jesus.
4. We can have a high degree of confidence in a hypothesis about a past event when that hypothesis is the best explanation of the available data.
5. We can discover real historical facts about people who lived in ancient times—including Jesus.

6. Truth is something we discover, not something we invent.
7. A historical fact is a past event that researchers discover through verification.

When a strongly evidenced event approaches historical bedrock, historians inquire as to the cause of the event. How should one investigate the reasons a given event occurred? Our orientation to the world of professional historians now moves from theoretical conversations to practical methods for doing the detective work required to uncover the truth about Jesus' divine claim. It's time to head back down the spiral staircase and explore the ground level of our turret library.

Rules of Evidence

INVESTIGATING THE HISTORICAL JESUS

The first time someone challenged my faith, I was a senior in high school. I had taken a flight from Manila, Philippines, to visit my grandpa in the United States. While I was visiting a midweek youth group gathering in Maryland, I got into a conversation about Jesus with another guy who was about my age. I was surprised at how skeptical he was about the Bible—especially since we were in a church setting. In the middle of our conversation, he stopped me and said, "Look, I'm not gonna base my life on a book. There isn't a shred of evidence outside the Bible that Jesus is even real." He shot me a look that signaled our conversation was over. For him, it was a mic-drop moment. Game over.

As a teenager, I had no idea what to say. I tried to respond with some generalities about history and archaeology corroborating some biblical details, but he shrugged it off with a flippant retort. "So what if someone digs up a pot?" Again, I had no idea what to say. I wished I knew how to talk about Jesus with someone who was so skeptical about the Bible. That was a moment when I began to get curious about how professional historians studied Jesus. Even in a church setting, this skeptical senior didn't see the Bible as the answer. For him, the Bible was the question. He didn't see Jesus as anything more than a character in a work of fiction. How could I help someone like him consider the historical reality of Jesus' claims? Are there "best practices" for studying Jesus as a figure in ancient history?

THE STAGING AREA (PART TWO)

Our orientation to the world of professional historians now takes us to the lower level of the elegant library in our mental construct. Welcome back to the staging area. As you descend the spiral staircase and step into the open workspace, you are reminded that the philosophical considerations we discussed on the upper level make a practical difference in the way we proceed with our investigation of Jesus' divine claim. You step onto the plush dark green carpet of the lower level and approach the large oak desk you first saw from the upper level. Next to the magnifying glass and antique banker's lamp is a large open codex written in Greek. It's an ancient handwritten copy of the Bible. Seeing the Scriptures in this context is a reminder that investigating the text as a historian is very different from the way Bible studies are conducted in church small group meetings.

Again, think of this lower level as the methodological space where we work to accurately reconstruct past events. Can we investigate Jesus' words and deeds using the same tools that historians employ to study any other figure in ancient history? Yes, we can. But working in a highly skeptical context means making a corroborative case for Jesus' words and deeds. We cannot merely appeal to faith or the inspiration of the Scriptures if we are to gain the right to be heard by the very people with whom we are seeking to engage. So, we will work to carefully establish common ground with those who do not see the Bible as an authority. Think of your skeptical friends, family, coworkers, and neighbors who have historical questions about Jesus. We need to do this so that we can have better conversations with them about the meaning, truth, and significance of Jesus' claims.

In this chapter, we will survey seven methodological considerations in building a credible historical case for Jesus' divine claim:

1. methodological approaches
2. making an argument to the best explanation
3. the spectrum of historical certainty

4. the role of historical bedrock
5. ancient sources and the question of authenticity
6. the criteria of authenticity
7. investigating sayings and events in the life of the historical Jesus

Along the way, you'll learn how to make the right moves in the world of historians. Think of this as best practices for studying Jesus as a figure in ancient history. You'll also learn the rules of evidence—rules that were not invented by the church. At the end of this chapter, I'll lay out the procedure for our study and put all my cards on the table so you are fully aware of my personal biases (and perhaps begin to consider your own biases as well).

What's the Word? The Bible in Historical Research

Forgive me for my need to state the obvious at this point. Atheists believe that God does not exist. If God does not exist, then the Bible is not the Word of God, and it is no more authoritative or inerrant than any other collection of ancient documents. Many Christians are puzzled by those who read the Bible and ask, "Why was the text written this way? How did it really happen?" However, it is important to put ourselves in someone else's shoes in order to understand them and the issues they raise so that we can have better conversations about Jesus—even if they're hesitant to see him as more than a figure in ancient history.

For those who don't see the Bible as the Word of God, there are three basic ways to approach the text. The first is a more generous approach, similar to the way a friend who first becomes interested in going to church might read the Bible and generally give it the benefit of the doubt—even the friend is not sure whether it is reliable. The second is a more skeptical approach, similar to the way that an atheist friend may be hesitant to believe the Bible. The third is a moderating position between them both. This is how many respectful conversations can proceed, where the person who makes a claim also explains why they believe it.

Here's how this works in historical research. First, the more generous approach is called methodological credulity. Historians who operate this way tend to take texts at face value unless there are mitigating factors that suggest the source may be untrustworthy (e.g., contradictions with known facts of history). This is the most generous of the approaches. An example is the ancient document rule in American jurisprudence. The Federal Rules of Evidence 803(16) originally exempted documents twenty years old and older from being excluded in a court proceeding or trial by the rules of evidence. The court generally treats these documents as more reliable and trustworthy in legal proceedings. Why? Because it's unlikely that a document created decades ago was intended to influence a present-day controversy. In light of electronic texts, the current language states: "(16) *Statements in Ancient Documents.* A statement in a document that was prepared before January 1, 1998, and whose authenticity is established."[1] Still, it is prudent to apply what philosopher Richard Swinburne calls the "principle of credulity" when assessing testimony— that is, giving the witness the benefit of the doubt unless there are mitigating factors that call their perception into question.[2]

Most people who don't see the Bible as an authority are hesitant to apply this approach to the text. However, if we want to make our case for Jesus' divine claim from a common starting point, our investigation cannot assume the inspiration or infallibility of the Bible—regardless of our own convictions. Skeptics say that ancient authors embellished stories and that surviving copies of biblical texts were changed or corrupted. Beyond this, it might also be difficult to identify cultural conventions that affect the way we interpret Jesus' words or deeds. When engaging with skeptics, the challenge is to demonstrate what Jesus himself meant and what his audience believed about the kind of claims he made.

This brings us to the second, more skeptical approach. Historians who operate with what is called methodological skepticism tend to view the biblical accounts as unreliable until they discover data that is strongly supported by evidence. These critics are immediately suspicious of the Gospel portraits of Jesus and often seek to fact-check the Bible. The problem is that some may require such a high standard of corroboration

---

[1] Federal Rules of Evidence, "ARTICLE VIII. HEARSAY › Rule 803. Exceptions to the Rule Against Hearsay," www.law.cornell.edu/rules/fre/rule_803.

[2] Richard Swinburne, *The Existence of God*, 2nd ed. (Oxford: Clarendon, 2004), 303.

that we would have to throw out much of what we know about the past if we adopted their level of skepticism.

Third is the moderating position. Historians who operate with what is called methodological neutrality want to level the playing field. Now, the word *neutrality* doesn't mean that researchers who take this approach can ever be completely neutral (everyone has biases, and we should be honest enough to recognize them in ourselves). Rather, the approach places the burden of proof on the one who makes a claim about a historical detail or account. For example, when I argue that Jesus claimed to possess divine authority in Mark 2:1-12, I bear the burden of proof for this positive hypothesis. But, by the same token, a critical scholar who asserts that Jesus did *not* claim to possess divine authority in Mark 2:1-12 also bears the burden of proof for this negative hypothesis. It will not do for a skeptic to merely say that the healing account in Mark 2 is inauthentic, or that the scribal response in the text is inauthentic, or that Jesus' forgiving sins would have been heard merely as a claim to priestly authority rather than divine authority. No, a skeptic must produce evidence to demonstrate that one of these options (or another option) is more probable than the hypothesis that Jesus claimed to possess divine authority in Mark 2. So, this moderate approach says, "Let's favor the view that is more plausible than competing theories." This avoids an overly skeptical attitude toward the text while still employing the corroborative data needed to build a positive historical case. For our study on Jesus' divine claim, then, we will adopt the third way of methodological neutrality as an approach over credulity or skepticism.[3]

WHO DO YOU LISTEN TO? HOW TO DISCOVER
THE BEST EXPLANATION

Historians examine evidence and make inferences to the best explanation.[4] This is how we will build the case for Jesus' divine claim. My hypothesis is that Jesus made divine claims. After building a historical

---

[3]This follows Licona's conclusions and adoption of neutrality. Michael R. Licona, *The Resurrection of Jesus: A New Historiographical Approach* (Downers Grove, IL: IVP Academic, 2010), 99.

[4]This is preferable to arguments from statistical inference. See C. B. McCullagh, *Justifying Historical Descriptions* (New York: Cambridge University Press, 1984), 46-47, 57-58.

case for this, we will see how well it stacks up to alternative theories. Historians use five criteria to help adjudicate between theories and adopt the most likely view.

1. The first among the criteria is a prerequisite for considering the hypothesis alongside opposing views. It's called plausibility. This pertains to how much a hypothesis is implied by historical bedrock and other highly evidenced facts.

2. The second is called explanatory scope. This pertains to the number of known historical facts that are accounted for by a given hypothesis.

3. The third is called explanatory power. This pertains to how well the hypothesis can explain the known facts. For example, we ask, "Is the explanation a good fit for the facts? Or does it seem forced?"[5] Think of the second and third criteria as key supportive elements of a hypothesis.

4. The fourth is called "less ad hoc."[6] This applies when the hypothesis does not rely on poorly evidenced assumptions that go well beyond the known facts. It helps researchers determine the least problematic view among those under consideration.

5. The fifth is a bonus criteria related to any implications a hypothesis might have for other areas of research. This is called illumination. This pertains to how well a hypothesis helps us explain another historical matter or helps us clarify matters that are related to accepted facts. It's important to note that this should not count negatively against a hypothesis if it doesn't apply. But if it does, it gives us another reason to accept that hypothesis as the best one.

Historians weigh competing hypotheses to discover which one is best (or least problematic). For example, we would prefer a plausible hypothesis with a broad explanatory scope over one that seems only less ad hoc. The former

---

[5]"The bits and pieces of evidence must be incorporated, without being squeezed out of shape any more than is inevitable." N. T. Wright, *The New Testament and the People of God* (Minneapolis: Fortress, 1992), 99.

[6]Also called *simplicity*. See Wright, *New Testament and the People of God*, 100-101. This is a hypothesis with the least amount of seemingly ad hoc suppositions.

would be the better explanation of the two competing theories—especially if it could also counter challenges from competing theories. This is how historians weigh competing theories about Jesus and any other figure of ancient history.[7] After building our case for Jesus' divine claim, we will review this section as we weigh our hypothesis against competing theories.

How Sure Can We Be? The Spectrum of Historical Certainty

How sure can we be that something happened in the past? Historians describe the strength of their convictions using various degrees of certainty. Those who study Jesus have ranked competing theories about him on a spectrum of historical certainty.[8] For our study, we will use the following scale, with numerical values, for our investigation of the historical evidence for Jesus' claim to possess divine authority:[9]

(–4) certainly not historical

(–3) very improbable

(–2) quite improbable

(–1) more improbable than not

---

[7]McCullagh, *Justifying Historical Descriptions*, 37-38.

[8]E.g., E. P. Sanders lists facts surrounding the historical Jesus by degree of certainty: certain or virtually certain, highly probable, probable, possible, conceivable, and incredible. See Sanders, *Jesus and Judaism* (Philadelphia: Fortress, 1985), 326-27. N. T. Wright mentions "a scale from, say, 'extremely unlikely,' through 'possible,' 'plausible' and 'probable,' to 'highly probable.'" See Wright, *The Resurrection of the Son of God* (Minneapolis: Fortress, 2003), 687. John Meier mentions broader categories: "very probable, more probable, less probable, unlikely, etc." See Meier, *A Marginal Jew: Rethinking the Historical Jesus*, vol. 1, *The Roots of the Problem and the Person* (New York: Doubleday, 1991), 33. James D. G. Dunn: "almost certain . . . very probable, probable, likely, possible, and so on . . . 'probable' is a very positive verdict." See Dunn, *Jesus Remembered*, Christianity in the Making 1 (Grand Rapids, MI: Eerdmans, 2003), 1:103. Ben F. Meyer seems too broad: "historical, non-historical, and question-mark." See Meyer, *Critical Realism and the New Testament* (Allison Park, PA: Wipf & Stock, 1989), 135. Similarly, Dale C. Allison Jr.: "plausible but uncertain," "unlikely but still possible," "We just do not know." See Allison, *Resurrecting Jesus: The Earliest Christian Tradition and Its Interpreters* (New York: T&T Clark, 2005), 338.

[9]Sean McDowell uses a similar scale for evaluating historical evidence for the martyrdom of Jesus' apostles: not possibly true (certainly not historical), very probably not true (doubtfully historical), improbable (unlikely), less possible than not (slightly unlikely), possible (indeterminate but not impossible), more possible than not (slightly more possible than not), more probable than not (likely), very probably true (somewhat certain), and the highest possible probability (nearly historically certain). See McDowell, *The Fate of the Apostles: Examining the Martyrdom Accounts of the Closest Followers of Jesus* (Burlington, VT: Routledge, 2016), 122. This in turn was adapted from Licona's investigation of the historical data surrounding the resurrection reports about Jesus. See Licona, *Resurrection of Jesus*, 122.

(0) indeterminate (i.e., neither improbable nor probable)

(+1) more probable than not

(+2) quite probable

(+3) very probable

(+4) certainly historical (i.e., the highest possible probability)

Some theories about Jesus are better supported than others. For example, a historian may have more confidence that Jesus was known as a miracle worker than that he claimed to be divine in some sense. A hypothesis earns the rank of "historical" in one of two ways: either the data more strongly supports it over a competing hypothesis or there are more good reasons for accepting it than rejecting it.[10] In the scale above, such would receive a solid rating of at least *more probable than not* (+1).

While using a numerical scale can be helpful in terms of showing how sure we can be about something, we shouldn't think about it like a mathematical formula. Again, persuasion is always person-relative, and the strength of one researcher's conviction may differ from another—even when they are dealing with the same data set. Still, the scale at least signals the degree of certainty we are justified in having in light of the available evidence. This is similar to civil cases in a court of law where a jury weighs the data based on a preponderance of the evidence. In deliberations, members of the jury ask themselves, "Is it more probable than not that the defendant is guilty based on the facts presented in this case?" This is similar to assessing a historical hypothesis as well, where Jesus scholars view "more probable than not" as a strongly positive affirmation.[11]

ROCK SOLID: THE ROLE OF HISTORICAL BEDROCK

Historical bedrock is a common starting point for scholars regardless of their views about Jesus. For example, on one side of the scholarly spectrum is Paula Fredriksen, Aurelio Professor of Scripture emerita at Boston University. While she is skeptical of the reality of Jesus' miracles, she recognizes that Jesus was believed to be a miracle worker in his

---

[10]McCullagh, *Justifying Historical Descriptions*, 63, 103; C. B. McCullagh, *The Truth of History* (New York: Routledge, 1997), 23; Graham H. Twelftree, *Jesus the Miracle Worker: A Historical and Theological Study* (Downers Grove, IL: InterVarsity Press, 1999), 248.

[11]Dunn calls it "a very positive verdict" (*Jesus Remembered*, 1:103).

context. This is acknowledging what she calls "historical bedrock, facts known past doubting."[12] Indeed, highly evidenced facts are good anchors for building a credible position on Jesus' self-identity. We should first consider facts that are closest to historical certainty before considering facts in the "somewhat certain" to "very certain" range. On the other side of the scholarly spectrum is Gary Habermas, distinguished research professor of apologetics and philosophy at Liberty University in Virginia. He too begins with what he calls "minimal facts" in his historical defense of the reality of Jesus' resurrection. Like Habermas, we will adopt a method that allows the work of historians outside conservative biblical scholarship to serve as a starting point for discussions with those who approach the Bible with skepticism.[13] To find common ground, Habermas builds a case on core facts that meet this criteria:

1. Those that are established by more than adequate scholarly evidence and by more than one independent line of argumentation.
2. Those that are acknowledged by the majority of contemporary scholars in relevant fields.[14]

Again, it is very important to understand that this is not merely an appeal to authority. Habermas explains, "Of the two criteria, I have always held that the first is by far the most crucial, especially since this initial requirement is the one that actually establishes the historicity of the event."[15] Licona uses a similar method in his work defending Jesus' resurrection, adding, "If a hypothesis fails to explain all of the historical bedrock, it is time to drag that hypothesis back to the drawing board or to relegate it to the trash bin."[16]

RULES OF EVIDENCE: CRITERIA OF AUTHENTICITY

Whether you are playing a sport, a card game, a video game, or any other kind of game, it's important to know the rules. Rules tell us how the game

---

[12]Paula Fredriksen, *Jesus of Nazareth: King of the Jews* (New York: Vintage, 1999), 264.
[13]Gary R. Habermas, "The Minimal Facts Approach to the Resurrection of Jesus: The Role of Methodology as a Crucial Component in Establishing Historicity," *Southeastern Theological Review* 3, no. 1 (2012): 17.
[14]Habermas, "Minimal Facts Approach," 16.
[15]Habermas, "Minimal Facts Approach," 16.
[16]Licona, *Resurrection of Jesus*, 56.

works. They dictate the kinds of moves we can legally make. Rules are also important to lawyers who gather the relevant evidence and work to build a credible case for a jury in a court or law. In historical Jesus studies too, there are rules. These are rules of evidence that allow scholars across a range of religious commitments (as well as those who do not identify with any faith tradition) to examine biblical texts as ancient documents and investigate the words and deeds of the historical Jesus. Most historians recognize that when one or more of these rules applies to a certain saying or event, the probability that the saying or event accurately represents Jesus is significantly increased. Scholars call these rules the "criteria of authenticity."[17] Here are seven key rules that will be important for our study.

Rule one: Multiple attestation. As historical Jesus scholarship is most often concerned with corroboration, multiple attestation is the chief criteria. Historians pay careful attention to reports to a given event that come from different sources, even if their authors hold different perspectives on the same event. Why? Because if more than one independent source tells us about something, that's generally a good sign that it probably happened. For example, imagine that four college students saw a hit-and-run in the parking lot after class. Even if four eyewitnesses couldn't agree on exactly how it happened, a campus police officer responding to the scene would be able to see the damaged vehicle and take their statements about the fact of the incident as a plausible explanation. In terms of studying the historical Jesus, virtually every critical scholar who publishes professionally agrees that Jesus of Nazareth was a real person and that he was executed by crucifixion under the Roman government.

So, multiple attestation applies when a saying, event, or theme is present in more than one source. What counts as a source? Historians do not treat the Bible as one book but recognize that it is a collection of individual ancient texts. But scholars do not count Matthew, Mark, Luke, and John as four individual sources. Again, these rules were not written by the church.

The key source for understanding the historical Jesus is the Gospel According to Mark (which most Jesus scholars see as the first Gospel

---

[17]These seven criteria are adapted from Darrell L. Bock, *Who Is Jesus? Linking the Historical Jesus with the Christ of Faith* (New York: Howard, 2012), 16-24.

written). This is a good place to begin any study of the narratives of Jesus' life because almost all of Mark's content is in Matthew or Luke and the other Gospels often follow Mark's outline of the events in Jesus' life.

A second source is a hypothetical one. Scholars call it Q (because the German word for "source," *quelle*, starts with the letter *q*). This merely stands for a body of data that helps explain why Matthew and Luke share about 220 verses of Jesus' teaching between them. Most scholars believe that the authors of these two Gospels did not use each other's work when they wrote their own accounts (e.g., Matthew and Luke have different genealogies). Rather, they likely utilized another source (or a mixture of oral and written sources), and this explains the overlap between them. This shared material between Matthew and Luke is treated as a single independent source, called Q.

Other key sources for the narratives of Jesus' life include the source behind the unique material in the Gospel According to Luke (called L), the source behind the unique material in the Gospel According to Matthew (called M), and the Gospel According to John (which is often relegated to a supporting role, since over 80 percent of the text is unique and cannot easily be corroborated). The epistles of the apostle Paul can also be relevant, although there are limited points of corroboration with Gospel materials. In some cases, Gospels outside the Bible could be mentioned, although there is no clear evidence for a direct link between these and the apostles or the historical Jesus. General details such as the existence of Jesus, his reputation as a miracle worker, and crucifixion under the Roman government may include mentions of ancient, non-Christian sources such as first-century Jewish historian Josephus and second-century Roman historian Tacitus. However, multiple attestation mostly refers to material present in more than one of these: Mark, Q, L, and M. There are subcategories of this rule as well.

Rule one (version A): Multiple attestation of theme. This applies when a theme in a saying or event is present in more than one source. This shows the theme is widespread in the tradition and more likely to represent an authentic theme in the sayings or events in the life of the historical Jesus. For example, the theme of specifically healing lame people is multiply attested in Mark 2:1-12; Matthew 21:14; John 5:1-9; and Q (the source behind Mt 11:2-6 and Lk 7:18-23).

Rule one (version B): Multiple attestation of forms. This applies when a saying or event appears in reports that represent more than one form, or literary category: sayings, reported miracles, controversies, pronouncement stories (where the key point of the story appears in a single saying at the end of the account), legends (stories that exalt Jesus), or myths (supernatural encounters).[18] These categories derive from skeptical scholarship. Still, they can be helpful in building common ground by demonstrating that the saying or report is widespread in the tradition and more likely to represent an authentic saying or event in the life of the historical Jesus. For example, multiple stories about Jesus doing miracles appear in each canonical Gospel in various literary forms.[19]

Rule two: Dissimilarity. Variations of this rule have been debated. For example, the criterion of double dissimilarity has come under fire.[20] This older version pertains to a saying or event in Jesus' life that is very different from Jewish teaching and very different from the early church's teaching. Here is the problem: Jesus was certainly influenced by his Jewish context, and he also influenced the early church. Looking for double dissimilarity results in a concept of Jesus that artificially disconnects him from both his own Jewish culture and the movement he began. So this version of dissimilarity gives us an unhelpful image of a threadbare, minimalistic Jesus who doesn't seem very Jewish and doesn't seem like the founder of Christianity either.

There is a more refined version of dissimilarity, however. This reformulation seeks Jesus material that is not *quite* like Judaism and not *quite*

---

[18]See C. H. Dodd, *The Parables of the Kingdom* (London: Nisbet, 1935), 26-29; also Dodd, *History and the Gospel* (London: Nisbet, 1938), 91-102. For a discussion of form as a literary tool, see Darrell L. Bock, *Studying the Historical Jesus: A Guide to Sources and Methods* (Grand Rapids, MI: Baker Academic, 2002), 185-87.

[19]J. P. Meier, *A Marginal Jew: Rethinking the Historical Jesus*, vol. 2, *Mentor, Message, and Miracles* (New York: Doubleday, 1994), 622; Gerd Theissen and Annette Merz, *The Historical Jesus: A Comprehensive Guide* (Minneapolis: Fortress, 1998), 304-9.

[20]Anthony Le Donne, "The Criterion of Coherence: Its Development, Inevitability, and Historiographical Limitation," in *Jesus, Criteria, and the Demise of Authenticity*, ed. Chris Keith and Anthony Le Donne (London: T&T Clark, 2012), 108.

like Christianity, while still allowing for a Jewish influence on Jesus and Jesus' own influence on the church. Indeed, we should pay close attention to Jesus' sayings that are somewhat similar to Judaism while recognizing his subversion of Jewish conceptions.[21] Jesus is the transitionary figure between Judaism and Christianity. Data that shows this can help us appreciate how Jesus utilized and developed Jewish thought in his own message. So, the best formulation of the dissimilarity rule applies when a reported saying or event includes two things: a concept that is similar to but not exactly like Jesus' Jewish context and a concept that is similar to but not exactly like the early Christian church's context. In this case, the historical Jesus can be seen as the continuum or hinge between two ideas.

Rule three: Rejection and execution. This applies when a saying or event sheds light on how Jesus was rejected by Jewish religious leaders (e.g., scribes, Sanhedrin) and how it came to be that Jesus was crucified under the Roman government. This has been seen as one of the most reliable criteria.[22] Coherence with the other events surrounding the death of Jesus is a strong indication of authenticity. This takes us to the next rule—coherence more broadly understood.

Rule four: Coherence. This applies when a saying or event is consistent with highly evidenced data that is widely accepted as authentic on the basis of the weightier rules of evidence. While this can be somewhat subjective, it can also prove useful for considering material that appears in only one witness, such as the Gospel According to John.

Rule five: Embarrassment. This applies when a saying or event contains embarrassing elements, as it is unlikely that the early church would

---

[21]N. T. Wright, *Jesus and the Victory of God* (London: SPCK, 1996), 132-33. For a discussion of Jesus' adaptation of rabbinic parables, see Paul Barnett, *Finding the Historical Christ*, After Jesus 3 (Grand Rapids, MI: Eerdmans, 2009), 224-27.

[22]Meier, *Marginal Jew*, 1:177. This does not establish that a past event has occurred but rather notes that it coheres with other events surrounding the death of Jesus at the rejection of some Jewish leaders and the hands of the Roman government. See also Stanley E. Porter, "How Do Know What We Think We Know? Methodological Reflections on Jesus Research," in *Jesus Research: New Methodologies and Perceptions—the Second Princeton-Prague Symposium on Jesus Research, Princeton 2007,* ed. James H. Charlesworth, Brian Rhea, and Petr Pokorny (Grand Rapids, MI: Eerdmans, 2014), 97.

create sayings or invent details that would be considered embarrassing to the early church or cast Jesus in a negative light. For example, the crucifixion of Jesus associates him with criminals who suffered capital punishment. Jesus calling the apostle Peter "Satan" (Mk 8:33 // Mt 16:23) paints Peter, one of the pillars of the early church, in a negative light. Still, the rule should not be used negatively. While embarrassing details could help increase probability, the lack of embarrassing details should not count against the authenticity of a saying or event. Due to the somewhat subjective nature of this rule, it often plays a supporting role rather than a primary one in historical investigations.

Rule six: Contextual plausibility. This applies when a saying or event realistically corresponds with Jesus' cultural context, although there may be some aspects that are not quite like the normative cultural expectation. This is similar to what some call the criterion of historical or cultural plausibility—something that is plausible in its Jewish context and can also explain Jesus' influence on the early church.[23] There is some overlap with dissimilarity here, as authentic material should fit Jesus' setting in the early first century and the religious context of Second Temple Judaism while still having some influence on early Christianity that may not neatly fit the tendencies of the early church.

Rule seven: Inherent ambiguity. This applies when a saying or event contains inherent ambiguity or vagueness, as it is less likely that the early church would likely create sayings or event details that are vague rather than clear about something Jesus said or did. This rule is helpful in discussing the authenticity of Jesus' implicit claims. This is especially true when it comes to sayings or events related to the kind of authority that Jesus claimed to possess.

In general, the more criteria that apply to a saying or action, the stronger the corroboration and consequently the conviction of historians that the saying or action is authentic. However, observing these rules of

---

[23]Gerd Theissen and Dagmar Winter, *Saving the Quest*, trans. M. Eugene Boring (Louisville, KY: Westminster John Knox, 2002), 126. Theissen also proposes a criterion of historical plausibility. See Theissen, "Historical Skepticism and Criteria in Jesus Research," in *Handbook for the Study of the Historical Jesus*, ed. Tom Holmen and Stanley E. Porter (Leiden: Brill Academic, 2011), 554.

evidence does not guarantee that a virtual consensus can be reached among researchers. Think of the criteria more as guides that can help keep our study within the bounds of responsible historiography.

OLD, NOT OBSOLETE: USING THE CRITERIA

Not everyone likes the criteria. In fact, the use of these criteria in historical Jesus research is debated. On one hand, some critical scholars call the criteria of authenticity "outdated," saying that we should either seriously revise them or simply abandon them.[24] For example, some question how useful the rules really are in a book called *Jesus, Criteria, and the Demise of Authenticity*.[25] On the other hand, some biblical conservatives resist skeptical methods that are focused on fact-checking the Bible. Most disagreements regarding the criteria stem from expectations placed on the criteria.[26] Skeptics often expect the criteria to help distinguish supposedly unmediated (and therefore "authentic") data from mediated (and therefore "inauthentic") products of the early church. But this is unrealistic. For example, the crucifixion of Jesus is well-recognized as authentic, historical bedrock that is preserved by the church in the canonical Gospels.

Additionally, there are two key non-Christian sources that corroborate the Gospel reports of Jesus' crucifixion. First century-Jewish historian Josephus wrote about the Jewish role in Jesus' death in his work *The Antiquities of the Jews* (18.63-64): "Now there was about this time Jesus, a wise man. . . . Pilate, at the suggestion of the principal men among us, had condemned him to the cross."[27] Early second-century Roman historian Cornelius Tacitus wrote about the Roman role in Jesus' death in *The Annals of Imperial Rome*. This is in the context of

---

[24]Jonathan Bernier, *The Quest for the Historical Jesus After the Demise of Authenticity: Toward a Critical Realist Philosophy of History in Jesus Studies*, Library of New Testament Studies 540 (New York: T&T Clark, 2016), 41n6, 1.

[25]Keith and Le Donne, *Jesus, Criteria*, 94-114.

[26]See Licona's review of Keith and Le Donne, *Jesus, Criteria*. Michael R. Licona, "Is the Sky Falling in the World of Historical Jesus Research?," *Bulletin for Biblical Research* 26, no. 3 (2016): 353-68.

[27]Josephus, *The New Complete Works of Josephus*, trans. William Whiston and commentary by Paul L. Maier, rev. and expanded ed. (Grand Rapids, MI: Kregel, 1999), 590.

mentioning how Nero blamed Christians for the fire in Rome (*Annals* 15.44): "Nero fastened the guilt and inflicted the most exquisite tortures on a class hated for their abominations, called Christians by the populace. Christus, from whom the name had its origin, suffered the extreme penalty during the reign of Tiberius at the hands of one of our procurators, Pontius Pilatus."[28]

So, Jesus' crucifixion is multiply attested across a range of literary forms, including those written by unsympathetic sources. It also coheres with Jesus' rejection by some Jewish leaders and execution at the hands of Rome. Further, the passion accounts include embarrassing elements, including Jesus' crucifixion itself.[29] It is because of such evidence that Ehrman, an agnostic atheist historian, and Crossan, a postmodern historian, agree with biblical conservatives on the crucifixion of Jesus. Indeed, there is virtual consensus that Jesus was crucified. We can rank the crucifixion of Jesus as +4 or certainly historical (i.e., the highest possible probability) on our scale of historical certainty.

In light of this, it would seem difficult for those who reject the criteria to justify the basis for their conclusions on historical bedrock such as Jesus' crucifixion. This is why most researchers have not outright rejected these tools. To what could we appeal if we abandon the criteria? As Licona says, "For those who would call for the abandonment of the criteria or regard them as having little value, I would want to hear from them whether they think Jesus died by crucifixion and, if so, on what basis they have arrived at this conclusion."[30]

Johnathan Bernier is the director of the Lonergan Research Institute, an institute affiliated with Regis College at the University of Toronto. In his book *The Quest for the Historical Jesus After the Demise of Authenticity*, he says we should reject the criteria and instead "focus upon asking

---

[28]Tacitus, *The Complete Works of Tacitus*, trans. Alfred John Church, William Jackson Brodribb, and Sara Bryant (New York: Perseus, Random House, 1942).

[29]For a discussion of the evidence leading to this virtual consensus, see Licona, *Resurrection of Jesus*, 303-18.

[30]Michael R. Licona, "Jesus's Resurrection, Realism, and the Role of the Criteria of Authenticity," in *Jesus, Skepticism and the Problem of History*, ed. Darrell L. Bock and J. Ed Komoszewski (Grand Rapids, MI: Zondervan, 2019), 301.

which texts are more likely to provide us with the most usable data." He rejects the very notion of authenticity but makes a distinction between using the criteria and incorporating insights that may have led to the formulation of specific criteria. Even he admits that his own reasoning appears to use the criteria of dissimilarity.[31] Incorporating insights from the development of other criteria may be helpful as well—even for those who are wary of the criteria. There seems to be little practical difference in employing the logic behind the criteria and using the criteria themselves. So, even scholars who reject the rules of evidence find the logic behind specific criteria helpful.

While the criteria have not allowed scholars to arrive at a consensus about Jesus' self-identity, a similar point could be made in regard to the criminal procedure in the case of a hung jury. Think about what goes on in a jury deliberation. Various perspectives on the same evidence are discussed. When a jury can't reach a unanimous verdict, it doesn't mean that we should throw out the rules of evidence for criminal procedures. In a case where the police mishandled evidence, a jury could reach a verdict without access to all the relevant data. Even this, however, does not suggest the rules of evidence should be rejected. Similarly, we shouldn't confuse someone's use or misuse of the criteria from the criteria themselves. These are merely historiographical tools and, as Princeton New Testament professor Dale Allison puts it, "Tools do not dictate how they are used; the hands that hold them do that."[32] So, the various ways scholars use the criteria don't make them worthless. We don't need to throw them out. We just need to be aware of their limitations. They may be old—but they are not obsolete.

Yes, the individual criteria are not perfect. They certainly have limitations and may fail to give us an accurate understanding of the past when used in isolation. However, using the rules together as a group can help us build a strong cumulative case for the authenticity of a saying or event. When we use stronger criteria alongside others and reduce our

---

[31]Bernier, *Quest for the Historical Jesus*, 41, 75n5.
[32]Dale C. Allison Jr., "It Don't Come Easy: A History of Disillusionment," in Keith and Le Donne, *Jesus, Criteria*, 197.

expectations of the criteria, these tools can help us uncover data that sheds light on the words and deeds of the historical Jesus. This is what we must do in order to have a seat at the table of historical Jesus conversations.

TRUE ENOUGH: UNCOVERING THE SAYINGS OF THE HISTORICAL JESUS

When my son was in elementary school, one of his friends came over to watch the original 1977 movie *Star Wars* (a.k.a. episode IV, *A New Hope*). The boy had never seen the classic film before and was enthralled by the famous scene where a small robot or droid named R2-D2 is playing a game against Chewbacca, a large and imposing creature called a Wookiee. Upon learning that Wookiees can get violent upon defeat, the small droid's companion, C-3PO, says, "I suggest a new strategy, R2. Let the Wookiee win." My son's friend laughed, turned to share the levity of the moment with my son, and exclaimed, "He said 'Let Chewbacca win!'" This is an example of gist and variation. The boy didn't quote the movie verbatim, even just a moment after hearing the famous line. However, because Chewbacca is the Wookiee in this scene, this boy's report was accurate even if his quotation was not precise. We see a similar phenomenon when reading ancient authors. While they wanted to accurately communicate the gist of a saying, they were not generally concerned with meticulously recording the person's precise words.

For example, we can see the gist of Jesus' question preserved with variation across the Synoptics: "Who do people say that the Son of Man is?" (Mt 16:13), "Who do people say that I am?" (Mk 8:27), and "Who do the crowds say that I am?" (Lk 9:18). "The Son of Man" was Jesus' favorite way of referring to himself, so it's not surprising to see this rendered synonymously across the accounts. Because Jesus is the Son of Man in this scene, the reports in Mark and Luke can be accurate even if they are not as precise (assuming Jesus used "the Son of Man" rather than "I" when the event occurred). Similarly, there is no dramatic change in referent from "people" and "the crowds." Regardless of whether the differences reflect Aramaic to Greek translation, stylistic adaptation by the author, or a kind of summary, it is not difficult to understand the point of the question. Even in a dialogue, ancient authors could be accurate without being precise.

What does this mean for "red-letter Bibles" that print the words of Jesus with red ink? While this practice can be helpful in terms of seeing where Jesus is speaking in the narrative, it can give some people the false impression that they are reading an exact transcript of Jesus' words. However, this is not what the Gospel writers intended to record. Like most Jews in the first century, Jesus most often spoke in Aramaic. The earliest manuscript evidence of his teachings contain Greek translations of Jesus' words (except on rare occasions where the Greek text preserves a few Aramaic sayings). So, how do critical scholars go on a quest to uncover the words of the historical Jesus?

On one side of the spectrum, those concerned with precision search for examples of what is called *ipsissima verba*—the very words of Jesus. The problem is that there are variations in reported speech throughout the Gospel accounts. So, the text isn't giving us access to the exact words Jesus said in most places. On the opposite side of the spectrum are those concerned with the differences among Gospels. Think back to the colored beads you saw next to the bottom of a spiral staircase in our construct. In the 1980s and '90s, a skeptical group of scholars known as the Jesus Seminar used beads like these. They popularized the idea that the majority of the sayings attributed to Jesus were edited, embellished, or outright created to meet the needs of early Christian communities.[33] Members of the group voted on the sayings of Jesus using colored beads: red meant definitely historical, pink meant probably historical, gray meant probably not historical, and black meant definitely not historical. They declared, "Eighty-two percent of the words ascribed to Jesus in the gospels were not actually spoken by him."[34] But this is misleading. First,

---

[33]The seminar's "Scholar's Version" of the text (SV) was the result of a secret vote among seminar members on the authenticity of over 1,500 sayings attributed to Jesus. Robert W. Funk, Roy W. Hoover, and the Jesus Seminar, *The Five Gospels: What Did Jesus Really Say? The Search for the Authentic Words of Jesus* (San Francisco: HarperOne, 1996), ix. The text reflects this via color-coded sayings of Jesus in the Gospels: black (0-25 percent, or he did not say this), gray (26-50 percent, or the ideas rather than the words are close to his own), pink (51-75 percent, or he probably said something like this), red (76-100 percent, or he undoubtedly said this or something like it) (36-37).

[34]Funk, Hoover, and the Jesus Seminar, *Five Gospels*, 5.

the group rejected the burden of proof and apparently presupposed that the Gospels were unreliable right from the beginning.[35] Second, it also seems like some skeptics informally created an implicit criterion of limited Christology—that is, a tendency to reject the authenticity of sayings that indicate that Jesus is more than a sage or storyteller.[36] Can we avoid the extremes on either side of the spectrum?

Once again, there is a third way. And that is to recognize that the Gospels usually do not intend to supply more than what is called *ipsissima vox*—the very voice of Jesus. This means an accurate summary that preserves the gist of a saying but without the level of precision you might expect from a twenty-first-century court stenographer. Indeed, the Gospel authors were not trying to provide a literal transcript of Jesus' teachings. Rather, they were content with a reduced summary. It's more like watching an engaging highlight reel than an entire livestreamed event. For example, one of Jesus' longer speeches, the Sermon on the Mount in Matthew 5–7, takes just minutes to read. But it was probably a much longer sermon, as Jesus could hold his audience for hours.[37] Remember, all historical reporting is necessarily selective. While accounts may have been edited, it is unlikely that the Gospel authors created sayings out of whole cloth. Why? The earliest disciples respected Jesus' words and the narrative context of key sayings they felt were worth preserving and contemplating.[38] Rather than the tradition relying on an individual's memory alone, apostles, elders, eyewitnesses, and others were involved in guarding the accuracy of narrative accounts performed in corporate settings. Indeed, faithfully remembering and preserving the words and deeds of Jesus were key concerns of the early Christian community.[39]

---

[35]Funk, Hoover, and the Jesus Seminar, *Five Gospels*, 4-5.

[36]Darrell L. Bock, "The Words of Jesus: Live, Jive, or Memorex?," in *Jesus Under Fire: Modern Scholarship Reinvents the Historical Jesus*, ed. Michael J. Wilkins and J. P. Moreland (Grand Rapids: Zondervan Academic, 1995), 92-93.

[37]E.g., Mk 6:34-36. See Bock, "Words of Jesus," 77-78.

[38]For example, Jesus' sayings in texts such as Mk 2:1-12; 14:53-65 seem tightly connected to the events being portrayed.

[39]James H. Charlesworth, *Jesus Within Judaism: New Light from Exciting Archaeological Discoveries*, Anchor Bible Reference Library (New York: Doubleday, 1988), 20. See also Henry Wansbrough's comment: "The evidence we have been examining attests in itself a concern on the part of the earliest Christians to recall the ministry of Jesus, including not least his words and actions,

Many of Jesus' sayings in Mark's Gospel are closely linked to their narrative context. Here, Jesus' words are the focal point of each passage. For example, the forgiveness saying in Mark 2:5, "Son, your sins are forgiven," makes little sense apart from the narrative of the healing of the paralytic in Mark 2:1-12. Why preserve such a saying apart from a context? This increases the likelihood of its authenticity. Only a few dispute the authenticity of this saying. For example, Jesus Seminar members took a vote using colored beads to categorize this saying as black (0-25 percent certainty or "he did not say this"). They concluded:

> The dispute that occurs in Mark 2:5b-10 over the forgiveness of sins appears only in the synoptic version (Matthew, Mark, Luke). The controversy interrupts the story of the cure—which reads smoothly if one omits vv. 5b-10—and it is absent in the parallel in John. Scholars usually conclude, on the basis of this evidence, that Mark has inserted the dispute into what was originally a simple healing story.[40]

Still, they give no further reasons for rejecting the forgiveness saying itself, which appears in the triple tradition (all three Synoptic Gospels: Matthew, Mark, Luke). It is unclear why the seminar members saw this as a special case and required support from John's Gospel as a criterion for authenticity. Although the saying contains variation in Luke 5:20, "Man, your sins are forgiven you," and in Matthew 9:2, "Take heart, my son; your sins are forgiven," an authentic saying does not need to be an explicitly direct quotation or appear identical in its wording across the Gospel witnesses. Rather, the gist of the saying can be "true enough," to borrow a phrase from Christopher Pelling's evaluation of highly evidenced data in Plutarch's *Lives* (Plutarch was a first- and second-century Greco-Roman historian who wrote a series of ancient biographies on the lives of Roman emperors).[41] So, we can see a certain Gospel text as "true enough" to adequately represent what Jesus was remembered as

---

and to preserve and pass on these traditions." Wansbrough, *Jesus and the Oral Gospel Tradition* (New York: T&T Clark, 2004), 12.

[40]Funk, Hoover, and the Jesus Seminar, *Five Gospels*, 43-44.

[41]Christopher Pelling, *Plutarch and History: Eighteen Studies* (Swansea: Classical Press of Wales, 2011), 152.

communicating—and something his followers felt compelled to preserve and contemplate. Voting on the words of Jesus with colored beads is not the most credible way forward.

This Is How We Do It: The Procedure of This Study

What are the best practices for investigating surviving traces of past events and using the data to reconstruct Jesus' claims and his intended meaning? There are three main phases: The first is concerned with gathering and interpreting surviving traces in order to determine how the data may function as evidence. The second is concerned with using hypotheses to interpret and explain the data, preferring a hypothesis that best explains the evidence. The third concludes the process by producing a narrative account of the most plausible representation of the past event under consideration.[42] Two key questions will guide our study:

1. What key sayings of the historical Jesus can best be demonstrated as being at least probably historical (earning a rating of at least 1, "more probable than not")?
2. In light of Jesus' cultural context, what is the most likely significance of each saying?

The next two major parts of this book will examine two events, present the evidence for the general authenticity of sayings tied to each event, and pay careful attention to the cultural context and its significance with reference to Jesus' claim to possess divine authority. In doing this, we will be following best practices that have proved helpful in the work of the Institute of Biblical Research Jesus Group.[43]

Full Disclosure: A Disclaimer from the Author

Before we begin to build our historical case for Jesus' divine claim, let me put my cards on the table. As part of managing my personal biases, I give

---

[42]Darrell L. Bock and Robert L. Webb, eds., *Key Events in the Life of the Historical Jesus: A Collaborative Exploration of Context and Coherence* (Grand Rapids, MI: Eerdmans, 2010), 33-37.

[43]Adapted from the procedure of the Institute of Biblical Research Jesus Group. See Bock and Webb, *Key Events in the Life*, 83.

the following disclaimer:[44] My interest in historical Jesus studies arose both from my personal faith commitment and a desire to defend essential Christian truth claims with regard to my Lord, Jesus Christ. My educational background includes three advanced degrees earned at conservative evangelical institutions: Biola University in La Mirada, California (MA), and Dallas Theological Seminary in Dallas (ThM, PhD). Today, I am a professor of Bible and theology at Moody Bible Institute in Chicago. In sum, every school with which I am associated holds to the full deity and divine authority of Jesus. Additionally, I host a podcast called *The Apologetics Guy Show* (https://apologeticsguy.com) to help Christians explain their faith with both courage and compassion.

Just as all historical reporting is selective, so all historical studies of Jesus' claims must be selective. When I embarked on this project, I immediately recognized the limits of my study. I was intentionally restricting my investigation to a minimalistic body of highly evidenced data related to Mark 2:1-2; 14:53-65. When I looked at these texts, I asked, "What does the data tell us about the historicity of Jesus' divine claim?" and "Do any recent theories about the kind of authority Jesus claimed to have make the best sense of this data?"

I knew that if my findings were not strong enough to demonstrate that it is at least more likely than not that the historical Jesus claimed to possess divine authority, this would not necessarily mean that Jesus never made any divine claims. Rather, it could indicate a problem with the limits of my approach (e.g., perhaps my sample size of texts was too small, and more than two key scenes must be investigated). In light of this, I never believed that my personal conviction in the deity and divine authority of the real Jesus was at stake during my research. Being cognizant of this was liberating. I was able to proceed freely with a kind of detached interest in the outcome of my investigation. I really did wonder whether it was possible to adequately build a case for Jesus' divine claim that could answer the toughest critics by using highly evidenced data from just a couple of scenes in Jesus' life. By the end of my investigation, I was pleased to find

---

[44]This section is inspired by confessions in Licona, *Resurrection of Jesus*, 130-32.

that it is very possible. I'm excited to walk you through the process step by step as we go on a journey to examine the evidence together.

CONCLUSION

Your orientation to the world of professional historians and the procedure for studying Jesus as a figure in ancient history is complete. What are the top takeaways from our staging area? First, let's recap what we learned in the upper story of the library—the theoretical space where we discussed key philosophical considerations of our study. History is a narrative account of a past event based on a certain interpretation of surviving traces. Historiography relates to the means by which one discovers facts about a past event. Despite hermeneutical challenges, historians can have knowledge of past events by studying surviving traces, since at least some of an author's meaning is accessible to the researcher. Still, conclusions are provisional. When we come to historical conclusions, we should be careful to talk about the probable truth of a hypothesis rather than proclaiming 100 percent certainty. Despite the challenges of postmodernity, historians can still produce narrative accounts that adequately corresponds to past events. Correspondence theory seems most helpful, pragmatic, and true: historical facts are discovered, not created. We should pay close attention to the data resulting in a majority view or near consensus across a spectrum of scholarship, as this can help establish historical bedrock that all theories must take into account.

Next, let's apply what we learned in the upper story to the lower story of the library—the practical, methodological space where we work to accurately reconstruct past events. In light of everything we discussed, our study will operate according to methodological neutrality. We will make an argument to the best explanation and evaluate theories regarding Jesus' divine claim. If the data under consideration more strongly supports a given hypothesis over competing ones or there are more good reasons for accepting it than rejecting it, we'll call that hypothesis "historical" and give it a rating of at least +1 (on a scale of –4 to +4).

Despite its limitations, the criteria of authenticity are not obsolete. These rules of evidence can help us build a cumulative case for the authenticity of a saying or event. Even though the Gospel authors did not intend to provide an exact transcript of Jesus' literal words, an authentic saying may reflect variation in the tradition while retaining the gist of what Jesus meant to communicate. We must also appreciate the importance of the events that provide a context for Jesus' sayings. These events were preserved by people with a high regard for Jesus' words and deeds. While some question both the ability to learn facts about past events and the usefulness of the rules of evidence, it seems too hasty to give up on historical Jesus research. We can still discover things about Jesus using the tools of historical inquiry. Gospel texts based on the memories of those who had experiences of Jesus can inform our investigation and contribute to an accurate, though not exhaustive, representation of the core of key sayings and events in Jesus' life.

PART TWO

The First Blasphemy Accusation Scene

HOW JESUS CLAIMED TO HAVE DIVINE AUTHORITY TO FORGIVE SINS

The Healing of the Paralytic (Mark 2:1-12)

Look, I'm not gonna base my life on a book. There isn't a shred of evidence outside the Bible that Jesus is even real." The words of the skeptical senior stuck with me throughout my college years. I walked away discouraged, with so many thoughts in my head. "How can I find common ground with someone who doesn't see the Bible as an authority?"

Years later, I discovered one way that Christians can have conversations with people who approach the Bible with skepticism: talking about Jesus' claims while engaging critical scholarship on its own terms. Even playing by key rules of evidence that emerged out of twentieth-century skepticism, we can make a historical argument for the biblical portrait of Jesus (e.g., his existence, his reputation as a miracle worker). I've seen this approach open doors to healthy conversations with people who have never thought about Jesus as a real historical figure.

Today, even in church settings, you can encounter people like the skeptical senior, people who don't see the Bible as the answer. For them, the Bible remains the question. How well do the Gospels reflect the words and deeds of Jesus? Having completed our staging area, we are now equipped with the tools we need to build a case for Jesus' divine claim that can stand up to the toughest challenges—even when operating according to standard historical practices and studying Jesus by the rules.

In part two, we will begin our investigation of the historical evidence for Jesus' divine claim, focusing on two blasphemy accusation scenes in the Gospel According to Mark. Our first case study is a story about Jesus known as the healing of the paralytic in Mark 2:1-12.

The Core Scene

A MIRACULOUS HEALING

Sometimes I get into conversations about Jesus with Uber drivers. It often begins with a common question about my trip or my line of work and quicky turns to their own views on religion or Jesus. One snowy day in Denver, an Uber driver asked me about the event I was attending at a large convention center: an annual meeting of the Evangelical Theological Society. Part of my answer had to do with the very book you are now holding in your hands! I told him that I studied Jesus as a figure in ancient history and I was meeting with an editor about the possibility of publishing my research. That got his attention. He told me that he wasn't religious but that he liked history. What turned into a forty-five-minute conversation all the way to the airport began with questions about how to understand Jesus as a miracle worker in his cultural and historical contexts. He asked questions such as, "Didn't people believe in all sorts of miracle workers back in the day?" and "Was Jesus really any different?" He seemed genuinely interested in a historical approach to his questions, especially because he had heard people say that miracle workers were a dime a dozen in the ancient world. We eventually focused on the way critical scholars investigate whether Jesus said anything that made him stand out from other miracle-working figures of the ancient world.

This conversation takes us straight to our first blasphemy accusation scene: the healing of the paralytic in Mark 2:1-12 (paralleled by Mt 9:1-8; Lk 5:17-26). Critical scholars who search for historical bedrock about Jesus tend to pay close attention to stories that make sense of his reputation as a miracle worker and healer—especially narratives in the earliest Gospel accounts. That's why the healing of the paralytic is an important scene to investigate. It's the first miracle story in the earliest Gospel, which is the Gospel According to Mark. It's a beautiful story about how Jesus had compassion on a paralyzed man and healed him. But before doing so, he said, "Son, your sins are forgiven" (Mk 2:5), and we read that the scribes who were present believed that only God possessed authority to forgive sins. This reveals an often-overlooked data point that supports Jesus' uniqueness as a miracle worker. Indeed, the part of the data that tells us that Jesus was known as a miracle worker also tells us that he was known as a unique kind of miracle worker. What makes him stand out among the others? His claim to forgive sins. This is key to building a historical case for his claim to possess divine authority.

ANSWERING SKEPTICISM IN CHURCH AND SOCIETY

Building a historical case for this scene gives us a way into a conversation about Jesus' claims when talking with people who doubt that biblical stories accurately reflect events that happened in the past. It is not surprising that scholarly skepticism toward the Bible can lead many people outside the church to doubt the historicity of Jesus' divine claims. However, this kind of skepticism is gaining ground even in the church.

Remember that study called the State of Theology conducted by Lifeway and Ligonier Ministries? In 2022, it noted "a rising disbelief in the Bible's literal truth," reporting that 26 percent of American evangelicals agree with the idea, "The Bible, like all sacred writings, contains helpful accounts of ancient myths but is not literally true."[1] What contributes to this? Ideas discussed in academic journals and scholarly

---

[1] See statement 16 in the 2022 State of Theology, https://thestateoftheology.com/.

literature often influence popular objections to the historicity of the Gospel accounts. This is why we need to pay attention to the questions being raised by critical scholars.

In his popular book *How Jesus Became God*, Bart Ehrman mentions the possibility that reported activities in the Gospels "*may* not even go back to the historical Jesus" and "*may* be traditions assigned to Jesus by later storytellers in order to heighten his eminence and significance" (emphasis added). While historians might agree that almost anything *may* possibly be the case, researchers must ask questions about plausibility and probability when evaluating the evidence. For Ehrman, many Gospel traditions "cannot pass the criterion of dissimilarity."[2] We noted this criterion in our discussion of the rules of evidence commonly used in historical Jesus studies. Can our first scene pass this test? What about other tests?

Ehrman is not alone in questioning this scene. Among the critics is a professor named Tobias Hägerland. His work brings the strongest historical challenge to the authenticity of the scribal reaction and Jesus' response in our first blasphemy accusation scene. Hägerland is a senior lecturer in religious studies and theology at the University of Gothenburg in Sweden and the author of a scholarly monograph called *Jesus and the Forgiveness of Sins: An Aspect of His Prophetic Mission*. In his monograph, Hägerland calls the historical accuracy of the healing of the paralytic into question on the grounds that Jewish scribes could not have believed that Jesus usurped a divine prerogative. Why? Because, he asserts, nondivine figures were also believed to have forgiven sins committed against God.[3]

This is an argument we cannot ignore. The integrity of our quest leads us to engage the best arguments against the historicity of this scene. In order to do honest research and follow the evidence where it leads, we must engage with Hägerland's bold challenge as we work to build a historical case for Jesus' divine claim. The conclusions we draw will be much

---

[2]Bart D. Ehrman, *How Jesus Became God: The Exaltation of a Jewish Preacher from Galilee* (New York: HarperOne, 2015), 127 (emphasis added).
[3]Tobias Hägerland, *Jesus and the Forgiveness of Sins: An Aspect of His Prophetic Mission* (Cambridge: Cambridge University Press, 2011), 137.

stronger after we journey through a difficult path and meet this challenge head-on.

OUR ITINERARY

As we begin our journey, we will consider a positive case for the plausibility of the core scene and examine key challenges against its historicity in light of Hägerland's theory. We have five stops on our itinerary before drawing our conclusions.

First, we will discuss the positive evidence for the plausibility of the core scene. Second, we will examine the authenticity for Jesus' forgiveness saying, "Son, your sins are forgiven" (Mk 2:5). Third, we will respond to objections to the historicity of the scribal response. Fourth, we will examine the significance of the forgiveness saying in light of Jewish concepts of blasphemy and miraculous healing. Fifth, we will assess challenges to Jesus' authority saying in this scene: "that you may know that the Son of Man has authority on earth to forgive sins" (Mk 2:10). Could this have been added to the story?

After these five stops, we will weigh the evidence and use the scale of historical certainty from chapter one to answer the question, Was the historical Jesus accurately remembered as a unique miracle worker who claimed to possess authority on earth to forgive sin? How well can we demonstrate that the answer is yes, on purely historical grounds?

THE RULES

As we investigate the data that supports Jesus' claim to possess divine authority on earth to forgive sins, we need to remember the seven rules of evidence from our briefing in the staging area. These rules allow scholars across a range of religious commitments (as well as those who do not identify with any faith tradition) to examine biblical texts as ancient documents and discuss what the historical Jesus likely claimed about himself. Most historians recognize that when one or more of these rules apply to a certain saying or event, the probability that the saying or event accurately represents Jesus is significantly increased. Let's review the criteria of authenticity (we'll call them "rules" for short) using examples (see table 3.1).

Table 3.1. Rules of evidence

Rule Number	Rule Name	Description	Example
1	multiple attestation	A saying, event, or theme is present in more than one source. Key sources: • Mark • John • M = unique material in Matthew • L = unique material in Luke • Q = material shared by Matthew and Luke that does not appear in Mark	Jesus' crucifixion: e.g., • Paul[4] • Q[5] • Canonical Gospels[6] • Josephus[7] • Tacitus[8] • Lucian of Samosata[9] See versions A and B below for more examples.
1 (version A)	multiple attestation of theme	A theme in a saying or event appears in more than one source.	Jesus' working miracles is a theme supported by Mark, Q, M, L, and John. Also sources outside the Bible: Justin Martyr, Josephus, Celsus, the Jewish Talmud.
1 (version B)	multiple attestation of forms	A saying or event appears in reports that represent more than one form, or literary category: • pronouncement: report where the climax is Jesus' authoritative statement • controversy • saying • legend: report that exalts Jesus • myth: report of supernatural encounter • miracle	Jesus' reputation as a miracle worker is supported by various literary forms in each Gospel. E.g.: • pronouncement: Mark 2:10-11 • controversy: Mark 3:22 • legend: Mark 5:41-42 • myth: Mark 6:49-50 • miracle: Mark 10:52
2	dissimilarity	A saying or event is both • similar to but not quite like Judaism • similar to but not quite like Christianity	Jesus' use of "the Son of Man" as a self-reference employs the definite article, distinguishing it from the common "son of man" used in Judaism. However, the early church did not commonly refer to Jesus as the Son of Man.
3	rejection and execution	A saying or event sheds light on how Jesus was rejected by Jewish religious leaders and crucified under Rome.	Jesus' clash with Jewish religious leaders, such as Sabbath controversies (e.g., Mk 2:23-28; 3:1-6) over his claimed authority

---

[4]E.g., Gal 3:1; 5:11; 6:12-14; 1 Cor 1:17-18, 22-23; 2:1-2.
[5]Mt 10:38; 16:24 = Lk 14:27.
[6]E.g., Mk 15:24; Jn 18:18.
[7]Josephus, *Jewish Antiquities* 18.63-64.
[8]Tacitus, *Annals* 15.44.
[9]Lucian, *The Death of Peregrinus* 11-13.

4	coherence	A saying or event is consistent with highly evidenced data that is widely accepted as authentic.	Jesus' saying "The Son of Man has authority on earth to forgive sins" (Mk 2:10) coheres with Jesus' consistent self-identification as the Son of Man throughout the Gospels, which is widely accepted as authentic.
5	embar-rassment	A saying or event contains embarrassing elements.	Jesus' crucifixion was a shameful method of execution in the ancient world and is unlikely to have been invented by his followers.
6	contextual plausibility	A saying or event realistically corresponds with Jesus' cultural context.	Jesus' use of "the Son of Man" aligns with both a cultural self-reference and Jewish reflection on a transcendent figure (see Dan 7:13-14).
7	inherent ambiguity	A saying or event that contains vagueness is more likely to be authentic, as the church would have invented a more explicit reference to deity.	Jesus' use of "the Son of Man" allowed more than one interpretation, from a simple self-reference to a transcendent figure (see Dan 7:13-14).

Jesus' Reputation as a Miracle Worker

Before building a positive case for the plausibility of the core scene, let us consider how just the first couple of rules support Jesus' reputation as a miracle worker. This reputation is the historical foundation on which we will begin an investigation of our first blasphemy accusation scene—the healing of the paralytic.

First, consider rule one: multiple attestation. Jesus' reputation as a miracle worker is multiply attested in Mark, Q, M, L, and John. Further, the idea that Jesus was remembered as a miracle worker is also corroborated by Greek apologist Justin Martyr and non-Christian sources, including first-century Jewish historian Josephus, a second-century Gentile opponent of Christianity named Celsus, and even the central text of rabbinic Judaism, the Talmud.[10] Second, consider rule two:

---

[10]Justin Martyr: "He [Jesus] compelled the men who lived at that time to recognize Him. But though they saw such works, they asserted it was magical art. For they dared to call Him a magician, and a deceiver of the people." *Dialogue with Trypho* 69, trans. Marcus Dods and George Reith, New Advent, accessed June 21, 2021, www.newadvent.org/fathers/01286.htm. Jesus is

multiple attestation of forms. Multiple miracle stories also appear in each Gospel in various literary forms.[11]

This is why there is a virtual consensus among New Testament scholars that Jesus performed unusual acts that many Jews perceived as miraculous healings. Indeed, Jesus' identity as a miraculous healer and exorcist is often recognized as among the bedrock facts regarding the historical Jesus. In fact, most critical scholars agree that Jesus did unusual things that many people at least interpreted as legitimate miracles and exorcisms. Recall how Fredriksen can be skeptical of the reality of miracles while acknowledging that "Jesus probably did perform deeds that contemporaries viewed as miracles."[12] Crossan cofounded the Jesus Seminar, a group of critical scholars who reject the authenticity of many Gospel sayings and deeds attributed to Jesus. However, even he agrees that "Jesus was both an exorcist and a healer."[13] This bears mentioning yet again. This sampling of scholars is not an appeal to authority but rather a demonstration that scholars across a wide range of backgrounds, religious commitments, and those of no faith can hold that Jesus' reputation as a miracle worker is a bedrock fact because they recognize the strength of the evidence based on key rules of evidence. This is how even critical scholars can agree with biblical conservatives on certain facts about the historical Jesus. Jesus' reputation as a miracle worker, then, may be used as a foundation from

---

likely reported as performing unusual, wonderful deeds in the earliest reading of Josephus, *Jewish Antiquities* 18.63-64. For a discussion on interpolations in the extant copies of this text, see Darrell L. Bock, *Studying the Historical Jesus: A Guide to Sources and Methods* (Grand Rapids, MI: Baker Academic, 2002), 55-57. Origen notes Celsus's assertion that Jesus obtained magical powers in Egypt in *Against Celsus* 1.28. The Babylonian Talmud charges Jesus with practicing sorcery in Sanhedrin 43a.

[11]Meier sees "three major literary forms: exorcisms, healings (including stories of raising the dead), and nature miracles." J. P. Meier, *A Marginal Jew: Rethinking the Historical Jesus*, vol. 2, *Mentor, Message, and Miracles* (New York: Doubleday, 1994), 622. See also Gerd Theissen and Annette Merz, *The Historical Jesus: A Comprehensive Guide* (Minneapolis: Fortress, 1998), 304-9.

[12]Paula Fredriksen, *Jesus of Nazareth: King of the Jews* (New York: Vintage, 1999), 264.

[13]John Dominic Crossan, *The Historical Jesus: The Life of a Mediterranean Jewish Peasant* (San Francisco: HarperSanFrancisco, 1991) 332. See also Robert Walter Funk and the Jesus Seminar, *The Acts of Jesus: What Did Jesus Really Do?* (San Francisco: HarperSanFrancisco, 1998), 527. Regarding exorcisms, Ehrman notes that Jesus' "ability to cast the demons out was seen as a characteristic aspect of his ministry. Moreover, the controversy over him was not about whether he had this ability but whether he had this power from God or the devil." Bart D. Ehrman, *Jesus: Apocalyptic Prophet of the New Millennium* (New York: Oxford University Press, 1999), 198.

which we can engage with critical scholarship and show that the healing of the paralytic represents an event in the life of the historical Jesus. With the recognition of historical bedrock, let us begin our journey.

THE HISTORICITY OF THE CORE SCENE

Our first stop lands us in the first century AD. We come upon an ancient home in the Galilean town of Capernaum. Like many homes in the area, the roof is constructed from beams and branches of trees covered with a mixture of earth and straw. Our first blasphemy accusation scene is ground zero for building a historical case for the divine claim of Jesus. It is the very first controversy in Mark's Gospel. It appears not only in Mark's Gospel but in the triple tradition (Mk 2:1-12; Mt 9:1-8; Lk 5:17-26). The existence of these three texts suggests that each author considered such a historic event memorable and worthy of contemplation. In each account, we find three core elements: Jesus (1) heals a paralytic, (2) tells him that his sins are forgiven, and (3) explains the significance of the healing. Every single account portrays the healing as proof that the Son of Man has authority on earth to forgive sins. Historians pay special attention to the earliest form of any story when gathering data. Why? Because they reason that the earliest form is less likely to contain the kind of embellishments that might develop over time. In light of this practice, let's follow suit and focus our investigation on Mark's account of our first blasphemy accusation scene.

MULTIPLE ATTESTATION OF KEY THEMES

Let's think about version A of rule one: multiple attestation of theme. The narrative has three key themes that are multiply attested throughout the Synoptic Gospels: Jesus working miracles, healing the lame, and pronouncing forgiveness. We already mentioned Jesus' reputation as a miracle worker—a bedrock fact from which we can begin to discuss the scene. Second, Jesus' healing of lame people (Mk 2:1-12; Mt 21:14; 11:2-6 // Lk 7:18-23 = Q 7:22-23; Jn 5:1-9) and his clash with the Pharisees and their scribes is also multiply attested (Mk 3:22; Mt 23:13-14; Lk 11:53; the tradition behind Jn 8:3). Third, Jesus' announcing forgiveness also exists in the triple tradition of the Synoptics and in L (Mk 2:5 // Mt 9:2; Lk 5:20).[14] Hägerland agrees that this increases the probability that Jesus was known as a miracle worker, was believed to have healed lame people, and pronounced forgiveness with regard to specific people.[15] In light of this, historians can see the healing of the paralytic as worthy of investigation. It coheres with the data that drives a virtual consensus among critical scholars that Jesus was at least remembered as a miracle worker. But was he remembered as more than a miracle worker?

THE AUTHENTICITY OF JESUS' FORGIVENESS SAYING IN MARK 2:5

In the mid-twentieth century, researchers working on the Yale-French Excavations in Syria discovered a wall painting from around AD 232 above the baptistry of a house church in an ancient city called Dura-Europos. This is believed to be the earliest surviving artistic depiction of one of Jesus' miracles.[16] Seeing the image on plaster reminded me of the way a comic book tells a story, although there are no clearly defined panels on the artifact. It depicts one scene where a man is lying on a mat alongside another scene where the man is carrying his mat. Jesus is depicted as standing above both scenes. The art gallery at Yale University displayed this 57″-by-34″ piece as "Baptistery wall painting: Christ Healing the Paralytic."[17] Archaeology contributes physical evidence to

---

[14]The core of narrative context surrounding Lk 7:47-48 is distinct from the healing of the paralytic in the Synoptics. Although Hägerland holds that Lk 7:36-50 is dependent on Mark and Lk 7:48-50 was likely Luke's creation, he grants that at least Lk 7:36-43, 47 are not derived from Mark and may be "invoked as an independent witness . . . [verse] 47 stems largely from a source (L) or from a pre-Lukan tradition. . . . Independently of Mark, Luke 7:47 therefore attests to Jesus' announcement of forgiveness for specific individuals." Hägerland, *Jesus and the Forgiveness of Sins*, 57-59, 83.

[15]Hägerland, *Jesus and the Forgiveness of Sins*, 84.

[16]Daniel Esparza, "The First Painting of Any of Jesus' Miracles Dates from the 3rd Century," Aleteia, October 12, 2019, https://aleteia.org/2019/10/12/the-first-painting-of-any-of-jesus -miracles-dates-from-the-3rd-century/.

[17]See "Baptistery Wall Painting: Christ Healing the Paralytic," Yale University Art Gallery, accessed September 1, 2023, https://artgallery.yale.edu/collections/objects/34498. Some have also linked this to a separate miracle story described in Jn 5:2-19. See "Wall Painting of Christ Healing the Paralytic," New York University Institute for the Study of the Ancient World, accessed January 25, 2025, https://isaw.nyu.edu/exhibitions/edge-of-empires/highlights/christ-healing -paralytic.

Figure 3.1. Baptistery wall painting: Christ healing the paralytic (AD 232)

our study by showing how early Christian communities created art to preserve and contemplate the meaning of this beautiful and deeply profound scene from the life of Jesus.

Our second stop focuses on the strength of the historical evidence for Jesus' intriguing saying tied to this scene: "Son, your sins are forgiven" (Mk 2:5). It is this saying and the scribal response that attracts the most debate in terms of understanding Jesus' claims. Let's begin thinking through how the rules of evidence apply. Jesus' forgiveness saying is supported by at least three criteria: dissimilarity (rule two), rejection and execution (rule three), and coherence (rule four).

First, the saying is dissimilar to Christian views on forgiveness, faith, and salvation. While the earliest Christians closely linked faith and salvation, they focused on christological and soteriological aspects rather than physical healing.[18] They also did not clearly ascribe forgiveness to Jesus but to God. Outside the Gospels, it is difficult to find a Scripture text that clearly identifies Jesus as the agent of forgiveness.

Second, the criterion of rejection and execution applies. Jesus' forgiveness saying generated a strong reaction in the minds of the scribes who believed Jesus was blaspheming (Mk 2:6-7). Further, it prefigures Jesus' rejection at his Jewish examination (Mk 14:64) and contributes to the explanation of his rejection and execution.[19]

Third, the saying coheres with Jesus' words in Luke 7:47-48: "'Therefore I tell you, her sins, which are many, are forgiven. . . . ' And he said to her, 'Your sins are forgiven.'" This represents a saying theme that is multiply attested in both Markan and L material. Even Hägerland agrees that Mark 2:5 is coherent with Jesus' sayings in the context of his miracles (Mk 5:34; see Mk 10:52 // Lk 18:42; 7:50; 17:19).[20] In light of these criteria, most scholars hold that this saying goes back to the historical Jesus.

---

[18]Hägerland cites Rom 10:9; Acts 16:31 (*Jesus and the Forgiveness of Sins*, 190).

[19]In Lev 24:15-23, blasphemy is shown to be a capital offense punishable by stoning. Cranfield notes the response implies "the scribes were already contemplating his destruction." C. E. B. Cranfield, *The Gospel According to St Mark: An Introduction and Commentary* (New York: Cambridge University Press, 1959), 98.

[20]Mark's narrative comment in Mk 2:5a makes explicit the connection between faith and forgiveness, which was already implicit in Jesus' saying in Mk 2:5b.

But some who admit that Jesus' forgiveness saying is historical may still wonder, "Did Jesus really mean to represent himself as forgiving sin by his own authority? Or was he just saying that God forgave the man?" Ehrman suggests the latter is what is going on here. He writes, "When Jesus forgives sins, he never says '*I* forgive you,' as God might say, but 'your sins are forgiven,' which means that *God* has forgiven the sins."[21] This is a fair challenge to raise. So, who's doing the forgiving? It's easy to wonder whether Jesus' use of the passive voice in "your sins are forgiven" might best be understood grammatically as a "divine passive," referring to God and not Jesus as the source of forgiveness. However, it is the narrative itself that must guide our understanding of the grammar. In fact, the so-called divine passive is not itself a syntactic category in Greek grammar.[22] The agent of forgiveness must be determined by context rather than by uncritically appealing to a presumed "divine passive" category.[23] In other words, we should look to the story itself—not a Greek grammar textbook—to verify the agent. In fact, passive verbs without an explicitly stated agent do not always imply divine agency. For example, there are four examples of apparently divine passives in Mark's miracle tradition that allow Jesus as the subject (Mk 1:40-42; 3:5; 5:27-30, 32-35).[24] Something many scholars miss by focusing exclusively on Mark's account is the fact that Jesus follows the way God is portrayed as using the passive "forgiven" when declaring the forgiveness of sins in the Hebrew Scriptures (e.g., Lev 4:31, "he shall be forgiven") and in Jewish texts outside the Bible.[25] Thus, the very ambiguity of the passive construction

---

[21]Ehrman, *How Jesus Became God*, 127, emphasis added.

[22]Wallace notes that "the divine passive is simply a specific type" of an existing category that is "obvious from the passage, due to focus on the subject, otherwise obtrusive, or for rhetorical effect." Daniel B. Wallace, *Greek Grammar Beyond the Basics: An Exegetical Syntax of the New Testament with Scripture, Subject, and Greek Word Indexes* (Grand Rapids, MI: Zondervan, 1997), 438.

[23]Sigurd Grindheim, *God's Equal: What Can We Know About Jesus' Self-Understanding?* (London: A&C Black, 2011), 66. D. A. Carson and Stanley Porter conclude the idea of a "divine passive" category is speculative and confuses grammar and theology in Stanley Porter, *Idioms of the Greek New Testament*, 2nd ed. (London: Bloomsbury T&T Clark, 1992), 65-66.

[24]Beniamin Pascut, *Redescribing Jesus' Divinity Through a Social Science Theory: An Interdisciplinary Analysis of Forgiveness and Divine Identity in Ancient Judaism and Mark 2:1-12*, Wissenschaftliche Untersuchungen zum Neuen Testament 2/438 (Tübingen: Mohr Siebeck, 2017), 158-63.

[25]"Jesus' use of the passive voice therefore followed the pattern of the Hebrew Bible when God declares that someone's sins are forgiven (Lev. 4.31, 35; 5.10, 13,16, 18, 26)." Grindheim, *God's*

bolsters the case for the authenticity of the saying. Why? Because a later invention or development by the early church would probably want to clarify the agent of forgiveness—not make it vague.[26] If the early church wanted to create a saying out of whole cloth and put it on the lips of Jesus, they would likely produce a clearer statement like, "I forgive your sins." So, we find that inherent ambiguity (rule seven) seems to apply here.

Beyond this, the evidence supporting the authenticity of the saying also bolsters the case for the authenticity of our blasphemy accusation scene itself. Think about it. Why would a saying be preserved all by itself, without a context? Think back to the original 1977 movie *Star Wars*. Among the most famous lines from classic Hollywood movies is this phrase from the film: "May the force be with you." Why has this saying been preserved for decades in the popular culture? This phrase doesn't mean much apart from the Star Wars universe—a franchise imbued with such cultural cache that its influence continues to shape twenty-first-century movies, video games, theme park attractions, and innumerable cultural artifacts. It is the story that fills the phrase "May the force be with you" with meaning, and it is the story on which the phrase depends for its continued remembrance in the popular culture.

My point is that while the phrase lives on in our shared cultural memory, it was not preserved in isolation, apart from a cinematic context. This reasoning also applies to true stories as well and helps when investigating questions of ancient history. We are considering a saying of Jesus supported by historical data, and memorable quotations generally arise from memorable contexts. It seems unlikely that Jesus' highly evidenced saying, "Son, your sins are forgiven," would be preserved in isolation, apart from the story of the healing of the paralytic. Indeed, Jesus' forgiveness saying wouldn't mean much without a narrative context. It is not just a generic saying. It's a specific one. This is another reason to

---

Equal, 67. As an example of a Jewish text outside the Bible, God's response to David's plea for forgiveness is passive in Babylonian Talmud Shabbat. 30a. See also Avot of Rabbi Nathan 9:2; Midrash Psalm 19:13; Rabbati Leviticus 5:8; Babylonian Talmud Sanhedrin 107a; Hermann Leberecht Strack and Paul Billerbeck, *Kommentar zum Neuen Testament aus Talmud und Midrasch* (Munich: Beck, 1922–1961), 2:585.
[26]It is perhaps this ambiguity that Mk 2:10 clarifies.

consider the core of our first blasphemy accusation scene as representative of a real historical event.

THE GREATEST CHALLENGE

Back to my Uber ride. The driver seemed fascinated by how historical Jesus studies as a discipline could bring together researchers from a variety of religious backgrounds and even those of no faith tradition to discuss what history could tell us about the sayings of Jesus and the key events of his life. As we were talking about the healing of the paralytic, he asked, "But not everyone agrees with what the Bible says about the story, right?" I said, "Yes, there are scholars who say that part of the story couldn't have happened. In my dissertation research, I actually found what I think is the biggest challenge that critics have brought against this particular story. One thing I found interesting is that it's not actually the miracle that's contested. It's the reaction of some of the Jewish scribes who heard what Jesus said." He gave me a curious look using the rearview mirror. He nodded, and his expression indicated that he wanted me to continue. This was shaping up to be an interesting ride.

I explained that some critical scholars such as Hägerland question the authenticity of our first blasphemy accusation scene. Why? Mark 2:6-7 tells us that the scribes who heard Jesus were thinking, "Why does this man speak like that? He is blaspheming! Who can forgive sins but God alone?" That's a good question. It's a rhetorical question that assumes a response of "no one." However, Hägerland insists that the scribes could not have assumed that Jesus usurped a divine prerogative. He asserts that it was not merely "God alone" who could forgive sins. He asserts that some nondivine figures of the ancient world forgave sins as well.[27] This is the very foundation of his objection to the credibility of the Markan narrative. This could potentially be the greatest challenge raised against the historicity of our first blasphemy accusation scene. But what about this? Can we really find examples of ancient figures in earlier texts who claim to forgive sins?

---

[27]Hägerland, *Jesus and the Forgiveness of Sins*, 137.

Discovering the answer will take us on a fascinating excursion through texts about Greco-Roman miracle workers and ancient Jewish figures, including a little-known fragment from the Dead Sea Scrolls that even some conservative Christian scholars say could present the very best argument against the claim that Jesus was a unique miracle worker. The next chapter brings us to the third and fourth stops on this leg of our journey.

4

A Blasphemy Accusation

WHO CAN FORGIVE SINS?

Why does this man speak like that? He is blaspheming!
Who can forgive sins but God alone?

MARK 2:7

Our third stop is like a long layover. In this part of our investigation, we'll examine texts from around the ancient world in order to answer a couple of key questions: Is there any record of other ancient figures claiming to forgive sins like Jesus did in the broader Greco-Roman world? What about in Jesus' own Jewish culture? Answering these historical questions is an important part of coming to an informed conclusion about the uniqueness of Jesus' forgiveness saying. This chapter will help us work through the challenges to our first blasphemy accusation scene by presenting evidence for the authenticity of the scribal response.

WHO COULD FORGIVE SINS IN THE ANCIENT WORLD?

Some critical scholars raise the question, "Was it really 'God alone' who could forgive sins?" This question refers to forgiveness in general. That's the kind of forgiveness that goes beyond the way you or I can forgive others if they intentionally offend us. When we talk about forgiving sins in this context, we are talking about third-party forgiveness. Who can legitimately claim to forgive you for something you did to your mother? People in the ancient world had the same question.

Let's get started by considering one of the ancient world's most dysfunctional relationships. In *The Life of Nero*, Roman historian Suetonius tells us the twisted tale of the Emperor Nero and his mother—and perhaps the one time this sadistic ruler ever felt a compelling need for forgiveness.

Divine forgiveness in Greco-Roman texts. To say that Nero had a bad relationship with his mother would be an understatement. She got on his nerves by constantly monitoring him and criticizing much of what he did. Eventually, he kicked her out of the palace. He even bribed people to harass her with lawsuits until she left the city. When she threatened him back, he tried to poison her—three times! She apparently knew about his attempts to poison her and began taking antidotes. So, Nero built a mechanical device that would make the panels of her bedroom ceiling fall on her as she slept. However, his plot was exposed by a coconspirator. Then he tried a new tactic. He pretended to reconcile with his mother by inviting her to attend the feast of Minerva with him. But this was all part of an elaborate plan to get her onto a boat he had sabotaged so that she would be killed in a shipwreck en route to the event. But Nero's plan failed yet again as his mother swam away to safety! In the end, he simply had her killed. Afterward, he framed her and her associate for plotting to assassinate him, painting her death as a suicide brought about by the discovery of her supposed conspiracy.[1]

Despite his reputation for the merciless murders of thousands of people, Nero carried a guilty conscience for what he did to his mother. He reports being haunted by her ghost and tormented by the Furies (ancient goddesses of vengeance). To alleviate his guilt, he asked the magi to perform a kind of séance so that he might beg his mother's ghost for forgiveness.[2] Nero did not seem to view religious figures such as the magi

---

[1]Suetonius, *Nero* 34.

[2]Suetonius, *Nero* 34.4. "He was hounded by his mother's ghost and by the whips and blazing torches of the Furies. He even had rites performed by the Magi, in the effort to summon her shade

as having authority to forgive sins, and there is no evidence that they purported to forgive Nero's sins against his mother.

Apart from this, it is unlikely that other Greco-Roman rituals included people pronouncing forgiveness—even in connection with sacrifices.[3] We can discover some details about such sacrifices by reading Homer's portrayals in *The Iliad* and *The Odyssey*.[4] While these stories depict priests offering up prayers to deities, the priests are never presented as announcing forgiveness. Even miracle-working accounts of Hellenistic "divine men" do not describe any human mediation of divine forgiveness. Whether you read the tales of deified healers such as Asclepius; his two superhuman sons, Machaon and Podarlirius; Machaon's own four sons; Menecrates of Syracuse; or Pyrrhus, you won't find anything like Jesus' forgiveness saying.[5]

While some Romans probably understood the notion of asking a certain deity for forgiveness after somehow offending the deity, there is no mention of any human being claiming to forgive sins in general. In fact, forgiveness seems to be ascribed to deities. For example, Greek writer Dionysius of Halicarnassus wrote a twenty-book series called *Roman Antiquities* around 7 BC. This includes a text describing the Trojan hero Aeneas explaining his aggressive actions to King Latinus. Here, the king says that he would "ask the gods and daimones (lesser spirits) that rule this very land to be forgiving to us and of the things we do out of necessity, and we will try to fend you off as assailants in this war."[6]

---

and entreat it for forgiveness." Translated by J. C. Rolfe, "The Life of Nero," Lexundria, https://lexundria.com/suet_nero/33-39/r.

[3]For a description of sacrificial rituals, see Hans-Josef Klauck, *The Religious Context of Early Christianity: A Guide to Graeco-Roman Religions*, trans. Brian McNeal, Studies of the New Testament and Its World (Edinburgh: T&T Clark, 2000), 24.

[4]In *Iliad* 1.458-68, an old priest of Apollo asks the deity to remove a curse from the Greek army and to stop punishing them: "When they had offered up prayers and sprinkled the barley grains . . ." In *Odyssey* 3.445-63, Nestor offers a cow to the goddess Athene, and an additional detail, the shouting of women present for the sacrifice, is also mentioned: "Nestor started the ritual. . . . When they had prayed and sprinkled the barley meal . . . the women raised their celebratory cry."

[5]For a summary of the ancient traditions surrounding these pre-Christian healers, see Barry Blackburn, *Theios Anēr and the Markan Miracle Traditions: A Critique of the Theios Anēr Concept as an Interpretative Background of the Miracle Traditions Used by Mark* (Tübingen: Mohr Siebeck, 1991), 24-28.

[6]Dionysius of Halicarnassus, *Roman Antiquities* 1.58.3-4, in Zsuzsanna Várhelyi, "'To Forgive Is Divine': Gods as Models of Forgiveness in Late Republican and Early Imperial Rome," in *Ancient*

The closest story to Jesus' healing of the paralytic may be an inscription from an ancient healing center called the Asclepieion of Epidaurus. Located in a small, secluded valley, it is considered a masterpiece of Greek architecture. It was built for Asclepius, the god of healing, and people traveled long distances longing for a miraculous cure to their aliments. When they arrived, they entered the building and read this cure inscription: "Nicanor, a lame man. While he was sitting wide-awake, a boy snatched his crutch from him and ran away. But Nicanor got up, pursued him, and so became well."[7] While this may be the closest Greco-Roman story to the healing of the paralytic, there is no meaningful parallel to Jesus. Here the boy does not even speak, and he certainly does not pronounce forgiveness.

When I first came across this sparse text with very little context, I wondered whether it even described a healing at all. It reminded me of a modern-day news report from the Philippines, around the area where I grew up. A 2021 headline in the *Manila Bulletin* read, "Look It's a Miracle! Crippled Beggar Chases, Tries to Stab Coast Guard Man on EDSA Bus Stop." According to the report:

> Commuters and a marshal of the Philippine Coast Guard (PCG) got a [*sic*] surprise of their lives after they witnessed how a beggar on crutches suddenly began to walk and even ran later at the EDSA Carousel Ortigas Avenue stop. No, it wasn't a miracle but a man pretending to be disable[d] who suddenly forgot his acting skills over intense anger when PCG Marshal . . . attempted to escort him away from the busway. . . . The man was threatening the commuters with a knife if they would not give him money.[8]

Forgiveness: Classical, Judaic, and Christian, ed. Charles L. Griswold and David Konstan (Cambridge: Cambridge University Press, 2011), 128. It is a noteworthy piece of background information that Aristotle did not list humility among the virtues; as Alasdair MacIntyre notes, "Aristotle finds no place among the virtues for either humility or charity." MacIntyre, *Whose Justice? Which Rationality?* (Notre Dame, IN: University of Notre Dame Press, 1988), 163.

[7]M. Fraenkel, ed., *Inscriptiones Graecae Aeginae, Pityonesi, Cecryphaliae, Argolidis* (Berlin, 1902), 121-22; stela 1.16 in Wendy Cotter, *Miracles in Greco-Roman Antiquity: A Sourcebook for the Study of New Testament Miracle Stories* (London: Routledge, 1999), 20; see also 21-23, 42-45.

[8]Richa Noriega, "Look It's a Miracle! Crippled Beggar Chases, Tries to Stab Coast Guard Man on EDSA Bus Stop," *Manila Bulletin*, June 3, 2021, https://mb.com.ph/2021/6/3/look-its-a-miracle-crippled-beggar-chases-tries-to-stab-coast-guard-man-on-edsa-bus-stop.

I wouldn't compare this report to the healing the paralytic. Similarly, I wouldn't suggest that Nicanor's account represents a meaningful parallel either. Again, what is significant for our investigation is that the writings of Dionysius and the Nicanor inscription include no pronouncement of forgiveness.

While few have heard about these figures, a name that often comes up when potential parallels to Jesus are discussed on a popular level is Apollonius of Tyana. In the third century, a Greek philosopher from Athens named Philostratus wrote about a miracle-working figure whom he presented as a contemporary of Jesus. Philostratus's *Life of Apollonius* includes a miracle story about the healing of an injured lion hunter. "There also arrived a man who was lame. He [was] already thirty years old and was a keen hunter of lions; but a lion had sprung upon him and dislocated his hip so that he limped with one leg. However, when they massaged with their hands his hip, the youth immediately recovered his upright gait."[9] Interestingly, there are no existing mentions of Apollonius before the third century AD—about 150 to 200 years after the time of Jesus. Regardless, no human beings are depicted as pronouncing forgiveness in the midst of healing the lion hunter. Apollonius doesn't even have any speaking parts in this miracle story. Even though skeptics often like to bring up alleged parallels between Apollonius and Jesus, these texts do not depict Apollonius claiming to forgive sins.

These stories present no data suggesting that any human beings were ever depicted as forgiving sins in general. In light of this, Jesus' claim to forgive sins appears to be a unique aspect of his miracles—even when compared with religious figures and miracle workers in the broader Greco-Roman world. Now, let's turn to Jesus' immediate Jewish context.

Divine forgiveness in Jewish texts. Did the Jewish scribes who heard Jesus really believe that only God could forgive sins? Hägerland insists

---

[9]Philostatus, *The Life of Apollonius of Tyana* 3.39, trans. F. C. Conybeare, Livius.org, www.livius .org/sources/content/philostratus-life-of-apollonius/philostratus-life-of-apollonius-3.36 -40/#3.39.

that it is impossible that the Jewish scribes would have thought that Jesus was usurping an exclusively divine prerogative: "'Your sins are forgiven' cannot possibly have been taken as a blasphemous violation of God's prerogative."[10] To say something is impossible is a bold claim, especially when historical studies are careful to use language that allows for degrees of certainty. Still, he says that other human figures such as prophets were believed to have forgiven sins. The strongest part of Hägerland's argument, however, relies on a partial, fragmentary text discovered among the Dead Sea Scrolls—the Prayer of Nabonidus (scholars call this text 4Q242 because it was found in Cave 4 at Qumran). All that remains of the original parchment are four small fragments. Still, we will pay close attention to the data arising from this text in order to fairly analyze the strength of Hägerland's theory. But first, let's set the stage by noting that God is the God of Israel.

The God of Israel. The scribes' apparently rhetorical question, "Who can forgive sins but God alone?" seems to point to the God of Israel's self-revelation as the one who forgives sin (e.g., Ex 34:6-7; see also Ps 103:2-5; 2 Chron 7:14). Jewish prophet Nehemiah describes him as "ready to forgive, gracious and merciful, slow to anger and abounding in steadfast love" (Neh 9:17). Beyond Jesus' immediate context, we find a similar idea represented in Jewish texts outside the Bible. For example, the Dead Sea Scrolls are a series of ancient texts that were discovered between 1947 and 1956 in eleven desert caves on the northwestern shores of the Dead Sea (about thirteen miles from Jerusalem).[11] One of the texts found in Cave 1 includes a Jewish prayer that identifies God as the one who forgives and judges (1QH 6:24).[12] Since only the one offended can forgive the offense, the ultimate right to forgive sin seems

---

[10]Tobias Hägerland, "Prophetic Forgiveness in Josephus and Mark," *Svensk Exegetisk Årsbok* 79 (2014): 137.

[11]"The Dead Sea Scrolls," Israel Museum, Jerusalem, accessed July 26, 2024, www.imj.org.il/en/wings/shrine-book/dead-sea-scrolls; UNESCO World Heritage Centre, "QUMRAN: Caves and Monastery of the Dead Sea Scrolls," accessed July 26, 2024, https://whc.unesco.org/en/tentativelists/5707/.

[12]In 1QH (Hodayot or Thanksgiving Hymns) 6:24, God "forgives those who turn from sin, but judges the iniquity of the wicked." For discussion, see Michael O. Wise, Martin G. Abegg, and Edward M. Cook Jr., *The Dead Sea Scrolls: A New Translation* (San Francisco: HarperOne, 1997), 88.

to be a uniquely divine function (see Ps 32:1-5; 51:1-4, 7-11; 103:3; 130:4; Is 43:25; 44:22; Dan 9:9; Zech 3:4; 1QS 2:9).[13]

Potential human mediators of divine forgiveness. Remember, Hägerland rejects the historicity of the healing of the paralytic because he says that the scribes would not have accused Jesus of blasphemy. The reason Hägerland is so insistent on this is that he says that Jewish prophets like Samuel and Daniel claimed to forgive sins. Let's examine the key texts he cites in defense of his idea.

Did the prophet Samuel forgive sins? Hägerland brings up a story that appears in 1 Samuel 12:16-25, where some people ask Samuel to pray for them.[14] They said, "Pray for your servants to the LORD your God, that we may not die" (1 Sam 12:19). Samuel agrees: "Far be it from me that I should sin against the LORD by ceasing to pray for you" (1 Sam 12:23). But notice that Samuel does not forgive sins here. He just says he will pray for them. But Hägerland wants to focus on a much later text: Josephus's retelling of this story in *Jewish Antiquities* 6.92-93. Josephus was a first-century Jewish historian who wrote over one thousand years after the time of Samuel, who lived in the eleventh century BC. Still, this is the text that Hägerland cites to assert that Samuel forgave sins. Hägerland translates Josephus's version of the story like this. "They began to implore *the prophet* . . . to make God benevolent towards them and *to forgive* this sin. . . . He for his part promised to beg and persuade God to pardon them for these things."[15] Here, the subject of "to forgive" is debated by scholars. Sir Isaac Newton's student William Whiston (1667–1752) was an English historian who rejected the deity of Jesus.[16] Still, Whiston's important translation of Josephus renders this text as: "besought the

---

[13]Otfried Hofius notes an explicit affirmation that appears in a later text, Midrash Psalm 17:3, as part of David's prayer: "No one can forgive sins but you alone." Cited in Simon J. Gathercole, *The Preexistent Son: Recovering the Christologies of Matthew, Mark, and Luke* (Grand Rapids, MI: Eerdmans, 2006), 60.

[14]Tobias Hägerland, *Jesus and the Forgiveness of Sins: An Aspect of His Prophetic Mission* (Cambridge: Cambridge University Press, 2011), 146-50.

[15]Hägerland, *Jesus and the Forgiveness of Sins*, 147, emphasis added.

[16]See Adam Shear, "William Whiston's Judeo-Christianity," in *Philosemitism in History*, ed. Jonathan Karp and Adam Sutcliffe (Cambridge: Cambridge University Press, 2011), www.cambridge .org/core/books/abs/philosemitism-in-history/william-whistons-judeochristianity/1E0FA2091 AC0FA860A5FAAD88343617B.

prophet . . . to render *God* so merciful as to forgive this their sin."[17] Either way, Samuel does not actually forgive sin but instead promises to pray that God will forgive them. This idea best fits with the biblical tradition behind Josephus's account.

Here is the key problem with Hägerland's theory: It is dependent on a metaphorical definition of prayer. He writes, "When Samuel 'forgives a sin,' *he prays* for the people in order to placate God and to avert temporal punishment for the sin committed."[18] Indeed, Samuel does not claim to forgive sins at all. For Hägerland's theory to work, he has to expand the definition of forgiveness of sins to included merely praying for people.[19] But prayer is not forgiveness.

We must avoid *parallelomania*—a tendency to see parallels behind every bush. Even when critical scholars are more nuanced, some of their readers can seem all too eager to make much of weaker connections to Jesus in order to undermine the historicity of the Gospel accounts. I've been in conversations with skeptics who desperately seize on any similarities as if to say, "You see? Jesus isn't unique after all!" However, we must also avoid the opposite tendency to reject any similarities between Jesus and prophets who operated in a similar Jewish context. Hägerland is right to note that Jesus had a prophetic dimension to his ministry. But he ignores key differences when he insists that nothing in Mark 2:1-12 "indicates that Jesus forgives in a sense that differs significantly from what Samuel is expected to do in Josephus."[20] While people appealed to Samuel for forgiveness, the paralytic did not appeal to Jesus for forgiveness. Although the paralytic came to Jesus for healing, Jesus brought up the idea of forgiveness seemingly out of nowhere. It was a totally unexpected move on his part. Even if we take Hägerland's view of forgiveness as Samuel's

---

[17]Paul L. Maier, *The New Complete Works of Josephus*, rev. ed., trans. William Whiston (Grand Rapids, MI: Kregel Academic & Professional, 1999), 205, emphasis added.

[18]Hägerland, *Jesus and the Forgiveness of Sins*, 149, emphasis added.

[19]I am indebted to Daniel Johansson's doctoral dissertation for this observation: "Samuel does not forgive in the sense Jesus does. . . . Rather than providing evidence that prophets forgave sins in the place of God, the Josephus passage is an example of a prophet interceding with God." Johansson, "Jesus and God in the Gospel of Mark: Unity and Distinction" (PhD diss., University of Edinburgh, 2012), 52.

[20]Hägerland, "Prophetic Forgiveness," 136-37.

prayer, there is still no comparison. Jesus did not pray or promise to pray before or after telling the paralytic, "Son, your sins are forgiven." Instead, Jesus appears to forgive by his own authority. All things are similar if you ignore the differences. There is no meaningful parallel here.

Perhaps the more interesting part of Hägerland's work is his discussion of an ancient fragment most people have never heard about—a text that even some biblical conservatives suggest could be the strongest argument against the idea that Jesus was a unique miracle worker. This is the part I was most intrigued to investigate: Hägerland's claim that the prophet Daniel forgave sins.

Did the prophet Daniel forgive sins? Like Samuel, Daniel is not portrayed as forgiving sins in the Hebrew Scriptures. However, Hägerland brings up the idea that Daniel might have forgiven sin in a fragmentary Aramaic text that is part of the Dead Sea Scrolls: the Prayer of Nabonidus (a.k.a. 4Q242). This contains part of a narrative attributed to Nabonidus, the last king of the Neo-Babylonian Empire, who reigned 556–539 BC.[21] According to Nabonidus's prayer in this text, he suffered from an ulcer for seven years and prayed to idols for healing. But then the king met a Jewish seer or prophet, and his sins were forgiven. The Jew tells the king to honor God by documenting the event in gratitude for the forgiveness that coincided with the healing.[22]

Now, here's where it gets controversial. Aramaic experts disagree on the most accurate way to translate this text. It could be that the king says that the Jew forgave his sin, or it could be that the king says it was God who forgave his sin.[23] For example, a noted Jewish scholar by the name of Geza Vermes was one of the first to study the Dead Sea Scrolls. In what became the standard English translation of the Scrolls, Vermes renders Nabonidus's prayer like this: "*An exorcist pardoned my sins.* He was a Jew."[24] However, another expert on the Dead Sea Scrolls, Michael O.

[21]Michael A. Knibb, *The Qumran Community* (Cambridge: Cambridge University Press, 1987), 205.

[22]Eric Eve, *The Jewish Context of Jesus' Miracles* (London: A&C Black, 2002), 83.

[23]For a discussion of translation issues, see Eve, *Jewish Context of Jesus' Miracles*, 186-87.

[24]Geza Vermes, *The Complete Dead Sea Scrolls in English* (New York: Penguin, 2004), 614, emphasis added.

Wise, believes a more accurate translation indicates that it was God who forgave his sin. He translates the text, "I prayed to the *Most High,]* and *He forgave my sins.* An exorcist—a Jew, in fact, a mem[ber of the community of exiles—came to me."[25] Regardless of the disagreement among translators, there are key differences between this text and Daniel's interaction with a Babylonian king in the biblical book of Daniel. In this fragment, the king is Nabonidus. But in the Bible, the king is Nebuchadnezzar. In this fragment, Nabonidus suffers from an ulcer. But in the Bible, Nebuchadnezzar suffers from insanity. It seems best, then, to talk about the Jew in the fragmentary 4Q242 text as an unknown seer, not the biblical prophet Daniel.[26]

So, did the Jew forgive the king's sins, or did God forgive his sins? Even for Aramaic scholars, this is unclear. Because of disagreement on the grammatical subject of the verb "to forgive" and the manuscript's fragmentary nature, scholars find no conclusive evidence that the Jew had the authority to forgive sins. This is why professor of New Testament at Atlanta Christian College Barry Blackburn says, "Varying interpretations of the Nabonidus text by competent Aramaic scholars certainly caution us against unequivocally judging that Jesus' words of forgiveness [in Mk 2:5] were not 'outstandingly novel or unique.'"[27]

Even if Vermes is right to say that the Jew forgave the king's sin, what are the chances that scribes in Capernaum knew of this text? And how accurately does a Babylonian king's prayer reflect Jewish views of forgiveness? Not only is it unlikely that this text was widespread in Capernaum, but it also seems unlikely that the king accurately reflects the views of the seer in the text or the scribes who heard Jesus. The Prayer of Nabonidus, then, does not challenge the idea that Jesus' claim to forgive sins in Mark 2:5 was *at least* heard as extremely unusual, highly exceptional, and as Blackburn puts it, "outstandingly novel and unique." Again, all things are similar if you ignore the differences. Let

---

[25]Wise, Abegg, and Cook, *Dead Sea Scrolls,* 266, emphasis added.
[26]Eve, *Jewish Context of Jesus' Miracles,* 185. Contra Hägerland, *Jesus and the Forgiveness of Sins,* 155.
[27]Blackburn, *Theios Anēr and the Markan Miracle Traditions,* 139.

us note the key differences between this text and Jesus' encounter with the paralytic.

First, King Nabonidus focuses on sickness and healing, not on sin and forgiveness. The story about his idolatry does not emphasize sinfulness. Rather, the text mentions the futility of appealing to idols. Whether the Jew or God forgave Nabonidus, the focus is on the result of the forgiveness—the miraculous healing that removed the consequences of his sin. In Mark 2, however, the focus is on sin and forgiveness. Jesus' claim and healing miracle are distinguished. In the healing of the paralytic, the paralyzed man is not healed when he receives forgiveness but only after Jesus tells him to get up. Further, Jesus does nothing to imply that the scribes were wrong to think that only God could forgive sins. Jesus presents his healing miracle as evidence for his claim to possess "authority on earth to forgive sins" (Mk 2:10).

What this tells us is that any parallel between the Jewish seer and Jesus is insignificant. Note that Hägerland presumes the Jewish seer or prophet effected Nabonidus's forgiveness via prayer: "The prophet, it seems, acts quite similarly to Samuel in Ant VI.92-3: he 'forgives' the penitent sinner by averting the temporal punishment for his sin, presumably by prayer to God, although this is not stated in the text."[28] Once again, we note that Hägerland must expand the definition of prayer for his theory to work (hence the quotes around the word *forgives*). Once again, we note that Jesus does not pray in Mark 2:1-12. Prophets who pray for people, like Samuel and Daniel, may be classified as "petitioners of numinous power." In contrast to these figures, Mark 2:1-12 presents Jesus as a "bearer of numinous power" who acts directly, without petitioning God or utilizing intermediary elements.[29] The absence of prayer in Jesus' healing of the paralytic is worth noting once again. Even though Hägerland suggests

---

[28]Hägerland, *Jesus and the Forgiveness of Sins*, 158.

[29]Werner Kahl explains that bearers of numinous power "incorporate healing power in themselves." Kahl, *New Testament Miracle Stories in Their Religious-Historical Setting: A Religionsgeschichtliche Comparison from a Structural Perspective*, Forschungen zur Religion und Literatur des Alten und Neuen Testaments 163 (Göttingen: Vandenhoeck & Ruprecht, 1994), 76. With the exception of Apollonius of Tyana—a figure 150 years after Jesus—Eve notes that Jesus is "virtually unique" in being presented as an immanent bearer of numinous power (*Jewish Context of Jesus' Miracles*, 16).

that the prophets Samuel and Daniel forgave sins, our study of the data indicates that prophets merely prayed for people. There is no compelling reason to believe that Samuel or Daniel (or the anonymous Jewish seer in 4Q242) forgave sin.[30] Still, some critical scholars object to the uniqueness of Jesus' claim for other reasons.

Priests. Ehrman recognizes the prophetic dimension of Jesus' ministry but writes that Jesus may have been claiming a merely human, priestly prerogative when he claimed to forgive sins. In *How Jesus Became God*, he says that Jesus' forgiving sins is "compatible with human, not just divine, authority. . . . This prerogative for pronouncing sins forgiven was otherwise reserved for Jewish priests in honor of sacrifices that worshippers made in the temple. Jesus may be claiming a priestly prerogative, but not a divine one."[31] But here's the problem with this view: while Jewish priests performed atonement rituals and prayed for people, there is no evidence that they ever claimed the authority to forgive sin. Indeed, Hägerland's own study found that there is no reference to a priestly pronouncement of forgiveness in Jewish literature.[32] No text quotes a Jewish priest as saying, "Your sins are forgiven" even in connection with sacrifices.[33] We have indications in the Letter of Aristeas (a Jewish text from the second century BC) that Jewish priests sacrificed in total silence at the Jerusalem temple.[34] Even the sayings of the high priest that are

---

[30]Although Hägerland includes a discussion of angels in his work, I have restricted my investigation to potentially parallel human statements in Greco-Roman and Jewish sources in order to discover whether Mark presents Jesus as a unique kind of miracle worker who claimed to forgive sins. Still, some Jews may have believed that the angel of the Lord could forgive sins committed against God. However, the distinction between this figure and God himself is somewhat unclear in the Old Testament (Ex 3:1-6). In Ex 23:21, the angel of the Lord will not forgive the people's sins. This negative assertion seems to suggest that the angel of the Lord can actually do so because he possesses the authority to forgive sins (see Josh 24:19). While an investigation of the angel of the Lord as a potential mediator of forgiveness is beyond the scope of this book, there seems to be no significant parallel with Jesus' healing of the paralytic. See Johansson, "Jesus and God," 55-58.

[31]Bart D. Ehrman, *How Jesus Became God: The Exaltation of a Jewish Preacher from Galilee* (New York: HarperOne, 2015), 127.

[32]Hägerland, *Jesus and the Forgiveness of Sins*, 134.

[33]Johansson, "Jesus and God," 49.

[34]"The most complete silence reigns so that one might imagine that there was not a single person present, though there are actually seven hundred men engaged in the work, besides the vast number of those who are occupied in bringing up the sacrifices." *Letter of Aristeas* 95, R. H. Charles, ed. Oxford: Clarendon, 1913, Christian Classics Ethereal Library, https://www.ccel.org/c/charles/otpseudepig/aristeas.htm. For discussion, see E. P. Sanders, *Judaism: Practice and*

recorded in the Mishnah (the primary legal text of Judaism) show that when people expressed repentance from sin, all the priest did was pray for them.[35] No text indicates that priests ever purported to forgive sins—even on the Day of Atonement.

It's important to note that priestly atonement and divine forgiveness are related but distinct concepts. For example, in Leviticus 12, we read about purification rites for a woman who has given birth. Since giving birth was never viewed as sinful, atonement here is linked to ritual purification—not forgiveness of sin. Even the atonement rites themselves were not enough to obtain God's forgiveness if a person had not yet made peace with the offended party. This idea is reflected in the teachings of Rabbi Akiva (Mishnah Yoma 8:9) and in Jesus' own teaching in the Sermon on the Mount. "So if you are offering your gift at the altar and there remember that your brother has something against you, leave your gift there before the altar and go. First be reconciled to your brother, and then come and offer your gift" (Mt 5:23-24). The point is that in the Jewish mind, the God of Israel—not Jewish priests—forgave sins.[36]

Even if, for the sake of argument, we speculate that Jewish priests may perhaps have pronounced forgiveness on rare occasions in the temple, it is highly unlikely that Jesus' forgiveness saying was only a claim to have a kind of merely human, priestly authority.[37] Why? Because Jesus'

Belief, 63 BCE–66 CE (London: SCM Press, 1992), 109. On the Letter of Aristeas, see Robert Jones, "Aristeas, Letter Of," in *The Lexham Bible Dictionary*, ed. John Barry (Bellingham, WA: Lexham, 2016).

[35]Hägerland, *Jesus and the Forgiveness of Sins*, 135.

[36]"Whereas the high priest is the agent of purgation (The verb is *pi'el* active), the Lord alone is the agent of forgiveness hence the verb is *niph'al*, passive." Jacob Milgrom, *Leviticus 1–16: A New Translation with Introduction and Commentary* (New Haven, CT: Yale University Press, 1998), 245.

[37]Crispin Fletcher-Louis uses a priestly-cultic reading of Dan 7:13, linking Jesus' saying and action to the Son of Man as Israel's true eschatological high priest. See Fletcher-Louis, "Jesus as the High Priestly Messiah: Part 2," *Journal for the Study of the Historical Jesus* 5, no. 1 (2007): 58, 72. Dunn also sees Jesus' action as priestly. See James D. G. Dunn, *The Parting of the Ways: Between Christianity and Judaism and Their Significance for the Character of Christianity*, 2nd ed. (London: SCM Press, 2011), 59-62, 231. However, one must be cautious not to make too much of the potential priestly function here, as forgiveness could be procured apart from the involvement of priests performing the Levitical ritual. For example, moral contrition and repentance coupled with a direct petition of God, apart from temple rituals, is in view in Gen 20:6-7; Ex 10:16-18.

method of forgiveness did not conform to divinely established patterns for Jewish priests. He wasn't at the sacred temple in Jerusalem. He was in a home in Capernaum—standing under a partially dismantled roof! Further, the paralytic didn't have a sacrifice, and he did not explicitly indicate any kind of repentance. This looks nothing like the way Jewish priests were involved with repentant Jews who sought forgiveness of sins.

Maurice Casey was a British professor of New Testament languages and literature at the University of Nottingham who was an influential voice in historical Jesus research. Although he was skeptical of miracles and rejected the idea of Jesus' deity, part of his work shows that Jesus' encounter with the paralytic was very different from the way that Jewish priests related to those in need of healing. He observes, "Priests were not involved in the healing process. . . . They did not forgive the sins of the person involved. Their purpose was to get the sick person out of the way, not to do anything to cure them."[38] This further challenges Ehrman's speculation about the kind of authority Jesus claimed to possess. Jesus' claim to forgive sins was not a merely human, priestly kind of claim. Casey is an important voice in the scholarly conversation about Jesus' authority. We will return to his views when we discuss our second blasphemy accusation scene.

"Who can forgive sins but God alone?" The scribes' implied answer, "no one," is historically credible in light of Jesus' cultural context. Unlike Jewish priests and prophets, Jesus did not pray or refer to God in Mark's description of the healing of the paralytic. Outside Jesus' forgiveness saying, there is no clear evidence of a human being claiming to forgive sins in either Greco-Roman or Jewish texts. In light of this, Jesus' forgiveness saying was unique, striking, and memorable. Unlike accounts of priestly and prophetic pronouncements of forgiveness, the blasphemy accusation scene in Mark 2 includes no clearly expressed repentance on the paralytic's part and no prayer on Jesus' part. Rather than merely

---

Still, it is important to note that Jesus does not pray in Mk 2:1-12. I discuss this observation in the following section on prophets.

[38] Here he is talking about the way priests were involved in incidents such as the one in Lev 13:32-44, which describes ritual cleanliness for those suffering from dermatological issues. See Maurice Casey, *The Solution to the "Son of Man" Problem* (New York: Bloomsbury T&T Clark, 2007), 154.

announcing God's forgiveness, it appears Jesus implicitly claims to forgive the man's sins based on his own authority.

Jesus' forgiveness saying in Mark 2:5 contains the offense to which scribes respond in Mark 2:6-7. Jesus' unoccasioned, direct initiation of forgiveness appears unparalleled in both Judaism and Greco-Roman sources. So, there are historical reasons to see the scribal response to Jesus in Mark 2:6-7 as quite probable.

Jesus' disciples. It's not just critical scholars who question the uniqueness of Jesus' forgiveness saying in Mark 2. I remember presenting my initial research on Jesus as a unique miracle worker on a beautiful, sunshiny day in San Diego. It was 2019. It was memorable because it was my first time presenting research at the annual meeting of the Evangelical Theological Society, and it was also my last speaking engagement before the Covid-19 pandemic hit. After my session, a member of the society asked me, "Didn't Jesus' disciples claim to forgive sins, too?"

He was alluding to Jesus' words to his disciples in the context of a resurrection appearance: "If you forgive the sins of any, they are forgiven them; if you withhold forgiveness from any, it is withheld" (Jn 20:23). However, from a historical perspective, it is important to note that there is no biblical scene that actually depicts Jesus' disciples as claiming to forgive sins like Jesus did—either in the context of a miraculous healing or otherwise. It is also anachronistic to read this text back into the minds of the scribes who heard Jesus forgive the paralytic. Still, the idea that Jesus authorized his disciples to forgive sins does not change the fact that Mark 2 presents Jesus as independently forgiving the paralytic's sin. But the Evangelical Theological Society participant's question is one that tends to come up in conversations with Christians (and even Muslims) about Jesus' claim to forgive sins. As we talked, his theological concern behind the question was revealed: How does the authority the resurrected Jesus granted his disciples in John 20:23 differ from his own claimed authority to forgive sins in Mark 2:5?

Again, all things are similar if you ignore the differences. Jesus sent his disciples out to carry on his ministry as his official spokespeople. They had no authority to independently pronounce forgiveness like Jesus did. A closer reading of the New Testament shows that disciples' authority is presented as entirely dependent on Jesus' authority. In another saying from a resurrection appearance, Jesus connects forgiveness to his own authority as he explains what the Hebrew Scriptures predicated about the Messiah: "Thus it is written, that the Christ should suffer and on the third day rise from the dead, and that repentance for the forgiveness of sins should be proclaimed *in his name* to all nations, beginning from Jerusalem" (Lk 24:46-47). In Acts 10:43, the apostle Peter explains this connection to Gentiles—that forgiveness is based on Jesus' authority: "To him all the prophets bear witness that everyone who believes in him receives forgiveness of sins *through his name.*" "In his name" is the key to understanding the difference between Jesus' authority and the disciples' authority.

This resurrection saying in John echoes Jesus' earlier sayings in Matthew's Gospel. Jesus tells Peter, "I will give you the keys of the kingdom of heaven, and whatever you bind on earth shall be bound in heaven, and whatever you loose on earth shall be loosed in heaven" (Mt 16:19), and tells the disciples, "Truly, I say to you, whatever you bind on earth shall be bound in heaven, and whatever you loose on earth shall be loosed in heaven" (Mt 18:18). I like the translations that bring out the perfect participle *lelymena* in both verses: "shall have been loosed," as is rendered in the NASB and footnoted in the NIV, or "had already been loosed." Just a couple of verses later in Matthew 18:20, Jesus explains, "For where two or three are gathered *in my name*, there am I among them." That is, the disciples' authority is portrayed as totally dependent on Jesus' authority.

Think about it like the authority of a bailiff who is appointed by the judge. The bailiff serves at the will of the judge and can even exercise the judge's authority in a limited capacity "in his name," by performing duties required by the judge (but only in the courts of a given county; the bailiff's authority is not as comprehensive as the judge's authority). For example, the bailiff can announce courtroom rules or carry out the judge's orders to remove a witness from the courtroom. Even if the bailiff might in some sense share authority while maintaining order during a trial or supervising a jury, the bailiff does not purport to possess the judge's authority independently while exercising authority (sourced in the judge) in a limited capacity. In fact, it is possible for the bailiff to overstep their authority by making statements not authorized by the judge. For example, in the case *O'Brien v. Seattle*, the Supreme Court of Washington affirmed the trial court's decision to grant a new trial because the bailiff made statements outside of open court which were not authorized by the judge and therefore violated the law.[39]

In the end, texts in Matthew or John do not challenge the uniqueness of Jesus as a miracle worker in the earliest miracle story in the earliest Gospel, the Gospel of Mark. Each coheres with the idea that Jesus claimed to have authority to forgive sins in a unique sense—so much so that he could even authorize other humans to forgive sins with the caveat that their actions would be connected to his own approval and to God's own will. Indeed, the San Diego man's inquiry about Jesus' disciples also raises the question of the kind of authority Jesus was really claiming to possess in Mark 2. That's another reason our interaction was so memorable.

Our long layover is complete. This brings us to the fourth stop on this leg of our journey, where we consider the cultural significance of Jesus' forgiveness saying.

BLASPHEMY, HEALING, AND THE SIGNIFICANCE OF JESUS' FORGIVENESS SAYING

Hägerland actually acknowledges that Mark 2 presents Jesus as the primary cause of forgiveness and notes that this text was "implying a unity between God and Jesus that surpasses every instance of prophetic intimacy with the divine."[40] But what about this? What did the scribes really think about the kind of authority Jesus was claiming to possess? The significance of the saying also supports its uniqueness—especially in light of ancient Jewish concepts of blasphemy and miraculous healing.

Let us return our focus to where it all began—that mudbrick house in Capernaum with a partially deconstructed roof. Debris from the thatched

---

[39]It violated Revised Code of Washington 4.44.300. See *O'Brien v. Seattle*, no. 52, Wn.2d 543, The Supreme Court of Washington, Department One, July 3, 1958; "Bailiff Orientation—Interaction with Jurors," Washington Courts, accessed February 25, 2025, www.courts.wa.gov/training /global_printversion/bailiff_printversion.htm#bailresp.

[40]Hägerland, "Prophetic Forgiveness," 137.

roof is still freshly strewn on the floor as Jesus tells the paralytic, "Son, your sins are forgiven." You can imagine the crowd looking on as a moment of silence fills the air with anticipation. The scribes evaluate Jesus' claim with dubious expressions on their faces. This is the moment of the blasphemy accusation itself: "Why does this man speak like that? He is blaspheming! Who can forgive sins but God alone?" (Mk 2:7).

THE BLASPHEMY CHARGE IN MARK 2:7

Let's be clear on what *blasphemy* meant in Jesus' Jewish context. Blasphemy was seen as slandering God through a saying or an act that disrespected him, his unique honor, glory, authority, or power, by comparing oneself to him. The Mishnah's definition of blasphemy requires that the offender actually said the divine name out loud and in an inappropriate way. The offender could face capital punishment for this.[41] However, there was another socially perceived category of cultural blasphemy as well.[42] This was a broader definition of blasphemy that included claiming God's prerogatives for oneself.[43] The alleged offense in Mark 2:6-7 best fits this kind of offense—apparently disrespecting God's unique authority by usurping the divine prerogative of forgiving sins.[44]

The way that Jesus forgave the paralytic's sins was the central issue. To the scribes, Jesus' claimed authority disrespected God's authority—a sentiment reflected in their rhetorical question "Who can forgive sins but God alone?" This seems to allude to the Shema from Deuteronomy 6:4, "Hear, O Israel: The LORD our God, the LORD is one." While God had the prerogative to forgive sins in whatever manner he saw fit, the scribes recognized a divinely sanctioned protocol for any human mediation of

---

[41]Mishnah Sanhedrin 7:5. Note that this was considered a capital offense. See Lev 2:10-16; Mishnah Sanhedrin 6:4, 7:5; Philo, *On the Life of Moses* 2.203-6.

[42]Darrell L. Bock, *Blasphemy and Exaltation in Judaism: The Charge Against Jesus in Mark 14:53-65* (Grand Rapids, MI: Baker Academic, 2000), 111.

[43]E.g., Philo, *On Dreams* 2.130-31; *Decalogue* 13; 14.61-64. As Cranfield says, "The term was understood more widely so that to usurp God's prerogative would be blasphemy." C. E. B. Cranfield, *The Gospel According to St Mark: An Introduction and Commentary* (New York: Cambridge University Press, 1959), 98-99.

[44]See Adela Yarbro Collins, "The Charge of Blasphemy in Mark 14.64," *Journal for the Study of the New Testament* 26, no. 4 (2004): 379-401.

forgiveness. Repentant Jews needed a priest to perform sacrificial rituals at the temple in order to obtain divine forgiveness. What human being was authorized to deviate from this? Any legitimate exception would require the action of God himself. This realization exposes the error of Hägerland's theory that Jesus merely acted as a prophetic representative. It also exposes the error of Ehrman's theory in *How Jesus Became God* that Jesus may have merely claimed "a priestly prerogative, but not a divine one."[45] Indeed, these theories are at odds with the data regarding Jewish concepts of blasphemy.

Considering Jesus' forgiveness saying and the miraculous healing together as a unit further clarifies the significance of the scene in general. Imagine how uncommon it would be for anyone to dare to even think about saying anything like this in Jesus' Jewish culture. Because of the independent nature of his claim, Jesus was not heard as claiming to possess a merely human priestly or prophetic kind of authority. No, Jesus' enemies heard it as an implicit claim to somehow possess divine authority. The reason for the scribal offense and the blasphemy charge was his apparent usurpation of a divine prerogative. In other words, he was claiming to do something only God had the right to do.

The context of Jesus' saying further clarifies its profundity. Mark 2:10 makes the significance of the miracle explicit, linking the healing itself to Jesus' own authority to forgive: "But that you may know that the Son of Man has authority on earth to forgive sins." This clearly presents the healing miracle as a reason to believe that Jesus, as the Son of Man, does in fact have divine authority on earth to forgive sins—not merely mediate God's forgiveness. It's no wonder that the historicity of Jesus' authority saying has been hotly contested by critics as well.

WHAT IF THE SKEPTICS ARE RIGHT?

Before we come to our conclusion about the uniqueness of Jesus as a known miracle worker, we need to address skeptical challenges to the historicity of Jesus' authority saying in this scene. Was this part added to

---

[45]Ehrman, *How Jesus Became God*, 127.

the original story? Some critical scholars doubt that Jesus ever said "But that you may know that the Son of Man has authority on earth to forgive sins" in Mark 2:10. What if they are right? This part of my research made me pause and reevaluate my view of what Jesus really said in this verse. I remember looking down at my Bible, trying to imagine the implications for my view of the text if the skeptics turned out to be right on this point. I worked to avoid confirmation bias, trying to be as charitable as possible as I considered each argument. In the fifth and final stop on this leg of our journey, I'll help you see how giving even skeptical scholars the benefit of the doubt on Mark 2:10 doesn't have to wreck your faith or do any damage to the biblical portrait of Jesus' claim.

5

A Divine Claim

AUTHORITY TO FORGIVE ON EARTH

But that you may know that the Son of Man has
authority on earth to forgive sins . . .

MARK 2:10

We have arrived at the last stop on this leg of our journey. Here we immediately encounter what could be the biggest challenge to the precision of the report in Mark 2:1-12. It is something that challenges the way that virtually every Christian understands Mark 2:10. A straightforward reading leaves little doubt that Jesus said, "But that you may know that the Son of Man has authority on earth to forgive sins . . ." Imagine hearing this text read in the context of Sunday church service. It would seem very natural for the congregation to begin to contemplate the meaning and significance of Jesus' authority saying.

"Not so fast," some say. "What if Jesus never actually said this?" While it's not uncommon for skeptics to raise questions about Jesus' words, it's important to note that questions are not arguments. Historians don't base theories about what a person said based on what-ifs or mere possibilities. This is why questions shouldn't immediately strike doubt in our minds or fear in our hearts. Still, engaging with critical scholarship is one way to better understand people and their concerns about the Bible so that we can have better conversations about Jesus. So, let's consider what is plausible. Let's interact with the best arguments against this text and think carefully about how well theories about Jesus' claims fit the evidence. Hägerland probably presents the best argument in the scholarly literature against the authenticity of Mark 2:10. Let us engage with his theory.

THE AUTHENTICITY OF THE AUTHORITY SAYING IN MARK 2:10

Hägerland rejects the historicity of Jesus' authority saying in the first part of Mark 2:10 because he believes that Mark 2:1-5 and Mark 2:11-12 are the only historical parts of the story. What about the scribal blasphemy charge (Mk 2:6-7) and the healing miracle (Mk 2:8-10)? His theory is that those parts were added into the story and that Jesus never really said, "But that you may know that the Son of Man has authority on earth to forgive sins . . ." (Mk 2:10). For Hägerland, this saying doesn't pass two historical tests: contextual plausibility and coherence.[1] Remember the rules of evidence? To say that something is contextually implausible means that the saying fails to correspond with the cultural context. To say that something is incoherent means that it is inconsistent with highly evidenced sayings of Jesus that are widely accepted as authentic.

Our fifth stop focuses on the scholarly discussion around Jesus' authority saying. We will answer five key questions.

1. Does Jesus' authority saying pass the test of plausibility?
2. Does Jesus' authority saying pass the test of coherence?
3. Could the saying be an editorial comment?
4. What if Jesus never said this?
5. What is the significance of the healing miracle itself?

---

[1] Tobias Hägerland, *Jesus and the Forgiveness of Sins: An Aspect of His Prophetic Mission* (Cambridge: Cambridge University Press, 2011), 225.

THE CHALLENGE OF IMPLAUSIBILITY:
YOU CAN'T USE THE BIBLE TO PROVE THE BIBLE

Does Jesus' authority saying pass the test of historical plausibility? On Hägerland's theory, the scribal blasphemy accusation in Mark's account is not only historically unrealistic—it is impossible. This is a bold claim. He says that the scribes believed that Jesus was only acting on God's behalf and forgiving sins in some kind of a secondary way.[2] Because of this, Hägerland sees Jesus' authority saying in Mark 2:10 as a fictional part of the story. He explains it like this:

> For Mark, Jesus does not forgive in the secondary sense of that word, but in its primary sense, thus implying a unity between God and Jesus that surpasses every instance of prophetic intimacy with the divine. In *the narrative world of Mark*, then, "to forgive" invariably means to forgive in the primary sense, and any one who does so claims to do what only God can do. By contrast, in *the real world of early Judaism*, as far as it can be reconstructed, the phrase "Your sins are forgiven" cannot possibly have been taken as a blasphemous violation of God's prerogative, and any "authority to forgive sins" would naturally have been understood as an authority to forgive in the secondary sense. To argue for the historical realism of the scribes' criticism . . . by pointing to the uniquely controversial nature of Jesus' bestowal of forgiveness is in fact to engage in circular reasoning, since the narrated controversy is entirely dependent on the dichotomy implied by Mark 2:7 itself.[3]

Hägerland is contrasting what he says the fictionalized Jesus in the Markan story meant by "your sins are forgiven" with what he thinks the historical Jesus must have meant in the real world. Interestingly, Hägerland says that Mark's Gospel presents Jesus as having a kind of unity with God that no other Jewish prophet ever had. I agree. However, Hägerland also believes that it's wrong to think that the blasphemy accusation in Mark's Gospel means that the historical Jesus really usurped

---

[2] Hägerland, *Jesus and the Forgiveness of Sins*, 126-28.

[3] Tobias Hägerland, "Prophetic Forgiveness in Josephus and Mark," *Svensk Exegetisk Årsbok* 79 (2014): 137. In agreement with E. P. Sanders, *Jewish Law from Jesus to the Mishnah: Five Studies*, new ed. (Philadelphia: Trinity Press International, 1990), 63. See also Maurice Casey, *The Solution to the "Son of Man" Problem* (New York: Bloomsbury T&T Clark, 2007), 157.

a divine prerogative. Why? Because, he says, this idea only works if you already believe that the Bible is giving you accurate history. That is his main problem with Mark 2:10.

While many skeptics say, "You can't use the Bible to prove the Bible," Hägerland presents a more historically nuanced version of this objection. He is basically saying, "You can't use the scribes' blasphemy accusation in the story to prove that Jesus' alleged blasphemy actually happened. Why? Because real Jewish scribes would never have accused Jesus of blasphemy in first place." So, his rejection of Jesus' authority saying in Mark 2:10 is directly connected to his rejection of the scribal blasphemy accusation in Mark 2:7. Understanding where he's coming from is important. His rationale is a good example of how many critical scholars often see a huge chasm between "the Jesus of history" and "the Christ of faith." On this view, the real human being in ancient history called Jesus is a very different man from the portrait of Jesus in Bible.

Still, Hägerland's theory is wrought with difficulties. First, there is no clear evidence that ancient Jews thought about forgiveness of sins in categories such as "primary forgiveness" and "secondary forgiveness." Second, it seems presumptuous and beyond even the skepticism of most atheist historians to insist that the scribal blasphemy accusation must be impossible—especially because Jesus presumed to forgive the paralytic's sins apart from any prayers, references to God, or religious requirements such as a sacrifice. Jesus operated in a very direct way, assuming that his own authority was sufficient to declare a person's sins forgiven. No, Hägerland's theory presents no compelling reason to believe that Jesus' authority saying is implausible. Mark 2:10 passes the text of plausibility.

THE CHALLENGE OF COHERENCE:
WHAT WERE THEY THINKING?

Does Jesus' authority saying pass the test of coherence? Some people are suspicious of this scene because Mark does not report that the scribal charge was verbalized. How could Jesus know what they were thinking? Although it is a historical fact that Jesus was known as a miracle worker, some skeptics may balk at the idea and ask, "Are you saying that I have to believe that Jesus was a mind reader?" No, researchers can see the scribal blasphemy accusation as historical even if they doubt that Jesus employed supernatural means to know what the scribes were thinking. As one of the top British New Testament scholars of the twentieth century, Charles E. B. Cranfield, once wrote about the scribes' response, "No doubt their faces expressed it."[4] Regardless of how Jesus knew this information, the blasphemy accusation itself is plausible, as it fits the Jewish culture of Jesus' day. Remember that blasphemy refers to slandering God through a saying or an act that disrespected him, his unique honor, glory, authority, or power. To the scribes, Jesus' forgiveness saying fit the category of disrespecting God's unique authority by usurping an exclusively divine prerogative—forgiving sins.[5]

Hägerland reasons that if the accusation in Mark 2:7 is fiction, then Jesus' response in Mark 2:10 must be fiction too. He insists that data from rare, debated texts such as Josephus's *Jewish Antiquities* and the Prayer of Nabonidus must mean that Jewish prophets forgave sins in general. This assumption drives his conclusion that the blasphemy accusation is fictitious by reason of incoherence. However, these debated texts do not clearly indicate any human was believed to forgive sins. In fact, the scribal response coheres with Jesus' later sayings and actions that resulted in accusations of blasphemy (Mk 3:22; 14:64). Why would early Christians fabricate and circulate a blasphemy accusation against Jesus? This seems unlikely.

To say that the healing of the paralytic is really a combination of a healing (Mk 2:1-5, 10-12) and a clash with the scribes (Mk 2:5-10) misses the close connection between healing and forgiveness in Judaism.[6] Also,

---

[4]C. E. B. Cranfield, *The Gospel According to St Mark: An Introduction and Commentary* (New York: Cambridge University Press, 1959), 98.

[5]Adela Yarbro Collins, "The Charge of Blasphemy in Mark 14.64," *Journal for the Study of the New Testament* 26, no. 4 (2004): 379-401. See also Darrell L. Bock, "Jesus as Blasphemer," in *Who Do My Opponents Say That I Am? An Investigation of the Accusations Against the Historical Jesus*, ed. Scot McKnight and Joseph B. Modica, Library of New Testament Studies 327 (New York: T&T Clark, 2008), 83.

[6]Cranfield, *Gospel According to St Mark*, 96. It is perhaps William Wrede who first suggested that a polemical discussion about the Son of Man's authority to forgive sins was implanted into the original healing story. Wrede, "Zur heilung des Gelähmten (Mc 2, I Ff.)," *Zeitschrift für die neutestamentliche Wissenschaft und die Kunde der älteren Kirche* 5 (1904): 355.

Jesus' authority saying explains what has already happened, and it fits the context of a controversy.[7] The two key actions in this scene are combined in the saying, "'But that you may know that the Son of Man has authority on earth to forgive sins'—he said to the paralytic—'I say to you, rise, pick up your bed, and go home'" (Mk 2:10-11). Here Jesus appeals to the healing itself as evidence that his claim to possess the authority to forgive sins is legitimate. Thus, Jesus' saying in Mark 2:10 passes the plausibility test.

THE CHALLENGE OF INCOHERENCE: WOULD JESUS REALLY HAVE SAID THIS?

Another reason Hägerland rejects Jesus' authority saying is that it seems to contradict a couple of later sayings he sees as historically credible. This is why he believes that the saying must be fictitious by reason of incoherence. For him, the first part of Mark 2:10, "But that you may know that the Son of Man has authority on earth to forgive sins," is inconsistent with Jesus' words in Mark 8:12, "No sign will be given to this generation," and Mark 11:33, "Neither will I tell you by what authority I am doing these things." Hägerland says that this observation "seals the verdict on 2.6-10 as fictitious."[8]

But this misses the context of the later sayings and the challenges that prompted them in the first place. When Jesus says, "No sign will be given to this generation," he is talking about a heavenly sign—the kind of sign the Pharisees requested (Mk 8:11). When Jesus says, "Neither will I tell you by what authority I am doing these things," he is implicitly alluding to divine authority (Mk 11:29). There is no reason to believe that Jesus' refusal to answer in this case set a precedent that required him to refuse to respond in all settings. The key issue in the confrontation between Jesus and the religious leaders in Mark 11:27-33 was Jesus' authority. The same issue is at the heart of the clash between Jesus and scribes during the healing of the paralytic. Rather than being incoherent, then, Mark 2:10

---

[7]Darrell L. Bock, "The Son of Man in Luke 5:24," *Bulletin for Biblical Research* 1 (1991): 120. See also I. Howard Marshall, *The Gospel of Luke* (Grand Rapids, MI: Eerdmans, 1978), 215-16.

[8]Hägerland, *Jesus and the Forgiveness of Sins*, 225.

coheres with Jesus' clash with Jewish scribes over the kind of authority he claimed to possess.

THE CHALLENGE OF REDACTION: COULD SOMEONE ELSE HAVE SAID THIS?

Might this saying perhaps be an editorial comment? Maybe an editor added some text to speak directly to the first readers or hearers. This may well be a view we need to consider. However, it is worth noting that those who see Jesus' authority saying as either incoherent or implausible have a problem on their hands. They must try to explain where this saying came from. Cranfield once suggested that the Gospel writer or an editor may be responsible for the authority saying—not Jesus.[9] In this case, the text would communicate something like, "But so that you, O reader or listener, may know that the Son of Man has authority on earth to forgive sins, Jesus said to the paralytic, 'Son your sins are forgiven.'"[10] I found this to be an intriguing suggestion. After all, the Greek manuscript tradition does not contain quotation marks like our modern translations. But what if the critics are right? I held this potential conclusion loosely as I sought out the rest of the story.

First, Darrell Bock points out a grammatical problem with this theory: "The syntax of the verse makes the case for this awkward and quite unlikely."[11] Second, no one in the entire Gospel refers to Jesus as the Son of Man except Jesus himself. This makes the idea that the Gospel writer, an editor, or perhaps someone else created this statement more unlikely. Remember that Jesus' use of "Son of Man" passes the test of multiple attestation (rule one). It also coheres (rule four) with Jesus' other sayings that were accompanied by miracles and controversies involving his authority (e.g., Mt 12:32).[12] The last part of the phrase, "*on earth* to forgive sins," lends credence to the historicity of the saying as

---

[9]Cranfield, *Gospel According to St Mark*, 96. See also James Edwards, "The Authority of Jesus in the Gospel of Mark," *Journal of the Evangelical Theological Society* 37, no. 2 (1994): 231.

[10]Cranfield, *Gospel According to St Mark*, 96. See also Edwards, "Authority of Jesus," 231.

[11]Darrell L. Bock, *Blasphemy and Exaltation in Judaism: The Charge Against Jesus in Mark 14:53-65* (Grand Rapids, MI: Baker Academic, 2000), 225 n105.

[12]Further, "Son of Man" is related to Dan 7:13-14 in Lk 21:27; 22:69; Jn 5:27.

well via the criteria of dissimilarity. The early church did not chiefly focus on Jesus' authority to forgive sins on earth but rather on Jesus' authority as exercised in heaven. So, the authority saying passes the test of dissimilarity as well (rule two). In light of all this, the authority saying is both plausible and coherent.

IMPLICATIONS AND FUNCTION:
SO WHAT IF JESUS NEVER SAID THIS?

What should we think when we hear that the text may be an editorial comment and not a saying of Jesus? First, it's important to remember that challenges to the authenticity of Jesus' authority saying do not negate the historicity of the scene as a whole. When I first heard this, I decided to play devil's advocate. Let's think about the implications for historicity. What if the saying does not go back to Jesus? If that is the case, then Mark or another source would be responsible for highlighting the significance of the healing event—namely that Jesus' unprecedented forgiveness saying was a legitimate divine claim rather than a blasphemous one. However, what if the saying does go back to Jesus? If this is the case, then Jesus himself explicitly highlighted the same significance. So, what is being challenged is not the significance of the healing event but which source is historically responsible for expressing it. Either way, the miracle was meant to demonstrate the validity of Jesus' authority to forgive the paralytic's sins—not merely mediate God's forgiveness. As intriguing as it might be to imagine that the Gospel writer or an editor may be behind this text, there are stronger reasons to believe that the authority saying goes back to Jesus.

Jesus confirms the scribes' understanding that he was claiming to forgive sin by his own authority. The original audience was left to decide whether they believed that Jesus really possessed that kind of authority.[13] Interestingly, Jesus' authority saying in Mark 2:10 seems to echo the literary context of Isaiah 43, where God's self-declaration is made as a response to Jewish criticism of his announcement of Isaiah's new

---

[13]Darrell L. Bock and Benjamin I. Simpson, *Jesus According to Scripture: Restoring the Portrait from the Gospels*, 2nd ed. (Grand Rapids, MI: Baker Academic, 2017), 186.

exodus.[14] Jesus presented the healing miracle to validate his implicit claim to divine authority. The healing functions as a heavenly sign and demonstrates what would otherwise be undetectable: Jesus' forgiveness saying was legitimate and effective.

SIGNIFICANCE OF THE HEALING MIRACLE PROPER: RIDDLE ME THIS

In Mark 2:9, Jesus poses this riddle: "Which is easier, to say to the paralytic, 'Your sins are forgiven,' or to say, 'Rise, take up your bed and walk'?" The heart of the controversy is whether Jesus' pronouncements were legitimate and effective. On the one hand, merely saying the words "Your sins are forgiven" might seem easier because no one could physically see whether the man's sins were really forgiven by God. Was Jesus' forgiveness saying legitimate and effective? Indeed, telling the man, "Rise, take up your bed and walk" might seem like the harder thing to say because Jesus' success or failure in attempting to healing a lame man would be obvious.[15] If the man did not comply, Jesus' reputation as a miracle worker would be tarnished and the blasphemy accusation would be validated. Legitimately forgiving sins is more difficult because it requires genuine, divine authority. Perhaps the answer to the riddle is that neither is easier. Regardless, the scribes understood that both were equally easy for God. God could easily accomplish either forgiveness or healing via performative utterances because of his divine authority.

In Mark 2:11, Jesus tells the paralytic, "I say to you, rise, pick up your bed, and go home." Mark 2:12 explains the man's response: "And he rose and immediately picked up his bed and went out before them all, so that they were all amazed and glorified God, saying, 'We never saw anything like this!'"

The positive response of the general crowd suggests many onlookers understood the significance of the healing miracle was as a testimony

---

[14]The Targum glosses this in such a way that it includes Israel's rebellious teachers. See D. A. Carson and G. K. Beale, eds., *Commentary on the New Testament Use of the Old Testament* (Grand Rapids, MI: Baker Academic, 2007), 133.

[15]Darrell L. Bock, *Mark* (Cambridge: Cambridge University Press, 2015), 142. Contra Morna D. Hooker: "Neither one is easier." See Hooker, *Son of Man in Mark* (Montreal: McGill-Queen's University Press, 1967), 88.

that Jesus possessed authority on earth to forgive sins, not merely mediate God's forgiveness. Indeed, Jesus' hearers likely believed that only God could autonomously forgive sins and only God could heal to demonstrate that the performative utterance was efficacious.[16] While the idea that a regular human being could possess this kind of authority seems to stretch the limits of Jewish monotheism, many in the crowd may have reasoned that Jesus must at least have God's blessing. Perhaps some wondered whether he might be a unique kind of Son of Man, reasoning, "Why would God heal a paralytic in order to validate the audacious claims of a sinner—or even worse, a blasphemer?" In any case, it seems plausible that Jesus purported to somehow possess divine authority to forgive and meant to validate his claim by healing the paralytic. This was yet another reason for the scribal offense.

Understanding cultural backgrounds can provide deeper insight into the profound significance this event held for the Jews who experienced it. Many Jews saw a link between sin and illness as well as a link between healing and forgiveness (2 Sam 12:13; 2 Chron 7:14; Ps 103:3; Is 38:17; 57:18-19; Babylonian Talmud Nedarim 41a). In light of this, Jesus presented the healing miracle as a visible way to validate his implicit claim to possess divine authority to forgive sins. While a sick person who was miraculously healed might have reasoned that they were forgiven, it's worth noting that this is the only known healing miracle story where forgiveness comes first. Jesus presented the healing miracle in order to validate his implicit claim to possess divine authority to forgive sins. Here, the healing itself functions as a heavenly sign and demonstrates what would otherwise be undetectable: the legitimacy and effectivity of Jesus' forgiveness saying.

CONCLUSION

We have completed the first leg of our journey. Now we can synthesize our findings and come up with a historically defensible answer to the question, "How probable is it that the historical Jesus was accurately

---

[16]Barry Blackburn, *Theios Anēr and the Markan Miracle Traditions: A Critique of the Theios Anēr Concept as an Interpretative Background of the Miracle Traditions Used by Mark* (Tübingen: Mohr Siebeck, 1991), 139.

remembered as a unique miracle worker who claimed to forgive sins?" Data from the earliest healing miracle in the earliest Gospel (Mk 2:1-12) shows us that the Jewish scribes who heard Jesus' forgiveness saying believed that only God could forgive sins committed against him. While some such as Hägerland challenge the authenticity of the scribal response, a study of Greco-Roman texts and key mediators of forgiveness in early Judaism yielded no conclusive evidence suggesting anyone other than God was believed to forgive sins in general. Further, no meaningful parallels appear to exist between Jesus' encounter with the paralytic and ancient forgiveness texts involving human beings, including religious figures such as priests or prophets (e.g., Samuel, Daniel, or the Jew in the Prayer of Nabonidus).

Let us be reminded of the scale of historical certainty:

(−4) certainly not historical

(−3) very improbable

(−2) quite improbable

(−1) more improbable than not

(0) indeterminate (i.e., neither improbable nor probable)

(+1) more probable than not

(+2) quite probable

(+3) very probable

(+4) certainly historical (i.e., the highest possible probability)

The first leg of our investigative journey has uncovered five historical facts we can hold with the following degrees of certainty:

1. **Jesus' reputation as a miracle worker:** (+4) *certainly historical*

   - Multiple attestation: Mark Q, M, L, and John
   - Multiple attestation of literary forms in the Gospels, Josephus, Celsus, and the Talmud
   - Jesus' reputation as a miracle worker is the bedrock fact from which one can begin to assess the core scene.

2. **The core scene:** (+3) *very probable*

   - Recurrent attestation of key themes: Jesus working miracles, healing the lame, and pronouncing forgiveness

- The preservation of the forgiveness saying is unlikely without a narrative context.

3. Jesus' forgiveness saying: (+3) *very probable*

- Coherence with Jesus' later sayings
- Dissimilarity with regard to early Christian concepts of forgiveness, faith, and salvation
- Rejection and execution

4. The scribal response: (+3) *very probable*

- No clear evidence of another human claiming to forgive sins in either Greco-Roman or Jewish texts
- Coherence with Jewish views of blasphemy

5. Jesus' authority saying: (+3) *very probable*

- Multiple attestation of Jesus' use of "Son of Man"
- The expositional nature of the saying fits a controversy
- Coherence with Jesus' confrontations with leaders over his authority
- Coherence with other sayings accompanied by miracles and controversies surrounding his authority
- Dissimilarity with the early church's focus on Jesus' authority as exercised in heaven

Jesus' reputation as a miracle worker is certainly historical, and the second-order facts are also highly evidenced. These observations solidly anchor the idea that Jesus was accurately remembered as a unique miracle worker who claimed to forgive sins. These highly evidenced facts possess further weight when considered in light of other evidences: my view is supported by the scribal response, which is *very probable*, and the authenticity of the core scene represented in Mark 2:1-12, which is—at the very least—*more probable than not*. The uniqueness of the forgiveness saying coheres with the survey of human figures in Greco-Roman and Jewish texts in our study.

The authority saying in Mark 2:10 also seems *very probable*. However, even if this saying does not go back to the historical Jesus, it does not challenge the authenticity of the core scene but merely makes the significance of the miracle event explicit: the Son of Man has authority on earth to forgive sins, not merely mediate God's forgiveness. Those who may disagree with the strength of my convictions must recognize that the authenticity of the data points are linked to a certain extent as they appear in the same report, the details of which were deemed worthy of preservation and reflection by those who respected Jesus' words and deeds.

Beyond the uniqueness of Jesus' forgiveness saying, we may find in this scene the earliest traces of a category of divine authority beginning to emerge in the claims of the historical Jesus. The data we surveyed thus far suggests that Jesus' forgiveness saying does not seem to be a claim to merely possess a kind of merely human priestly or prophetic authority. Rather, in light of the Jewish belief that God alone is the forgiver of sins, and in light of the more general definition of blasphemy in the Second Temple period, the charge against Jesus fits the category of disrespecting God's unique authority. In the minds of the scribes, Jesus was comparing himself to God by usurping a divine prerogative. For now, we should be open to the idea that Jesus' forgiveness saying may suggest that forgiveness somehow came from both God and Jesus, who shared the same authority to forgive sins. Indeed, the implication that Jesus, as a special kind of human being, could somehow do something believed to be an exclusively divine action—autonomously forgiving sins—was at the heart of the blasphemy charge.

Therefore, I conclude that it is *very probable* that the historical Jesus was accurately remembered as a unique miracle worker who claimed to forgive sins. I give this fact a +3 on the scale of historical certainty. In light of Jesus' cultural context, his forgiveness saying was very probably heard as an implicit claim to somehow possess divine authority to forgive sins—an aspect of Jesus' ministry that was outstandingly novel among ancient figures who were believed to do miracles.

PART THREE

The Second Blasphemy Accusation Scene

HOW JESUS CLAIMED TO HAVE DIVINE AUTHORITY TO JUDGE SINS

Jesus' Jewish Examination (Mark 14:53-65)

Didn't people believe in all sorts of miracle workers back in the day?" "Was Jesus really any different?" I often hear these kinds of questions from people who say that miracle workers were a dime a dozen back in Jesus' day. However, you can be confident that Jesus was profoundly different. History tells us that he was a unique miracle worker because he

claimed to forgive sins in an ancient Jewish culture where people saw this as something only God could legitimately do. I've found this talking point to be a helpful conversation starter with atheists, agnostics, and people from various religious backgrounds who are generally skeptical of the Bible but might be open to discussing what history can tell us about Jesus of Nazareth.

As my Uber ride was coming to an end that snowy day in Colorado, my driver asked how he could discover the truth about Jesus' claims for himself. He had never read the Bible before. I recommended he begin with the Gospel According to Mark, since we had been discussing the healing of the paralytic. We pulled up to my destination and he thanked me for "the consultation" and "history lessons," as he put it. After I exited the vehicle, I prayed a short prayer for him and left the results of our encounter to God. Historical Jesus studies does not have to be a merely intellectual or scholastic activity in the life of a Christian. The confidence you gain can help you to engage with both courage and compassion and have better conversations with people who see Jesus differently.

The first leg of our journey was a profitable one. Our first blasphemy accusation scene has enough credibility to warrant serious consideration. We may submit exhibit A, the healing of the paralytic, as admissible evidence relevant to establishing the facts of our case.

Some may object that this does not automatically mean that Jesus claimed to be God. However, recovering the historicity of Jesus' divine claim does not rest on a single scene. Some of the ambiguity present in this scene will be clarified in the next. In part three, we will begin the second leg of our journey as we investigate our second blasphemy accusation scene. This will function as exhibit B in our historical case for Jesus' divine claim.

6

The Core Scene

A LEGAL INVESTIGATION

The skeptical senior I met in high school was a teenager who doubted Jesus' existence. He dismissed the value of history and archaeology with a flippant retort. "So what if someone digs up a pot?" Later, I met another kind of skeptical senior while I was in college—not another young man like me but an older woman. She was not a high school senior but a senior citizen. She went to church every single Sunday and even served in their children's ministry. But one day, she decided to express her frustrations with Christianity and doubts about the Bible while we were talking. When I brought up a biblical story about Jesus, she angrily blurted out, "What's the difference between the Bible and a fairy tale?" Again, I was stunned. To her, this was a mic-drop moment. She quickly walked away, and I never got a chance to respond.

I started to see a pattern in implied assertions like these. I've often encountered a kind of intellectual lethargy in conversations with people who raise challenges against the Bible but aren't interested in history. But then I began to wonder how critical scholars who reject the Bible might make a historical argument against Jesus' claims. That got me curious. "Don't scholars who reject the Bible have their own kind of apologetics and evangelism too?" Indeed, authors who insist that Jesus never claimed to be God can be highly technical and nuanced in their arguments against the historicity of the Gospel portraits of Jesus.

There was no Google when I first logged on to what was called "the information superhighway" in the mid-nineties. Exploring the young and uncharted internet as a Christian college student, I was overwhelmed by discovering a plethora of websites and discussion forums that challenged the idea of Jesus' deity or his divine claim. Some of them even cited the work of academics. Eventually, I discovered another category of "skeptical senior": the skeptical senior scholar. These are seasoned academics who challenge the authenticity of biblical accounts with more sophisticated and nuanced arguments. Compared to the little verbal jabs of the teenaged skeptical senior I'd met before, their scholarly arguments seemed like massive, imposing giants. After all, they were professors and published authors. While I never experienced a crisis of faith, I did wonder whether there were good answers to the intriguing questions raised by skeptical scholarship. As a teenager, I didn't realize that I was already becoming interested in the world of historical Jesus scholarship.

ANSWERING SKEPTICISM IN CHURCH AND SOCIETY

I saw how profoundly these critics could affect people in the church when a Christian man began to email me about his doubts. His father was a pastor, and he grew up around ministry in the church. Yet, after discovering a handful of books by skeptical senior scholars, he began to wrestle with doubts. "Does the Bible really tell us what Jesus actually said?" As an example, he brought up Jesus' meeting with the Jewish high priest. "Did any of this really happen?" To him, the historical challenges were huge challenges to his faith.

Some critics reject the authenticity of the meeting altogether. Others grant the possibility as a bare fact but doubt the details in Mark's account. During my graduate studies, I studied both kinds of concerns—not only to find answers for myself but to help people who come across popular versions of these challenges and wonder whether there are any good answers to the hard questions. Ehrman is one example of a skeptical senior scholar who says, "We don't know exactly what happened at the proceeding" of Jesus' Jewish examination.[1] His books played a key role in this Christian man's doubts about the historicity of Jesus' Jewish examination.

But what about this? Just as we discussed the best arguments against the historicity of the first blasphemy accusation scene, the integrity of our quest compels us to engage the best arguments against the historicity of this second blasphemy accusation scene as well. As this man wrestled with his doubts, he reached out for direction so he could do honest research and follow the evidence where it leads. As we build our historical case for Jesus' divine claim, you'll get "the rest of the story" that even skeptical senior scholars can overlook. But uncovering the rest of the story will take us down a difficult road. Still, our conclusions will be that much stronger after pushing through these potentially faith-shaking obstacles that threaten to undermine even a lifelong believer's trust in the Bible. By the end of part three, you will see that the strongest scholarly challenges to this scene—arguments that could seem like imposing giants in our way—don't have to shake your faith. After a careful historical investigation, the giants will fall.

OUR ITINERARY

The late Maurice Casey was an influential British scholar of New Testament and early Christianity who taught at the University of Nottingham in England. Although he was skeptical of Jesus' miracle stories and rejected the idea of Jesus' deity, he once wrote, "That Jesus spoke with authority is not to be doubted."[2] But the question is, "What kind of authority did he claim to possess?" This second leg of our journey investigates the data from Jesus' Jewish examination, focusing on this question and the nature of the blasphemy charge. Carefully analyzing this scene will help us clarify the evidence for Jesus' divine claim.

---

[1]Bart D. Ehrman, *Jesus: Apocalyptic Prophet of the New Millennium* (New York: Oxford University Press, 1999), 220-21.
[2]Maurice Casey, *Jesus of Nazareth: An Independent Historian's Account of His Life and Teaching* (New York: T&T Clark, 2010), 32.

Our investigation begins with considering data that makes sense of Jesus' rejection by Jewish leaders and the factors that contributed to his crucifixion under Rome. Here, the Jewish examination of Jesus is pivotal. Think of this second blasphemy accusation scene as exhibit B in our historical case for Jesus' divine claim. It pairs with exhibit A as bookends for Jesus' ministry in the Gospel of Mark (scholars call this an *inclusio*). In both cases, Jesus refers to himself as "the Son of Man," and his enemies believe he is a blasphemer.[3] Together, these charges drive our historical case: the blasphemy charge as a result of Jesus' claimed authority as the Son of Man in Mark 2:1-12 (exhibit A) and the blasphemy charge as a result of Jesus' claimed authority as the Son of Man in Mark 14:53-65 (exhibit B).

Part three demonstrates how this second blasphemy accusation scene sheds further light on the nature of Jesus' claimed authority. It also clarifies the alleged offense that resulted in Jesus being delivered to Pilate. Moreover, it can help explain the direct connection between Jesus' claims and his crucifixion. Making this connection is very important to historians, as Ehrman notes: "The link between Jesus' message and his death is crucial, and historical studies of Jesus' life can be evaluated according to how well they establish that link."[4] By the end of part three, you will be able to clearly make this connection for anyone who is interested in the historical evidence for Jesus' divine claim.

Our task is to build a positive case for the plausibility of the core scene and examine key challenges against its authenticity. First, we will discuss the authenticity of Jesus' rejection by Jewish leaders and crucifixion under Rome and use this as a starting point for building our case. Second, we will explore the positive evidence for the plausibility of the core scene. To do this, we will engage with five critics who represent the five strongest challenges to the idea that Jesus claimed to possess divine authority at

---

[3]Darrell L. Bock, "Blasphemy and the Jewish Examination of Jesus," in *Key Events in the Life of the Historical Jesus: A Collaborative Exploration of Context and Coherence*, ed. Darrell L. Bock and Robert L. Webb (Grand Rapids, MI: Eerdmans, 2010), 595. Nicholas Perrin: "That the evangelist intends the so-called trial scene as a climax to the disputes of Jesus' final week, while also creating an *inclusio* with the dialogues of Mark 2:1-3:6, is almost certain." Perrin, "Jesus as Priest in the Gospels," *Southern Baptist Journal of Theology* 22, no. 2 (2018): 86.
[4]Ehrman, *Jesus: Apocalyptic Prophet*, 208.

his Jewish examination. You've already encountered four of these names in our study: Crossan (from the Jesus Seminar), Ehrman, and Casey. We will also read about Crossan's late associate, Marcus Borg, and encounter another who brings an intriguing objection to my thesis, Daniel Kirk.

Along the way, we will drill down to the details and defend against challenges to the scene by presenting evidence for the authenticity of Jesus' reply and the blasphemy charge itself. We will clarify the significance of the data and weigh the evidence using the scale of historical certainty in order to answer the question, "Was the historical Jesus accurately remembered as a unique defendant who claimed to possess the authority to judge sin?" Again, how well can we demonstrate that the answer is yes, on purely historical grounds?

THE RULES

We have already noted seven rules of evidence that allow scholars across a range of religious commitments (as well as those who do not identify with any faith tradition) to examine biblical texts as ancient documents and discuss what the historical Jesus likely claimed about himself. When one or more of these criteria of authenticity apply, historians recognize that this increases the probability that a biblical saying or event goes back to Jesus. Let's recap the rules.

> Rule one, *multiple attestation*, applies when a saying, event, or theme is present in more than one source.

> Rule two, *dissimilarity*, applies when a saying or event includes a concept that is similar to but not exactly like Jesus' Jewish context and a concept that is similar to but not exactly like the early Christian church's context.

> Rule three, *rejection and execution*, applies when a saying or event sheds light on how Jesus was rejected by Jewish religious leaders and how it came to be that Jesus was crucified under the Roman government.

> Rule four, *coherence*, applies when a saying or event is consistent with highly evidenced data that is widely accepted as authentic.

> Rule five, *embarrassment*, applies when a saying or event contains embarrassing elements.

- Rule six, *contextual plausibility*, applies when a saying or event realistically corresponds with Jesus' cultural context, although there may be some aspects that are not quite like the normative cultural expectation.

- Rule seven, *inherent ambiguity*, applies when a saying or event contains inherent ambiguity or vagueness.

THE "MEAT JELLY" MAN

Our second journey begins with a twentieth-century discovery that points us back to the time of Jesus. On a cold November day in 1990, an accidental archaeological discovery was made in Israel—one that would bring worldwide attention to the historicity of the high priest who questioned Jesus at his Jewish examination and handed him over to Pilate.[5] From AD 18 to around 36 or 37, a man who is simply referred to as "Caiaphas" in the Bible was the high priest in Jerusalem.[6] First-century Jewish historian Josephus indicates that his name was actually Joseph and that "Caiaphas" was more of a nickname (perhaps related to the priestly duties of his ancestor).[7] Caiaphas means "the jelly or crust that forms on boiled meat."[8] While "Meat Jelly" might seem like an odd nickname, we rarely get to choose the nicknames people give us (who knows how he might have felt about it?).

It was during the construction of a water park in Peace Forest near Jerusalem that workers uncovered a crumbling cave carved out of the soft limestone bedrock. It was the family tomb of the high priest Caiaphas. Twelve limestone boxes, which housed human bones, remained untouched since the first century. One of these containers (called ossuaries) contained a variety of remains, including the bones of a sixty-year-old

---

[5]Zvi Greenhut, "Burial Cave of the Caiaphas Family," *Biblical Archaeology Review* 18, no. 5 (September/October 1992): 29-32, 35-36.

[6]C. A. Evans, "Caiaphas Ossuary," in *Dictionary of New Testament Background: A Compendium of Contemporary Biblical Scholarship*, ed. Craig A. Evans and Stanley E. Porter Jr. (Downers Grove, IL: IVP Academic, 2000), 522-24.

[7]Evans, "Caiaphas Ossuary." See also R. Bauckham, "The Caiaphas Family," *Journal for the Study of the Historical Jesus* 10 (2012): 12: "In *Ant.* 18.95 (τὸν ἐπικαλούμενον Καϊάφας) Josephus uses a standard way of indicating a second name. In *Ant.* 18.35 the simple ὁ Καϊάφας is evidently an abbreviated version of the more common form of indicating a second name: ὁ καὶ Καϊάφας."

[8]For discussion see Bauckham, "Caiaphas Family," 16.

man. It featured an ornate carving of rosettes and an inscription in two places: "Joseph, son of Caiaphas."[9]

Mainstream news outlets brought this to public attention and sparked a renewed interest in the biblical story of Jesus' Jewish examination. The *Los Angeles Times* quoted Ronny Reich of the Israeli Antiquities Authority saying that the find was "particularly striking since it represents the first archeological evidence of the remains of any major figure in the New Testament."[10] This discovery not only corroborates the existence of the high priest mentioned in the Bible but provides an archaeological backdrop to our second blasphemy accusation scene—a monumental meeting of two confirmed historical persons: a high priest called Caiaphas and Jesus of Nazareth. Along with Jesus' claim to forgive sins, Jesus' testimony before the high priest is a pivotal part of building our historical case for his claim to possess divine authority.

THE CORE SCENE

Jesus' Jewish examination may well represent the most important legal proceeding in ancient jurisprudence, especially in terms of understanding the intersection of Jewish and Roman law. This legal investigation played a pivotal role in Jesus' delivery to Pilate for the death penalty. According to the earliest text, the examination began with an unsuccessful attempt to charge Jesus with threatening the temple (Mk 14:55-59).

The core of this scene is consistent throughout the Synoptic tradition: the high priest asks Jesus whether he is the Christ, the Son of the Blessed One.[11] While this question may seem unrelated to the temple's destruction, recognizing the theme of authority in this case is key to understanding the transition in this line of questioning. The high priest isn't

---

[9]Greenhut, "Burial Cave."

[10]"Ancient Bones May Be of Priest Who Handed Jesus to Romans," *Los Angeles Times*, August 14, 1992, www.latimes.com/archives/la-xpm-1992-08-14-mn-5366-story.html.

[11]Variations in Gospel parallels are common in accounts that reflect oral tradition. Still, the gist and core elements are preserved: Mt 26:63-64 retains the high priest's question (albeit without the circumlocution "the Blessed") as well as Jesus' affirmation and allusions from the Markan text. In Lk 22:70, Jesus merely affirms his identity as the Son of God, and no further elaboration is present in the text.

as focused on the destruction or rebuilding of the temple but on the kind of authority Jesus presumed to have.[12]

Just imagine the foreboding atmosphere in this pivotal scene as the high priest asks Jesus his pointed question. Everyone leans in. The tension is palpable. All eyes are on Jesus. What is he going to say? Consider how this pivotal exchange might look if it were represented as a modern legal transcript.

Figure 6.1. Jesus before Caiaphas

JESUS OF NAZARETH was examined and testified as follows:

EXAMINATION BY HIGH PRIEST JOSEPH CAIPHAS

Q: Are you the Christ, the Son of the Blessed?

A: I am, and you will see the Son of Man seated at the right hand of Power, and coming with the clouds of heaven.

---

[12]Bock, "Blasphemy and the Jewish Examination," 630.

Both the question and the answer read like an authentic Jewish exchange. For example, both show a strong cultural sensitivity that avoided pronouncing the divine name. So, the circumlocutions for God in this text are consistent with a first-century Jewish context. The high priest's question is direct while referring to God as "the Blessed."[13] Similarly, Jesus' response is also direct while referring to God as the "Power." Further, Jesus continues his well-established practice of referring to himself as the Son of Man. But the way he uses this term clarifies the kind of authority he claims to possess. He indicates that he will be vindicated and seated at God's right hand.

These observations support the authenticity of the exchange at the core of this scene. In each Synoptic account, Jesus' response includes a reference to Psalm 110:1—an oracle to a Jewish king. "The LORD says to my Lord: 'Sit at my right hand, until I make your enemies your footstool.'" Further, Matthew and Mark both record Jesus' claim that he will be seen riding the clouds.[14] This is an allusion to Daniel 7:13: "With the clouds of heaven there came one like a son of man." This records the prophet Daniel's vision of God giving eternal ruling authority, honor, and sovereignty to "one like a son of man" who was escorted into his presence. Both Matthew (Mt 26:65) and Mark (Mk 14:64) also record the blasphemy accusation as a result of Jesus' claim. As we examine the details of this scene, more examples of contextual plausibility (rule six) will emerge to support the weightier criteria.

THE AUTHENTICITY OF THE CORE SCENE IN MARK 14:60-64

At least three criteria point us to the authenticity of the core scene: (1) multiple attestation of sources, (2) rejection and execution, and (3) coherence. Let us consider each of these before examining key challenges to the authenticity of the core scene.

---

[13]Matthew 26:63 makes the high priest's circumlocution explicit: "I adjure you by the living God, tell us if you are the Christ, the Son of God." Finally, Lk 22:67 attributes this challenge to the assembly, providing the shortest rendering of this inquiry: "If you are the Christ, tell us." I will respond to Casey's challenge to the authenticity of this question in my discussion of Mk 14:61.

[14]Although Matthew has "coming on the clouds of heaven" (Mt 26:64) and Mark has "coming with the clouds of heaven" (Mk 14:62), the gist of the saying is virtually the same. While the location of the speaker in relationship to the accompanying clouds is specified in the former, it is unspecified in the latter. Still, one who arrives *on* clouds also arrives *with* clouds.

Multiple attestation of sources. Version A of rule one, multiple attestation of sources, applies to this scene. That Jesus was examined and condemned by Jewish authorities is multiply attested across the Synoptic tradition (Mk 14:53-56; Mt 26:57-68; Lk 22:54-71).[15] Further, we know of three later texts that were never accepted as authentic by the early church but nevertheless acknowledge Jesus' examination and condemnation by Jewish authorities: the Gospel of Thomas, the Gospel of Peter, and the Gospel of Nicodemus.[16] Gospel of Thomas 66 includes Jesus' warning to the "builders," or the Jewish leaders, who rejected the cornerstone. This either represents an independent report of the parable of the wicked tenants or simply strengthens the case that the allegory is multiply attested. Gospel of Peter 1:1 reports, "But of the Jews none washed his hands, neither Herod nor one of his judges. And since they did not desire to wash, Pilate stood up," alluding to the leaders who delivered Jesus to Pilate.[17] The Gospel of Nicodemus 1:1 mentions that the Jewish leadership brought accusations against Jesus to Pilate.[18] That Pilate's name appears tells us that there is a tradition stream that is independent from the biblical accounts. It is a different event from Jesus' Jewish examination. Here Pilate considers how to proceed with the accusations brought against Jesus.[19]

Beyond these ancient texts, Josephus also wrote about the Jewish role in Jesus' death in *Jewish Antiquities* 18.64. Here he notes that some of the

---

[15]While John reports a brief dialogue between Jesus and the high priest Annas (Jn 18:19-24), his Gospel does not include a parallel scene. Still, this meeting would not have been surprising given that Acts 4:23-26 and 1 Thess 2:14-15 place at least some of the blame for Jesus' death on the Jews in general, alluding to the role of the Jewish leadership. This also seems to echo Jesus' parable of the wicked tenants (Mt 21:33-45; Mk 12:1-12; Lk 20:9-19), which warned Jewish leaders that rejecting him perpetuated a pattern of Israel's covenant unfaithfulness and mistreatment of the prophets, alluding to the rejection of the cornerstone in Ps 118. Bock, "Blasphemy and the Jewish Examination," 589.

[16]Bock also highlights these sources in "Blasphemy and the Jewish Examination," 589.

[17]Raymond E. Brown, trans., "The Gospel of Peter," Early Christian Writings, accessed April 7, 2021, www.earlychristianwritings.com/text/gospelpeter-brown.html.

[18]"The chief priests and scribes assembled in council, even Annas and Caiaphas . . . and the rest of the Jews, and came unto Pilate accusing Jesus for many deeds, saying: We know this man, that he is the son of Joseph the carpenter, begotten of Mary, and he saith that he is the Son of God and a king; more-over he doth pollute the sabbaths and he would destroy the law of our fathers." M. R. James, trans., "Gospel of Nicodemus," Early Christian Writings, accessed April 2, 2021, www.earlychristianwritings.com/text/gospelnicodemus.html.

[19]Bock, "Blasphemy and the Jewish Examination," 591.

Jewish leaders shared responsibility with Pilate for Jesus' execution under Rome: "And when Pilate, at the suggestion of the principal men among us, had condemned him to the cross; those that loved him at the first did not forsake him." Despite the discussions about textual corruption in our existing copies of Josephus, this detail about the Jewish leaders is very likely original based on our Greek manuscripts and Latin translations.[20] So, we have four ancient texts in addition to the biblical materials telling us the same thing: Jesus was examined and condemned by some Jewish leaders before being delivered to Pilate.

Rejection and execution. The criterion of rejection and execution (rule three) applies to the core of our second blasphemy accusation scene. This meeting explains how the Jewish leadership rejected Jesus and what resulted in his crucifixion—another piece of historical bedrock. While Mark's account is primary, this dispute between Jesus and the Jewish authorities would have been discussed, debated, and circulated among both Christian and Jewish stakeholders in Jerusalem.[21]

Coherence. This scene coheres very well with the known historical facts (rule four), including Jesus' involvement in a temple controversy, his clash with the Jewish leadership over the nature of his authority, and his being handed over to Pilate and crucified. The late E. P. Sanders was a liberal, secularized Protestant scholar who played a key role in historical Jesus studies across the late twentieth and early twenty-first centuries. He listed the idea that "Jesus was engaged in a controversy about the temple" among what he called the "almost indisputable facts" about Jesus and began his investigation with the temple controversy as bedrock.[22] Sanders later expanded this list to include the idea that Jesus "was

---

[20]John P. Meier, *A Marginal Jew: Rethinking the Historical Jesus*, vol. 1, *The Roots of the Problem and the Person* (New York: Doubleday, 1991), 56-88.

[21]New Testament mentions of Jesus' innocence (e.g., Lk 23:14-15, 41, 47; implied in Acts 2:22; 5:30) may represent a response to public square discussions of what took place at Jesus' Jewish examination. See also Darrell L. Bock, *Who Is Jesus? Linking the Historical Jesus with the Christ of Faith* (New York: Howard, 2012), 155.

[22]E. P. Sanders, *Jesus and Judaism* (Philadelphia: Fortress, 1985), 11, 61. Similarly, the Jesus Seminar recognized the authenticity of some kind of antitemple act in Robert W. Funk, *The Acts of Jesus: The Search for the Authentic Deeds of Jesus* (San Francisco: HarperSanFrancisco, 1997), 121-22, 231-32, 338-39, 373-74. The majority of Jesus Seminar members held that Jesus likely spoke against the temple. See Robert W. Funk, Roy W. Hoover, and the Jesus Seminar, *The Five

arrested and interrogated by Jewish authorities, specifically the high priest" in his list of facts "almost beyond dispute."[23] Similarly, Ehrman agrees that "Jesus did make some kind of disturbance in the Temple that led to his opposition by the Jewish authorities, eventuating in his death."[24] Mark's account of Jesus' Jewish examination fits these facts very well. It begins with a line of questioning about this very issue.[25] My own mentor, Darrell Bock, wrote the most thorough historical defense of this scene.[26] His conclusions were later tested and affirmed by the Institute of Biblical Research's Jesus Group after a decadelong study that paid careful attention to historical coherence.[27]

The Challenge of Implausibility

Despite the positive evidence, some skeptical senior scholars have raised serious questions concerning the authenticity of the core scene. But do these really represent gigantic challenges that threaten our core scene? Let us consider the two strongest objections represented in the scholarly literature: (1) literary aspects of the general scene and (2) the presence of legal irregularities for a capital trial.

Literary aspects of the general scene. Borg and Crossan's explanation of this account is that the scene must have been invented in order to set a courageous example for early Christians facing suffering and persecution.[28] But there's a problem with this assumption. This scene doesn't just give us an example of Jesus' courage. It is much more focused on

---

Gospels: What Did Jesus Really Say? The Search for the Authentic Words of Jesus (San Francisco: HarperOne, 1996), 98. In the twenty-first century, Klyne Snodgrass argues for the authenticity of this event in "The Temple Incident," in Bock and Webb, Key Events, 429-80.

[23]E. P. Sanders, The Historical Figure of Jesus (New York: Penguin, 1996), 10-11.

[24]Bart D. Ehrman, Jesus Before the Gospels: How the Earliest Christians Remembered, Changed, and Invented Their Stories of the Savior (New York: HarperOne, 2016), 165.

[25]Although the Markan text mentions inconsistencies among the false witnesses, it is plausible that even false accusations were based on Jesus' authentic involvement in a public controversy surrounding the temple. Indeed, N. T. Wright argues that Jesus' temple action was a key reason that the Jewish leadership pursued his execution. See Wright, Jesus and the Victory of God (London: SPCK, 1996), 405.

[26]Darrell L. Bock, Blasphemy and Exaltation in Judaism: The Charge against Jesus in Mark 14:53-65 (Grand Rapids, MI: Baker Academic, 2000).

[27]Bock and Webb, Key Events.

[28]Marcus J. Borg and John Dominic Crossan, The Last Week: What the Gospels Really Teach About Jesus's Final Days in Jerusalem (San Francisco: HarperOne, 2007), 133.

the saying about his personal identity as the apocalyptic Son of Man—
something that Christians could not repeat or emulate.[29] Others, such
as Fredriksen, are not convinced that this scene really took place due
to apologetic material that seems to blame the Jews for Jesus' execution.[30] The problem with her idea is that the ongoing debate between
the Jewish leadership and early Christians about Jesus' guilt or innocence necessarily contains apologetic material. Any defense of Jesus'
innocence is a direct response to a real blasphemy accusation that had
to have occurred. The blasphemy charge came immediately after Jesus
appealed to some kind of future evidence (his return as judge) as validation of his claim. This echoes our discussion of exhibit A, Mark 2:1-12,
where Jesus also appeals to future evidence (the miraculous healing of
the paralytic) as validation for his authority on earth to forgive sins.[31]
There appears to be no good reason to insist that the event was created
by the early church.

Legal irregularities for a capital trial. Others argue that the temporal
setting and motivation of the Jewish leadership appear unrealistic. They
raise the question of apparent legal irregularities for a capital trial present
in Mark's account. For example, Sanders notes that Jewish trials could
not normally be held in the evening or in the midst of holidays.[32] It is
important to note that such challenges are dependent on later sources
such as the Mishnah, which was compiled around AD 200. This reflects
Pharisaic rather than Sadducean regulations that were in place during
the time of Jesus.[33] Indeed, the rabbinical criminal code for capital cases
mentioned in tractate Sanhedrin in the Mishnah was not in force during
Jesus' lifetime.[34] Even Adela Yarbro Collins says, "The regulations regarding trials involving capital punishment in the Mishnah should not

---

[29]Bock, *Who Is Jesus?*, 158.

[30]Paula Fredriksen, *Jesus of Nazareth: King of the Jews* (New York: Vintage, 1999), 254-55. Here
she follow Sanders's concern in *Jesus and Judaism*, 298.

[31]This coheres with his attempts to validate his authority over the Sabbath and numerous forces
such as nature, sicknesses, demons, and death.

[32]Sanders, *Jesus and Judaism*, 298.

[33]Josef Blinzler, *Der Prozess Jesu*, 4th ed. (Regensburg: Friedrich Pustet, 1969), 216-29.

[34]Henry Danby, "The Bearing of the Rabbinical Criminal Code on the Jewish Trial Narratives in
the Gospels," *The Journal of Theological Studies* 21, no. 81 (October 1919): 51-76.

be used in historical studies of the trial of Jesus."[35] Regardless, special circumstances may have warranted a speedy examination for Jesus because his opponents saw him as a deceiver who may put the nation at risk in some way. The Jewish leadership probably did not want to hold Jesus in custody any longer than necessary. They needed to quickly prepare a case for Pilate and secure a judgment against Jesus before Pilate returned to Caesarea Maritima.[36]

But what was the nature of this meeting? Key scholars on both the left and the right of biblical scholarship recognize that this was probably not an actual trial. Even the late Borg (a skeptic who was a member of the Jesus Seminar) concluded that rather than a formal trial, this scene likely describes a preliminary hearing:

> In all probability, there was a collaboration on the part of a small circle of Jewish leaders centered around the high priest. As the official religious leader of the community, the high priest played a domestic political function. Appointed by Rome and accountable to the Roman governor, he was responsible for maintaining political order in Palestine. . . . To assist him in this responsibility, the high priest appointed his own "privy council" who functioned as his political advisors. . . . The story of the "Jewish trial" of Jesus is probably a preliminary hearing before this "political Sanhedrin" rather than a formal trial before a religious council.[37]

Bock also agrees that Jesus' examination was not a formal trial in a strict legal sense.[38] He sees this scene as an informal investigation—something akin to the American grand jury process.[39] Here, the Jewish prosecution was looking for evidence strong enough to accuse Jesus of a capital crime and take him to Pilate for a legal pronouncement of guilt. For example, the leadership dropped the accusation that Jesus spoke against the temple when it was determined that a compelling case could not be built on

---

[35]Adela Yarbro Collins, "The Charge of Blasphemy in Mark 14.64," *Journal for the Study of the New Testament* 26, no. 4 (2004): 380.

[36]Bock, "Blasphemy and the Jewish Examination," 194-95.

[37]Marcus J. Borg, *Jesus, A New Vision: Spirit, Culture, and the Life of Discipleship* (San Francisco: HarperCollins, 1987), 179-80.

[38]Bock, "Blasphemy and the Jewish Examination," 602.

[39]Darrell L. Bock and Benjamin I. Simpson, *Jesus According to Scripture: Restoring the Portrait from the Gospels*, 2nd ed. (Grand Rapids, MI: Baker Academic, 2017), 476.

conflicting testimony. Further, although the Jewish leadership found Jesus worthy of death (Mk 14:64), they did not legally condemn him to death.[40] So, our core scene stands up to historical scrutiny. The charge of implausibility based on legal irregularities based on later Mishnaic trial law fails once the event is understood as an informal examination and not a formal trial.

In the end, the setting of our second blasphemy accusation scene is very plausible in light of the ongoing conflict between Jesus and Jewish leaders. Their motivation was most likely to gather evidence to build a case against Jesus that would prompt a speedy decision by Pilate—in this case, the death penalty. While this objection raises the question of the nature of the meeting, it does not suggest that the event itself never happened. What some may consider gigantic challenges of implausibility have fallen, and there is no compelling reason to doubt that a real historical event lies behind Mark's report.

This chapter established two key data points: (1) the authenticity of Jesus' rejection by Jewish leaders and crucifixion under Rome and (2) the authenticity of the core scene. But can we really know what happened at the meeting? How plausible is the exchange between Jesus and the high priest (Mk 14:61-63)? This is the next concern that sets itself up as a gigantic obstacle to trusting the text and considering the idea that Jesus made a divine claim. And it brings us to consider the words of the "Meat Jelly" man himself—the man called Caiaphas whose family tomb and awkward nickname began our journey into the second blasphemy accusation scene.

---

[40]For discussion, see Bock, "Blasphemy and the Jewish Examination," 602-3.

Questioning Jesus

WHO DO YOU THINK YOU ARE?

*And Jesus said, "I am, and you will see the Son of Man seated at
the right hand of Power, and coming with the clouds of heaven."*

MARK 14:62

In his classic book *The God Delusion*, British evolutionary biologist
Richard Dawkins asserts, "There is no good historical evidence that
[Jesus] ever thought he was divine."[1] In the early 2000s, Dawkins gained
a following outside the sciences as one of the "Four Horsemen of New
Atheism"—a group of popular atheist authors who ignited a critique of
Christianity in the public square. The other horsemen of the new atheism
movement were Sam Harris, Daniel Dennett, and the late Christopher
Hitchens. In response to arguments for God's existence based on
Scripture, Dawkins quickly dismissed the New Testament as an unre-
liable source of historical data. Even more, he painted the Gospels as
being no different from modern works of fiction such as Dan Brown's
novel *The Da Vinci Code*: "The only difference between *The Da Vinci
Code* and the gospels is that the gospels are ancient fiction while *The Da*

---

[1]Richard Dawkins, *The God Delusion* (Boston: Houghton Mifflin, 2006), 92.

Vinci Code is modern fiction."[2] Today, many atheists and agnostics hold a similar kind of sentiment. They seem to reason, "If the Gospels are purely fictional works, then any argument for the divine claim of the historical Jesus based on the Gospels must be rejected." But is this the best way to view the sources?

As we have seen, this is not how historians and critical scholars of the New Testament approach ancient texts about Jesus. Even these researchers find value in carefully investigating the Gospels to uncover highly evidenced data about what Jesus said and did. Indeed, in the world of New Testament scholarship, critics who launch the strongest objections to the authenticity of Jesus' divine claim include more nuance with regards to the text. At times, the arguments can seem rather technical and very different from the kinds of objections we might encounter in conversations with those who reject the Bible. However, some of what is debated among scholars in academic journals and espoused in technical monographs can easily find its way into popular sources, which then influence public-square conversations about Jesus. This is why it's worth diving into the concerns of critical scholarship, including the objections of skeptical senior scholars who specialize in the study of the New Testament and the historical Jesus. We need to understand these kinds of arguments so that we can be prepared to engage the toughest challenges. This is especially important when talking about Jesus' divine claim with a skeptical friend, relative, or coworker who may have read books by critical scholars who are concerned with pinpointing the sources behind the text before considering the data arising from our scene.

THE AUTHENTICITY OF THE
HIGH PRIEST'S QUESTION IN MARK 14:61

How do historians consider the details of this scene when the source(s) behind the text seem uncertain? Specifically for this case, how plausible is the high priest's question as recorded in the text? Let us examine both of these concerns.

---

[2]Dawkins, *God Delusion*, 97.

The uncertainty of pre-Markan source(s). In 1985, a figure who could be considered the godfather of contemporary New Testament criticism, the late E. P. Sanders, launched scholars into a new era of investigation called the "third quest for the historical Jesus." He wrote the classic text *Jesus and Judaism*, which rightly calls for understanding Jesus in light of first-century Judaism. In it, however, he also questions the likelihood that any eyewitnesses sympathetic to the Jesus movement could have served as sources for the data we have regarding Jesus' Jewish examination.[3] This raises questions such as, "How could Mark possibly tell us what happened if he wasn't there?" "Which disciples could possibly have told him what happened?" and "Can we consider any data from this scene if we aren't sure about where the details came from?" These kinds of questions can lead some to doubt the historicity of the pivotal exchange between the high priest and Jesus. Crossan and the late Borg of the Jesus Seminar expressed similar concerns.[4] Here's how Ehrman popularized the challenge at the turn of the twenty-first century:

> Unfortunately, we have no reliable way of knowing what happened when Jesus appeared before Caiaphas. In part we are hampered by our sources: according to the accounts themselves, the only persons present were Jesus, who was to be executed the next morning, and the Jewish rulers. Where, then, did our sources get their information? There wasn't a court stenographer whose records could be consulted. . . . Jesus must have appeared before some body of Jewish rulers, who decided to hand him over to Pilate after an initial questioning, but . . . we don't know exactly what happened at the proceeding.[5]

---

[3]E. P. Sanders, *Jesus and Judaism* (Philadelphia: Fortress, 1985), 298.

[4]Marcus J. Borg and John Dominic Crossan, *The Last Week: What the Gospels Really Teach About Jesus's Final Days in Jerusalem* (San Francisco: HarperOne, 2007), 128.

[5]Bart D. Ehrman, *Jesus: Apocalyptic Prophet of the New Millennium* (New York: Oxford University Press, 1999), 220-21. Still, he does not consider implausible the idea of a pre-Markan tradition. He writes, "My hunch is that the trial narrative and the burial narrative come from different sets of traditions inherited by Mark," but then immediately asks, "Or did Mark simply invent one of the two traditions himself and overlook the apparent discrepancy [of Joseph condemning Jesus and then arranging his burial]?" Bart D. Ehrman, *How Jesus Became God: The Exaltation of a Jewish Preacher from Galilee* (New York: HarperOne, 2015), 152-53.

This idea, once discussed only among New Testament scholars, made its way into the popular culture in part through YouTube and other kinds of social media. More people are expressing such doubts online. For example, a woman who watched Ehrman's presentation on the reliability of the Gospels commented: "My biggest issue has always been with the Trial of Jesus. All the disciples had fled. Who was there to witness the event?"[6] But does this automatically mean that the Gospel writer could not have known what transpired at this historic meeting? If disciples such as Peter or John were not within earshot of the exchange, we can still ask, "Why does a reliable source have to be sympathetic to Jesus?" Why couldn't any eyewitness talk about the details from Jesus' exchange with the high priest—regardless of whether they thought Jesus was guilty or innocent?

The problem is that this challenge ignores the false witnesses in Mark 14:56-57 as well other potential observers. Eyewitnesses may include guards as well as servants who may have been present at the scene but are unmentioned in the text.[7] In fact, anyone present at Jesus' examination may have related details during public debates with his followers. Other plausible witnesses include Jews who followed Jesus, such as Nicodemus or Joseph of Arimathea (Mk 15:43). These two would likely have had access to any Sanhedrin records.[8] It is also likely that Saul of Tarsus (a.k.a. the apostle Paul) was aware of the Jewish position on Jesus' claims, the examination, and its role in Jesus' execution.[9] Other priests

---

[6]Comment posted by @pamcurtis2717 on Bart Ehrman, "Are the Gospels Historically Reliable? The Problem of Contradictions," June 27, 2020, YouTube, 59:18, www.youtube.com/watch?v=AymnA526j9U.

[7]While textual variants exist in Mk 14:65, none call the presence of the guards into question.

[8]Darrell L. Bock, "Blasphemy and the Jewish Examination of Jesus," in *Key Events in the Life of the Historical Jesus: A Collaborative Exploration of Context and Coherence*, ed. Darrell L. Bock and Robert L. Webb (Grand Rapids, MI: Eerdmans, 2010), 607. While the historicity of Joseph of Arimathea is sometimes questioned, Raymond Brown's study finds his existence "very probable," arguing that the church's disdain for the Jewish leadership would make the fabrication of a sympathetic and indeed a heroic figure among those who condemned Jesus "almost inexplicable." See Brown, *The Death of the Messiah, from Gethsemane to the Grave: A Commentary on the Passion Narratives in the Four Gospels*, Anchor Bible Reference Library (New Haven, CT: Doubleday, 1994), 2:1212-32, 1240. See also William Lyons, "On the Life and Death of Joseph of Arimathea," *Journal for the Study of the Historical Jesus* 2, no. 1 (January 2004): 29.

[9]Bock, "Blasphemy and the Jewish Examination," 607.

who joined the Jesus movement (Acts 6:7) would have had access to this important exchange as well.[10]

Also, why rule out the possibility that official records of the examination were produced? Claudius Lysias's letter to Governor Felix as reported in Acts 23:26-30 suggests that charges against an individual in custody may have been documented. If so, records regarding the alleged blasphemy may also have been accessible—even if only to a few. When we think about Jesus' clash with the Jewish leadership over the nature of his authority, it makes sense that those who opposed him would publicize what he said to incur a blasphemy charge. In fact, Peter's insistence of Jesus' innocence in Acts 2:22-36; 3:13-15 seems to imply public debates surrounding the Jewish leadership's pronouncement of Jesus' guilt. Bock notes: "There was an ongoing debate between the new [Jesus] movement and the [Jewish] leadership that ran for thirty years within Jerusalem. In the heated polemic that certainly emerged, discussion of what led to Jesus' demise would almost certainly have surfaced, at least in its most fundamental terms."[11] Moreover, a stream of transmission existed into AD 70, when Josephus, who apparently had access to records about James's trial, wrote about the stoning of James under a descendant of the high priest Joseph Caiaphas, called Annas II.[12] While it may not be possible to conclusively pinpoint the exact source or sources used to produce the report in Mark's Gospel, it is certainly plausible that one or more of these potential sources provided data present in the text.

The high priest's use of "Christ" and "the Blessed." In Mark 14:61, we read that the high priest asks whether Jesus is "the Christ" (the Messiah), and adding a synonym, "Son of the Blessed."[13] Casey writes that this question cannot pass the test of plausibility on two counts. First, he challenges the high priest's use of *Christ*, or its Aramaic equivalent, asserting that it "had not yet crystallized out into a title" and saying that therefore

---

[10]Darrell L. Bock, "Jewish Expressions in Mark 14.61-62 and the Authenticity of the Jewish Examination of Jesus," *Journal for the Study of the Historical Jesus* 1, no. 2 (2003): 148.

[11]Bock, "Jewish Expressions," 149.

[12]Josephus, *Antiquities* 20.200.

[13]"Son of God" carries this sense in Ps 2:2, 7; 1 Chron 17:13; 2 Sam 7:12, 14. These appear coherent with ideas from Qumran in 4QFlorilegium 3.11-12; 1QSa 2:11-12.

the word *Christ* doesn't fit the time period of the event. Thus, its inclusion in the text "must be due to the early church, or to Mark himself."[14] The problem is that he cites no evidence for his strong conclusion that this must be the case. In fact, the word *Christ* (or the concept of Messiah) comes from the Hebrew Scriptures, which are full of messianic expectation.[15] Indeed, both the concept and title of Messiah were not unfamiliar to those who inquired about Jesus' identity. In a tradition attributed to Q (the hypothetical source behind shared material in Lk 7:18-23 and Mt 11:2-6), we see that John the Baptist, his inquiring disciples, and Jesus himself were familiar with the Messiah's range of activities, such as healing the lame.[16] Jesus' appeal to his miracles echoes signs of the messianic era in a text among the Dead Sea Scrolls called Messianic Apocalypse.[17] Moreover, Peter's declaration of Jesus as "the Messiah" at Caesarea Philippi (Mk 8:27-30) is highly evidenced and suggests the force of a title was already present.[18]

It's important not to miss the royal dimension of the Messiah as a future Davidic king because this coheres with Jesus' crucifixion as king of the Jews, as the sign above his head noted: "And the inscription of the charge against him read, 'The King of the Jews'" (Mk 15:26). This coherence and Peter's declaration itself show that the high priest could certainly use "the Christ" as a kind of title in his question to Jesus. Indeed, many Jews expected Messiah to one day judge wicked unbelievers,

[14]Maurice Casey, *The Solution to the "Son of Man" Problem* (New York: Bloomsbury T&T Clark, 2007), 243.

[15]Messianic expectation also appears in extrabiblical texts such as the Dead Sea Scrolls, the Psalms of Solomon, and 1 Enoch. See Larry W. Hurtado and Paul L. Owen, eds., *"Who Is This Son of Man?": The Latest Scholarship on a Puzzling Expression of the Historical Jesus* (London: T&T Clark, 2012), 44. Further, Hurtado writes, "The 'anointed one' of Isaiah 61 appears to have provided something of a script for much of Jesus' work. According to Luke 4:16-21, Jesus seems to have taken Isaiah 61:1-2 as programmatic for his ministry." Larry W. Hurtado, "Christ," in *Dictionary of Jesus and the Gospels*, ed. Joel B. Green, Scot McKnight, and I. Howard Marshall (Downers Grove, IL: InterVarsity Press, 1992), 117.

[16]Darrell L. Bock, *Luke 1:1–9:50* (Grand Rapids, MI: Baker Academic, 1994), 658-59. While "Messiah" is implicit in Luke, it is explicit in Matthew. Both texts connect messianic expectation to "the one who is to come" (Lk 7:20 // Mt 11:3).

[17]Jesus' appeal to his miracles echoes signs of the messianic era in 4Q521, fragment 2, 2:1-14 (Messianic Apocalypse).

[18]For a defense of the authenticity of this scene and Peter's declaration, see Michael J. Wilkins, "Peter's Declaration Concerning Jesus' Identity in Caesarea Philippi," in Bock and Webb, *Key Events*, 293-382.

deliver the righteous, and reign.[19] In light of these observations, the saying seems to pass the text of contextual plausibility (rule six). Further, Casey's first challenge is incoherent with the known data.

Second, Casey says that the high priest's use of "the Blessed" shows us that this exchange must have been invented by the church. For him, although this "sounds like a circumlocution for God, it is not attested as such. . . . We must see here the hand of the early church."[20] But this assertion is guilty of the title-concept fallacy. Even if direct references to God as "the Blessed" are not widespread, the concept of God as blessed was not rare. References to God as the "Blessed One" are present in ancient synagogue prayers as well as Jewish texts such as 1 Enoch and the Mishnah.[21] Further, "Son of the Blessed" is dissimilar to Christian titles for Jesus.[22] How many Christian hymns or worship songs call Jesus "Son of the Blessed?" As far as I know, the answer is zero. That's because this is not a way that Christians refer to Jesus. Elsewhere in Mark's Gospel, we can find Jesus called "Son of God" but not "Son of the Blessed" (Mk 1:1; 3:11; 5:7; 15:39). So this doesn't seem like something the church made up. No, the high priest's words are likely from a pre-Markan tradition—not a product of the church.[23] Outside Caiaphas's question, Mark's Gospel contains no references to God as "the Blessed."[24] Bock argues, "It is highly unlikely that Mark would create a Jewish feel to this trial, because his

---

[19]Psalms of Solomon 17-18; 4 Ezra 12; 2 Baruch 40.

[20]Casey, *Solution to the "Son of Man" Problem*, 243. He seems to follow the thought of Hugh Anderson, *The Gospel of Mark* (Grand Rapids, MI: Eerdmans, 1981), 331. Bock clarifies that "this expression is a circumlocution, not because it replaces God's specific name, but because it avoids referring to him as God as an indication of respect by mentioning him more circumspectly" ("Jewish Expressions," 150).

[21]Bock observes that his examples in synagogue prayers appear in dependent adjectival constructions rather than as a title or name. Still, "This description of God as a Blessed One is part of the central prayer life of the nation—an old synagogue prayer. . . . Its widespread use in the liturgical tradition suggests an old practice. It shows that it is perfectly appropriate to speak of God as the "Blessed One." Bock, "Blasphemy and the Jewish Examination," 633. On 1 Enoch and the Mishnah, see Hurtado and Owen, "Who Is This Son of Man?," 44. Although Owen does not cite the text, he seems to allude to 1 Enoch 77.2 and Mishnah Bereshit 7:3, which are directly noted by Bock along with other examples of similar references to God as "the Blessed" in "Blasphemy and the Jewish Examination," 632-33, especially n100.

[22]Bock, "Blasphemy and the Jewish Examination," 638.

[23]Bock, "Blasphemy and the Jewish Examination," 634.

[24]Bock, "Jewish Expressions," 150.

audience lacked savvy of Jewish matters as his translation of Aramaic expressions and explanation of Jewish customs show."[25] His helpful study of Jewish expressions in Mark 14:61-62 concludes this way:

> [As] unprecedented as the expression "Son of the Blessed One" is, the concept of God as the one who is blessed is not rare at all. It is this combination of similarity and dissimilarity that speaks to the likelihood that what we have in Mark 14 is a trace of Jewish expression, not made up by Mark or the church, but retained from Jewish roots and the serious nature of the examination of Jesus.[26]

So, we have good reason to take this question seriously as a piece of historical data. It is contextually plausible (rule six). Casey's second objection ignores known data and is guilty of a logical fallacy: the title-concept fallacy. There is no compelling reason to reject the high priest's direct question to Jesus, "Are you the Christ, the Son of the Blessed?" as implausible (Mk 14:61). But what about Casey's objections to Jesus' answer?

THE AUTHENTICITY OF JESUS' ANSWER IN MARK 14:62

In Mark 14:62, we read Jesus' reply: "I am, and you will see the Son of Man seated at the right hand of Power, and coming with the clouds of heaven." While Casey launches a multifaceted challenge to the text, perhaps his strongest reason for rejecting this saying is based on his rejection of the high priest's question. He reasons, "If the early church is responsible for the question, it must also be responsible for the first part of Jesus' answer."[27] But even if, for the sake of argument, he admitted the likelihood of the question, he would still insist that Jesus' answer cannot pass the test of plausibility. His strongest challenges are related to the way

---

[25]See Bock, "Jewish Expressions," 150-53. Here Bock refutes Juel's "pseudo-Jewish expression" theory by identifying similar ideas in Mishnah Bereshit 7.3 and 1 Enoch 77:2, and discussing the common Mishnaic refrain "blessed is he," "blessed be he," and "blessed are you." Interestingly, these phrases remain in use in the present day even in the briefest of Passover Haggadahs, which are careful to include the essentials. E.g., Robert Kopman, *30 Minute Seder: The Haggadah That Blends Brevity with Tradition* (Scottsdale, AZ: 30 Minute Seder, 2007).

[26]Bock, "Jewish Expressions," 153.

[27]Casey, *Solution to the "Son of Man" Problem*, 243.

the text portrays Jesus using the term "Son of Man" and combining Psalm 110:1 and Daniel 7:13. Casey boldly declares this objection "a massive argument" for rejecting the authenticity of Jesus' words in this scene.[28] But are these really the gigantic, imposing obstacles he makes them out to be?

Jesus' use of "the Son of Man." Casey's approach treats anything beyond a generic use of "Son of Man" as a later creation of the church, at a time when it "was already a Greek title for Jesus seen in Dan. 7.13 interpreted as a prophecy of his second coming."[29] But if the church just made it up, then why is the term almost exclusively found on the lips of Jesus in the Gospels? And why don't we see Jesus called "Son of Man" anywhere else in the New Testament? Why wouldn't the church talk it up if they made it up?

Let us consider how rule one applies: multiple assentation. Jesus' use of "Son of Man" as a theme is multiply attested, so it passes the most weighty of the criteria of authenticity.[30] It occurs eighty-one times on the lips of Jesus in the Gospels and one time in a report about Jesus' own words (Jn 12:34). Beyond this, there is a special category of Son of Man sayings that scholars call "apocalyptic Son of Man" sayings, where Jesus makes some reference to his role in the eschaton (the end of the age; culmination of history). These kinds of sayings are also multiply attested.[31] They are also the most widely distributed.[32] If the criteria of multiple attestation is of any value to historical reconstructions

---

[28]Casey, *Solution to the "Son of Man" Problem*, 244. There is perhaps some tension in Casey's view. While he rejects an apocalyptic "son of man concept" being attached to the generic idiomatic expression "son of man," he seems to grant that its contextual use can point to apocalyptic ideas. E.g., Jesus uses the concept of the eschatological Son of Man as a self-reference while suggesting his pivotal role in the judgment (e.g., Lk 12:8-9 // Mt 10:32-33; Casey, *Solution to the "Son of Man" Problem*, 193-94). I discuss this text while assessing the coherence of the blasphemy charge with Jesus' death. Casey's general caution appears to be against automatically assigning an apocalyptic nuance to the generic idiom in every occurrence. Jesus' use of the generic idiom may have filled it with new meaning and significance for his hearers.

[29]Casey, *Solution to the "Son of Man" Problem*, 242.

[30]Recall our discussion on the authenticity of Jesus' Son of Man saying in Mk 2:10.

[31]Bock, "Jewish Expressions," 155-56.

[32]Darrell L. Bock, *Luke 9:51–24:53* (Grand Rapids, MI: Baker Academic, 1996), 1171. See also Bock, "Blasphemy and the Jewish Examination," 645-56. For a fuller discussion, see Scot McKnight, *Jesus and His Death: Historiography, the Historical Jesus, and Atonement Theory* (Waco, TX: Baylor University Press, 2005), 171-75.

of Jesus, we should not ignore the data supporting these kinds of eschatological sayings.

Jesus' use of Daniel 7 is also multiply attested.[33] So, there is evidence that the Son of Man concept was something Jesus had used beforehand. Although Casey assumes that Jesus could not have derived a Son of Man concept from Daniel 7, the data suggests otherwise.[34] Jesus' use of both the apocalyptic Son of Man theme and the text of Daniel 7 appears solidly in the tradition. But there is another problem with Casey's view that authentic Son of Man sayings must always be interpreted generically. His approach results in awkward interpretations of authentic sayings such as, "But that you may know that the Son of Man has authority on earth to forgive sins" in the healing of the paralytic (Mk 2:10). On the one hand, Casey admits this saying is authentic.[35] On the other hand, he insists that Jesus was just making an observation that God gave some human beings the ability to heal psychosomatic infirmities.[36] But other scholars note that this interpretive lens doesn't work. For example, Paul Owen coedited the first collection of scholarly essays in English on Jesus' use of "Son of Man" with the late Larry Hurtado. Owen rightly questions Casey's approach both on hermeneutical and historical levels:

> The incredible glosses Casey puts upon such sayings stand as their own refutation. . . . Why would the early church have bothered to preserve such mundane observations by their founder? Are we really to believe that the historical Jesus simply went about espousing general maxims about the human condition? How then did his message occasion so much controversy and subsequent religious transformation in the lives of his followers? Was Jesus really so utterly unwilling to make statements exclusively about himself, his divine vocation and his unique significance in God's

---

[33]Direct or indirect references to Dan 7: "Triple Tradition (Mk 13:26 and par.; Mk 14:62 and par.), M (Mt 13:41; 19:28; 25:31) and either Q or L (Lk 12:8)." Bock, "Jewish Expressions," 155-56. For a fuller discussion, see Bock, *Luke 9:51–24:53*, 1171-72.

[34]Casey, *Solution to the "Son of Man" Problem*, 82.

[35]"The Son of man saying at Mk 2.10 is part of a true narrative of a real healing event. . . . It was a real reference to himself in particular. . . . [It] must be classified . . . as a genuine saying of Jesus in which he used a particular Aramaic idiom." Casey, *Solution to the "Son of Man" Problem*, 167.

[36]Casey, *Solution to the "Son of Man" Problem*, 147, 165-67.

plan? When then did Casey's modest Jesus incur the wrath of the religious and political establishment?[37]

Indeed, Jesus' Son of Man sayings would make little sense if he were just talking about people in general and pointing to himself as just one example of a generality.[38] You don't have to be a scholar to realize that Jesus must have said something that got him in trouble with some of the Jewish leaders. Indeed, Jesus' answer in Mark 14:62 is plausible (rule six) and coherent (rule four) with the way he often spoke about himself. Despite Casey's first major challenge, we have no good reason to reject Jesus' words as inauthentic. But Casey has a second, more complicated challenge set before us.

Jesus' combination of Psalm 110:1 and Daniel 7:13. Jesus' answer is profound and multifaceted. It employs the term "the Son of Man," connecting it to Daniel 7:13 and combining it with "seated at the right hand of Power" from Psalm 110:1. Casey says this is implausible. Why? Because it doesn't sound like Jesus to him: "It was not characteristic of Jesus to deal with a topic only in such rigidly scriptural terms."[39] But why call Jesus' allusions to prophetic texts "rigidly scriptural," especially when virtually every critical scholar recognizes Jesus' ministry as having a kind of prophetic dimension? These two Old Testament texts were probably very significant to Jesus.[40] Bock says, "Foreseeing (or even hoping for) a vindication, texts like Ps. 110.1 and Dan 7.13 were likely a part of his thinking and self-understanding. Where else would Jesus turn for such self-definition and understanding but to Scripture?"[41]

Indeed, this is not the first time we see Jesus combing Old Testament texts in one of his answers. For example, when a scribe asks Jesus, "Which commandment is the most important of all?" Jesus'

---

[37]Hurtado and Owen, *"Who Is This Son of Man?,"* 45.

[38]John J. Collins, "The Son of Man in Ancient Judaism," in *Handbook for the Study of the Historical Jesus* (Leiden: Brill, 2010), 2:1567.

[39]Casey, *Solution to the "Son of Man" Problem,* 244.

[40]E.g., for Ps 110:1, see Mt 22:41-45; Mk 12:35-37; Lk 20:41-44. For Dan 7:13, see Mk 13:26 // Mt 24:30; Lk 21:27; Q: Mt 24:27 // Lk 17:22, 24.

[41]Bock, "Jewish Expressions," 158. For other arguments supporting the authenticity of this use of Ps 110:1 and Dan 7:13, see Darrell L. Bock, *Blasphemy and Exaltation in Judaism: The Charge Against Jesus in Mark 14:53-65* (Grand Rapids, MI: Baker Academic, 2000), 220-30.

answer links Deuteronomy 6:4-6 and Leviticus 19:18 in his famous ethical teaching on loving God and loving neighbors (Mk 12:29-31):[42] "Jesus answered, 'The most important is, "Hear, O Israel: The Lord our God, the Lord is one. And you shall love the Lord your God with all your heart and with all your soul and with all your mind and with all your strength." The second is this: "You shall love your neighbor as yourself."'" The way Jesus used the Old Testament in light of the Jewish culture in which he ministered (and of which he was a part) is not surprising. He knew that Jewish speculation about the exalted Son of Man figure connected to Daniel 7 was something he could use as he revealed his identity.[43] For example, 1 Enoch 62:1-6 is a Jewish text where "the Son of Man" sits on a throne as the eschatological judge. It's hard to paint this apocalyptic son of man imagery as a generic picture of humanity.[44] Bock notes:

> Dan 7 was a text that was present in the theologically reflective thinking of Judaism, and thus quite available to Jesus once he started thinking in terms of eschatological vindication. There is nothing here that requires a post-Easter scenario. The moment Jesus contemplated the possibility of vindication of a divinely given authority, this text would have become a prime candidate for consideration. . . . The availability of Dan 7 for reflection about the end, authority, and vindication seems clear enough. In fact, one can argue that the use of the title to point to vindication and authority lies closest to its explicit sense in Daniel.[45]

Jesus' use of Psalm 110:1 "sitting at the right hand of Power" is also very plausible. He previously quoted the same text while teaching in the temple: "How can the scribes say that the Christ is the son of David?"

---

[42]Further, Mk 7:6-10 / Mt 15:4-9 links honoring of parents with honoring with lips. See Is 29:13; Ex 20:12 [Deut 5:16]; Ex 21:17 [Lev 20:9]. See Bock, "Jewish Expressions," 157.

[43]E.g., Jewish thought in Ezekiel the Tragedian, as well as slightly later works such as 1 Enoch 62:2 and 4 Ezra 13. See Bock, "Blasphemy and the Jewish Examination," 642. See also John J. Collins, "The Son of Man in First-Century Judaism," *New Testament Studies* 38, no. 3 (July 1992): 448-66; and William Horbury, "The Messianic Associations of the Son of Man," *The Journal of Theological Studies* 36, no. 1 (April 1985): 34-55.

[44]Although this is exactly what Casey attempts to do. See *Solution to the "Son of Man" Problem*, 91-111.

[45]Bock, "Blasphemy and the Jewish Examination," 644.

(Mk 12:35).[46] This question assumes that his audience knew about the view that the Messiah would be a descendant of David. In fact, he affirms this view (Mk 12:37). Like many Jews, Jesus held that David authored the psalm by the Holy Spirit (Mk 12:36). Jesus' riddle highlights a paradox, implying the Messiah cannot merely be David's son. He must be something more. He must somehow be superior to David as well. He asks how David could honor the Messiah by calling him "Lord," since this person is his descendant—an awkward situation in a patriarchal culture.[47] Jesus highlights the king's connection to a coming Messiah who is descended from but somehow superior to David. His point is that David calling the Messiah "Lord" is much more profound than just calling the Messiah "Son of David."[48]

Here our rules of evidence come into play once again. Think about dissimilarity (rule two). On the one hand, downplaying the Davidic sonship of the Messiah is dissimilar from the emphasis of the early church.[49] On the other hand, relating two ideas to each other in this way appears continuous with Jewish style.[50] So, this saying has a strong claim to authenticity.[51]

If Jesus previously used this text to consider the Messiah's authority in light of David's respect even for his descendant, there is nothing implausible about Jesus' allusion to Psalm 110 in Mark 14:62. Psalm 110 had a long history of interpretation leading up to this point. During the postexilic period, some interpreters linked the text with an expectation of the Davidic dynasty's restoration after the return from exile and the rebuilding of the temple (Jer 33:14-26; Zech. 3:1-10; 6:9-15; see also

---

[46]See Mt 22:41-46. While Lk 20:41-44 is a simplified version of the core event, it retains the gist of Jesus' teaching, including his assumption of the Davidic authorship of Ps 110.

[47]Bock also argues that Ps 110:1 is suitable to the setting of Jesus' Jewish examination in *Luke 9:51–24:53*, 1630-41.

[48]If the divine name was not pronounced, it is plausible that the ambiguity introduced by a substitute word would exist in Aramaic as well as Hebrew. The ambiguity and Jewish nature of the query increases the probability of authenticity. See Bock, "Blasphemy and the Jewish Examination," 639.

[49]Bock, "Blasphemy and the Jewish Examination," 640. See Acts 2:30-36; 13:23-39; Rom 1:2-4; Heb 1:3-14.

[50]David Daube, *The New Testament and Rabbinic Judaism* (London: Athlone, 1956), 158-63.

[51]Bock, "Blasphemy and the Jewish Examination," 641.

Hag 2:20-23). When this did not happen, some saw an image of the Messiah ushering in the eschatological kingdom and sitting at God's right hand in Psalm 110. In light of this, Jesus' reply appears to be a fitting response to the high priest's questions. Moreover, Jesus' reply applies the language of the psalm to himself, suggesting an expectation to sit at God's right hand in heaven as the long-awaited Messiah and eschatological king.[52] Here, Jesus' self-reference is supported by the authenticity of the blasphemy charge (which we will turn to next). There is no evidence that the high priest thought that Jesus changed the topic by speaking of "the Son of Man" as a third party or that he was speaking about humanity in general. No, Jesus didn't use the indefinite "a son of man." Jesus always used the definite article with the term ("the Son of Man") almost like a title. This further supports Jesus' self-reference.

Still, Casey challenges the authenticity of Jesus' reply to the high priest based on the idea that Psalm 110 appears often in the New Testament.[53] Here Casey appears somewhat inconsistent in looking for dissimilarity. Although he argues that the widespread presence of Psalm 110 in the New Testament suggests that Jesus' words were a creation of the church, he also challenges the allusion to Daniel 7:13 on the basis of the opposite—its *rarity* in the New Testament: "Dan. 7.13 did not catch on in the rest of the New Testament, as it surely would have done if Jesus had used it in this clear way at such a climactic moment."[54] But why must this text "surely catch on" if the saying were authentic? After all, even Casey grants the authenticity of some of Jesus' Son of Man sayings (e.g., Mk 2:10) despite the fact that it doesn't appear anywhere in the New Testament outside the Gospels. It is this very dissimilarity that supports the authenticity of his allusion to Daniel 7.

In fact, if you are looking for dissimilarity to Mark's style, we have it in Jesus' answer when he refers to God as "Power." This is not used anywhere else as a circumlocution for God in Mark or the New Testament—even

---

[52]The self-reference is supported by the authenticity of the blasphemy charge. There is no evidence that the high priest perceived that Jesus in any way changed the topic by speaking of a third party or humanity in general. The definite article further supports a self-reference.

[53]Casey, *Solution to the "Son of Man" Problem*, 243-44.

[54]Casey, *Solution to the "Son of Man" Problem*, 244.

though Psalm 110 appears often. This suggests an exceptionally memorable expression—not something created by the early church.[55] Such a response fits the scene well, especially in light of Jewish sensitivities to the divine name suggested by the high priest's use of "the Blessed" in his question.

The dissimilarity present in Jesus' reply suggests the allusions to Scripture in this solemn setting are more than plausible. In light of the Jewish cultural sensitivities reflected in the overall exchange, we can also see the idea of contextual plausibility (rule six) as an additional criterion that bolsters the case for authenticity. Casey's multifaceted challenge does not offer a compelling reason to reject the historicity of Jesus' reply to the high priest. Casey's self-proclaimed "massive argument" does not provide compelling reasons to conclude that Jesus' reply in Mark 14:62 is inauthentic.

CONCLUSION

While many skeptics in the public square may outright dismiss biblical texts as sources for the life of the historical Jesus, this is not the way that historians approach the Gospels. In this, Dawkins shows that he is unfamiliar with the way historians approach Scripture—even though he refers to an atheist New Testament scholar, Ehrman, in this part of his book. Even Ehrman's work shows that there is value in engaging with the text and investigating the data. Indeed, it is important to analyze the objections of those who reject the authenticity of Caiaphas's question and Jesus' reply.

While our investigation has yielded useful data, we're not out of the woods yet. Casey and Ehrman say that the blasphemy accusation itself is the biggest problem with the scene in Mark 14. Does this pivotal part of the narrative demonstrate that we are not in touch with history when we read the text? Is the blasphemy accusation itself a fabrication of the early church?

---

[55]Consider how Matthew and Luke omit this language while retaining the idea of strength (Mt 26:64 // Lk 22:69).

A Blasphemy Accusation

YOU CAN'T JUDGE ME!

Bart Ehrman went to school here." That's what I thought one morning as I closed my laptop after teaching a class at the Moody Bible Institute's Chicago campus. Then I imagined Ehrman in his youth—a seventeen- to twenty-one-year-old evangelical, sitting in one of the gray auditorium seats as a college student who had a passion for learning about the Bible. Despite the resentment he feels toward the school, he says, "I was and still am grateful for the massive inundation that I received in the Bible."[1] After his time at Moody, he spent two years completing his under-graduate degree at Wheaton College before he experienced what he calls a "crisis of faith" at Princeton Seminary.[2] Today, the agnostic atheist New Testament scholar has made no secret of his departure from the faith of his college days in Illinois and now argues that the historical Jesus never claimed to be divine.[3] Still, his popular books not only introduce scholarly issues in New Testament studies to a wider audience but often serve as a catalyst for biblical conservatives to engage with critical scholarship. Like

---

[1]Bart Ehrman, "My Resentment at Moody Bible Institute," *The Bart Ehrman Blog*, May 21, 2015, https://ehrmanblog.org/my-resentment-at-moody-bible-institute/.

[2]Bart Ehrman, "My Resistance to Change at Princeton Seminary," *The Bart Ehrman Blog*, May 8, 2017, https://ehrmanblog.org/my-resistance-to-change-at-princeton-seminary/.

[3]Alex O'Connor, "Did Jesus Even Claim to Be God? Bart Ehrman Says No . . . ," June 19, 2023, YouTube, 1:31:12, www.youtube.com/watch?v=2STiabRV8TE.

Ehrman, some critical scholars read the high priest's accusation at Jesus' Jewish examination (Mk 14:63-64) and pause to ask, "Blasphemy? What blasphemy?" He argues that the blasphemy charge is incoherent with anything in Jesus' reply. This is why some doubt the historicity of the blasphemy accusation itself. Here is how he explains his problem with taking the text seriously as a historical account.

> It is difficult to understand the trial proceeding if it actually happened as narrated. In our earliest account, the high priest asked Jesus if he is in fact the Messiah, the Son of the Blessed (Mark 14:61). So far so good. But when Jesus affirms that he is, and says that he, the high priest, will see the Son of Man coming on the clouds of heaven—sayings that in themselves co-incide perfectly well with Jesus' teachings elsewhere—the high priest cries out "Blasphemy," and calls for his execution (Mark 14:62-64). The problem is that if this, in fact, is what Jesus said, he didn't commit any blasphemy. It was not blasphemous to call oneself the Messiah. . . . Nor was it blas-phemous to say that the son of man was soon to arrive.[4]

Ehrman is right that it wasn't blasphemy to call oneself the Messiah or to talk about Daniel's vision of a son of man. While this raises very fair questions about the nature of the blasphemy, it is Casey's prior work (which includes the concerns popularized by Ehrman) that develops these ideas and perhaps represents the most robust historical argumen-tation against the authenticity of the blasphemy accusation in Mark 14:63. In this chapter we will analyze each part of his three-pronged challenge.

THE AUTHENTICITY OF THE HIGH PRIEST'S RESPONSE IN MARK 14:63-64

Casey's triple threat. Would the high priest really have heard what Jesus said as a kind of blasphemy? Casey says no. This is why he rejects the blasphemy accusation as unhistorical. He argues that the high priest's re-sponse is historically problematic because of three things: (1) the prereq-uisite for garment tearing, (2) the justification for a blasphemy charge, and (3) the incoherence of a blasphemy charge with Jesus' crucifixion. For him,

---

[4]Bart D. Ehrman, *Jesus: Apocalyptic Prophet of the New Millennium* (New York: Oxford University Press, 1999), 220.

the accusation cannot pass the text of contextual plausibility (rule six). Here's how he explains his triple threat:

> [According to the text, the high priest] tore his garments and accused Jesus of blasphemy, after which the whole council judged Jesus worthy of death. The high priest should tear his garments after a conviction for the legal offence of blasphemy, a conviction unjustified by what Jesus is supposed to have said. Jesus was crucified for sedition, which would be very difficult to justify from this charge of blasphemy. All this is accordingly too much to believe as a historical account. We are dealing with the creativity of the early church, and probably that of Mark himself.[5]

This first part of Casey's objection is multifaceted. In order to engage with his concerns regarding garment-tearing rules, however, we need to carefully investigate Jewish concepts of blasphemy. Having a clear understanding of the cultural background is pivotal to understanding the historical discussion around this text.

Blasphemy in Judaism. For Jews, God's glory and honor were seen as unique and worthy of the highest protections. So what exactly constituted blasphemy in Judaism? Perhaps the most thorough investigation is Bock's *Blasphemy and Exaltation in Judaism*.[6] This work played a role in my interest in being mentored by Bock while I was a student at Dallas Theological Seminary. I was honored to share countless lunch conversations with him, over many years, at our favorite spot—the original, family-owned Dickies' Barbeque Pit location in Dallas (the oldest barbecue restaurant in Dallas). There we talked about a range of topics, including my seminary studies, our podcast (called *The Table*), and the historical Jesus. Studying the evidence for Jesus' divine claim became an area of special interest for me as we discussed the toughest challenges to the historicity of Jesus' Jewish examination. Bock's highly detailed work *Blasphemy and Exaltation in Judaism* enhanced my own research into what the high priest may have heard as the alleged blasphemy in Jesus'

---

[5]Maurice Casey, *The Solution to the "Son of Man" Problem* (New York: Bloomsbury T&T Clark, 2007), 244.

[6]Darrell L. Bock, *Blasphemy and Exaltation in Judaism: The Charge Against Jesus in Mark 14:53-65* (Grand Rapids, MI: Baker Academic, 2000).

reply. Here is a summary of what I discovered and how the data can be applied to our interaction with Casey's thought.

While data for formal judicial examples of blasphemy is scarce, the Mishnah specifies that the legal offense requires a verbal pronouncement of the divine name.[7] Interestingly, many Jews were careful even to avoid blasphemy against the names of foreign deities out of respect for the divine name.[8] This is because blasphemy was taken so seriously that the inappropriate use of the divine name was considered a capital offense.[9] While warnings were sometimes given for a first violation, a subsequent violation would certainly result in liability for such a grave offense.[10]

Apart from this narrow legal understanding of blasphemy, there was also a category of cultural blasphemy. This cultural category applied to the use of substitute titles or actions not covered by formal legal statutes. We already referenced this category in our discussion of the scribal blasphemy accusation in the healing of the paralytic (Mk 2:6-7). There the scribes perceived that Jesus disrespected God's unique authority and compared himself to God by usurping the divine prerogative of forgiving sins. For a mere man to say that he was somehow comparable to God was considered arrogant blasphemy.[11] Beyond this, another way to arrogantly disrespect God was to insult his people, presence, or power.[12] Insulting God's chosen leaders would be related to this as a violation of Exodus 22:28, "You shall not revile God, nor curse a ruler of your people." So, blasphemy referred to a range of insulting actions or things someone could say with reference to God. In light of this cultural background, let us consider each of Casey's claims. How well does the data align with his assertion that the high priest's response to Jesus was a fiction created by the church (or Mark)?

---

[7]Mishnah Sanhedrin 7:5.

[8]Josephus, *Jewish Antiquities* 4.207; Philo, *On the Life of Moses* 2.205; *Special Laws* 1.53.

[9]Lev 24:10-16; Mishnah Sanhedrin 6.4, 7.5; Philo, *On the Life of Moses* 2.203-6.

[10]Mishnah Sanhedrin 8.4.

[11]Philo, *On Dreams* 2.130-31; *Decalogue* 13; 14.61-64.

[12]E.g., Goliath's idolatry and disrespect for God's people (1 Sam 17; Josephus, *Jewish Antiquities* 6.183). Even speaking against God's people could be considered blasphemy (1QpHab 10.13). For more, see Bock, *Blasphemy and Exaltation*, 111.

CHALLENGE ONE: PREREQUISITE FOR GARMENT TEARING

Why would Caiaphas tear his garments? This was a cultural sign of mourning or grief for Jews who heard an insult to God.[13] Casey writes, "The high priest should only tear his garments after a conviction for the legal offense of blasphemy."[14] Here Casey may be alluding to the Mishnah (compiled around AD 200, 170 years after Jesus' time), which describes a blasphemy trial.[15] Today most scholars see the use of later rabbinical materials as problematic. Even in this later text, however, there is no mention of a conviction for the legal offense of blasphemy before the judges tear their garments.

According to the legal procedure for alleged blasphemy cases, witnesses should use a substitute for the divine name when quoting the defendant in their public testimony. After everyone else is excused, the witnesses may quote the defendant verbatim, including the blasphemy, exclusively for the judges, who then stand up and tear their garments.[16] There was a second-century rabbinical debate regarding pronouncement of the divine name. While some, like Rabbi Meir (AD 140), thought that insulting God via certain euphemisms, circumlocutions, or alternative names was a capital offense, others disagreed.[17] Still, let us remember Bock's idea that Jesus' Jewish examination was most likely not a trial in the legal sense but something more like a contemporary grand jury investigation in American jurisprudence. Although those present found Jesus "to be deserving of death," he was not legally convicted of a capital offense at this meeting. The text does not say, "They sentenced him to death." Rather, the opinion of those present was that Jesus deserved to die. This allowed some Jewish leaders to take

---

[13]E.g., Adela Yarbro Collins cites Is 1:4 and Deut 31:20 as examples of "despising" God. See Yarbro Collins, "The Charge of Blasphemy in Mark 14.64," *Journal for the Study of the New Testament* 26, no. 4 (2004): 383. First Maccabees 2:6 summarizes Mattathias's lament over the destruction of Jerusalem and the loss of the temple. Seeing the fall of Jerusalem as a blasphemy, the priest and his sons tear their garments in mourning. For discussion, see Bock, *Blasphemy and Exaltation*, 40-41, 49.

[14]Casey, *Solution to the "Son of Man" Problem*, 244.

[15]Martin Goodman, "Mishnah," in *Oxford Research Classical Dictionary*, July 6, 2015, https://doi.org/10.1093/acrefore/9780199381135.013.4222.

[16]Mishnah Sanhedrin 7:4-6.

[17]Bock, *Blasphemy and Exaltation*, 69-70, 89-90.

Jesus to Pilate for an official legal decision on a related sociopolitical charge.[18] We will return to this important point when we discuss whether the blasphemy charge coheres with Jesus' crucifixion.

The point of this legal discussion is simply to say that the later Mishnanic procedures in the rabbinical criminal code are not as relevant for assessing this meeting. So, it seems plausible that the high priest tore his garments because he believed that Jesus' reply fit at least the cultural category of blasphemy.

CHALLENGE TWO: THE JUSTIFICATION FOR A BLASPHEMY CHARGE

Some skeptics say that the blasphemy accusation itself is a telltale sign that we are reading fiction in Mark's Gospel. Why? Because, they insist, there was nothing in Jesus' answer to the high priest that could possibly be construed as blasphemy. This is the heart of Casey's second challenge to the authenticity of the blasphemy charge. To him, it appears "unjustified by what Jesus is supposed to have said."[19] Now, it's true that just claiming to be the Messiah was not considered blasphemy. In fact, Josephus, the Jewish historian, mentions several people who claimed to be the Messiah but were never accused of blasphemy.[20] So, is there something else in Jesus' reply that the high priest could have heard as blasphemy? Bock suggests three options for consideration: (1) pronouncement of the divine name, (2) claiming the authority to sit at God's right hand, and (3) disrespecting God's chosen leaders. Do any of these apply?

1. Pronouncement of the divine name. Some researchers begin with the assumption that a person had to verbally pronounce the divine name in order to incur a blasphemy charge. Since the text doesn't include the divine name in Jesus' reply, some critics are quick to reject the plausibility

---

[18]Darrell L. Bock, "Blasphemy and the Jewish Examination of Jesus," in *Key Events in the Life of the Historical Jesus: A Collaborative Exploration of Context and Coherence*, ed. Darrell L. Bock and Robert L. Webb (Grand Rapids, MI: Eerdmans, 2010), 602-3.

[19]Casey, *Solution to the "Son of Man" Problem*, 244.

[20]Josephus, *Jewish Antiquities* 18.85-57, 97-98; 20.167-88. This does not rule out the possibility that a messianic claimant may have also been charged with blasphemy for a separate or related statement.

of the blasphemy accusation altogether. A few scholars suggest that Jesus may have pronounced the divine name when alluding to Psalm 110:1, and Mark's Gospel substituted "Power" as a circumlocution to prevent Scripture readers from pronouncing the divine name in public readings.[21] But this seems unlikely. It's more likely that Jesus did not pronounce the divine name at all—just as the text depicts his reply.[22] Even if Jesus did say the divine name, however, it would still remain uncertain whether the high priest would have thought that Jesus said it in a disrespectful or arrogant way. That's the key. Many people do not realize that merely speaking the divine name out loud was not itself considered blasphemy. For example, priests could pronounce the divine name with reverence while giving a solemn benediction or confession that included a quotation of Scripture (e.g., Num 6:24-26; Lev 16:30).[23] So, just saying the divine name was not enough to incur a blasphemy charge. Whether or not Jesus said the divine name in his reply, there had to be something else about the way he alluded to Psalm 110—an audacious, offensive something that Caiaphas and the council could have heard as an arrogant blasphemy. The following are a couple of ways to explain what that "offensive something" could be.

2. Claiming the authority to sit at God's right hand. One contender for this "offensive something" is Jesus' claim that God would bring him as the Son of Man into the divine presence, have him sit at God's right hand (Ps 110:1), and allow him to ride the clouds (Dan 7:13-14). The best way to assess whether Caiaphas might have heard this as somehow denigrating God's unique honor or glory is to understand Jewish concepts of human exaltation and connect this to what we have already discussed

---

[21]Robert H. Gundry, *Mark: A Commentary on His Apology for the Cross* (Grand Rapids, MI: Eerdmans, 1993), 915-18. For discussion, see Craig A. Evans, *Jesus and His Contemporaries: Comparative Studies*, Arbeiten zur Geschichte des antiken Judentums und des Urchristentums 25 (Leiden: Brill, 1995), 915-18. See also Bock, "Blasphemy and the Jewish Examination," 610-13.

[22]Yarbro Collins, "Charge of Blasphemy."

[23]Consider the solemn pronunciation of the divine name in a priestly benediction including Num 6:24-26 noted in Mishnah Sotah 7:6: "In the Temple, the priest utters the name of God as it is written in the Torah, i.e., the Tetragrammaton," and the high priests' Day of Atonement confession including Lev 16:30, noted in Mishnah Yoma 6:2: "And the priests and the people standing in the Temple courtyard, when they would hear the Explicit Name emerging from the mouth of the High Priest, when the High Priest did not use one of the substitute names for God, they would kneel and prostrate themselves and fall on their faces." See Evans, *Jesus and His Contemporaries*, 413.

regarding concepts of blasphemy in Jesus' context. Understanding this connection requires a deep dive into Jewish speculation on potential human mediators of divine judgment.

Potential mediators of divine judgment. Who could sit at God's right hand? Not just anyone. Beyond mere entrance into heaven for the righteous, Jews believed that access to God's immediate presence was highly restricted.[24] Only God's own invitation could allow anyone to sit with him—a temporary privilege that even angels did not possess.[25] We find speculation about this in the way luminaries are depicted in a variety of texts. For example, Moses is described as enthroned during his vision in connection with his responsibility of leading God's people, and Abraham is depicted in a heavenly position of honor, sitting at God's left hand.[26] Both David and the Messiah are also spoken of as being seated to receive heavenly honor.[27] Beyond sitting with God, certain luminaries were believed to even share divine authority to rule and judge: Adam is portrayed as a highly exalted, ruling figure with a throne in heaven, and Abel is pictured in a temporary role, judging in an initial judgment.[28]

Perhaps most interesting among the extrabiblical texts are stories about Enoch, an Old Testament figure. In a Jewish pseudepigraphal book from the late third or early second century BC called 1 Enoch, he is transformed into the Son of Man, is seated on the throne of glory, and shares divine authority to judge.[29] Although he shares God's throne in this text,

---

[24]Bock, "Blasphemy and the Jewish Examination," 181. See especially n194 on the obstacles that some Jews believed hindered one's access to God's unique presence.

[25]While it is possible that some Jews believed the angel Gabriel sat next to God, at least as Enoch's escort, 2 Enoch 24:1-3 may include Christian interpolations that call its authenticity into question. See Bock, *Blasphemy and Exaltation*, 165n147.

[26]Moses is referred to in Exagoge of Ezekiel 68-89. Bock observes, "Moses is enthroned with great authority, but his exalted role is likely a metaphorical picture of his authority to establish the nation" (*Blasphemy and Exaltation*, 182). Abraham appears in Midrash Psalm 18.29.

[27]Bock, *Blasphemy and Exaltation*, 162.

[28]On Abel, see Testament of Abraham 11:10-12. Philo, *On the Creation* 148, portrays Adam as a "king" whom God made his viceroy to rule over the animals as his subjects. Wisdom 10:1-2 notes that God gave Adam "strength to rule all things." Life of Adam and Eve 47:3 mentions that Adam will "sit on the throne of him who overthrew him." In 2 Enoch, Adam is a second angel assigned to rule as king over the earth with God's wisdom.

[29]1 Enoch 45:3; 51:3; 55:4; 61:8; 62:2-8; 69:27, 29. See also 39–71, esp 70–71. On 1 Enoch, see Johnathan Alan Hiehle and Kelly Whitcomb, "Enoch, First Book Of," in *The Lexham Bible Dictionary*, ed. John Barry (Bellingham, WA: Lexham, 2016).

it is unclear whether God is simultaneously sitting as well.[30] Bock writes, "[Enoch] gets as close to God as any figure, sharing in his judgment in the end and being seated on a throne God uses. He assumes this role, because God himself extends the invitation to him to sit and receive such honor."[31] It is rare for texts to mention a human being seated at God's right hand. While a few portray human luminaries as potential mediators of divine judgment, many Jews were uncomfortable with traditions bringing even highly respected figures too close to God. For example, rabbis sharply disagreed on the question of whether any human being, even luminaries such as King David, could sit with God in heaven.[32] In light of this discussion, it is not difficult to see how Caiaphas and the council could easily perceive Jesus' unusual reply as presumptuously irreverent.

The uniqueness of Jesus' claim. How exceptional was Jesus' claim? Jesus' reply stands out as dissimilar even among potential mediators of divine judgment. There is no evidence depicting even highly revered Old Testament figures as ever predicting that they will be exalted by sitting at God's right hand or riding the clouds. Jesus' reply would have likely been heard as an audacious claim even if it came from Abraham, Moses, or Enoch themselves during their earthly lives.[33] None of these luminaries ever predicted that they would sit at God's right hand, ride the clouds as a deity does, or judge God's representatives. In light of this, Jesus' reply seems outstandingly novel and unique. This dissimilarity from what we find among Jewish luminaries increases the historical likelihood of its preservation and contemplation.

Beyond this, most of the Jewish leaders at Jesus' examination were Sadducees. Unlike the Pharisees (who had a lot more in common with

---

[30]1 Enoch 51:3; 55:4; 61:8.

[31]Bock, *Blasphemy and Exaltation*, 128-29.

[32]Babylonian Talmud Hagigah 14a; Babylonian Talmud Sanhedrin 38b.

[33]Perhaps one example of such hubris from outside Israel is an Egyptian prefect and governor whom Philo rhetorically called extraordinarily evil because he claimed to possess divine authority to overrule Jewish law, daring "to compare himself to the all-blessed God" and speaking "blasphemies against the sun." Philo, *On Dreams* 2.130-31. Yarbro Collins also notes that Philo applied the term *blasphemy* to "a human being claiming a greater degree of authority and power than he has a right to do and, directly or indirectly, claiming divine status for himself," in *Legatio ad Gaium* and *De somniis* ("Charge of Blasphemy," 395). For discussion, see 386-89. Still, no extant text records a human being claiming what Jesus did in his reply to the high priest.

Jesus, theologically), they rejected the concepts of an afterlife, bodily resurrection, the existence of angels, and heavenly exaltation and rewards.[34] To them, the idea of a mere human being of little stature predicting that he would sit with God in heaven in the role of an eschatological judge was not just laughable—it was outright offensive. You could imagine the high priest hearing Jesus' reply and thinking, "We are God's chosen representatives on earth. And who are you? How dare you!" Still, Jesus' extraordinary reply suggests that God will vindicate him. It also suggests a kind of elevated authority that seems to go beyond anything even human luminaries ever claimed. How elevated was this claim to authority? This is clarified in the second part of Jesus' reply.

After Jesus states that the leadership will see him sitting at God's right hand, he also says that they will see him "coming with the clouds of heaven" (Mk 14:62). Here Jesus alludes to Daniel 7:13-14, claiming that God will have him ride the clouds—something indicative of deity.[35] In the prophet Daniel's context, the Son of Man is seen going to God, portraying his vindication and his earthly return to rule—judging the wicked and vindicating the righteous. Jesus links his exaltation with God and suggests not only that he will share in both judging and ruling but that he possesses a kind of heavenly transcendence as well. Bock explains, "It is the juxtaposition of seating and coming on the clouds that makes clear the transcendent function that Jesus gives himself here, with the reference to clouds making it apparent that more than a pure human and earthly messianic claim is present."[36] In light of this, it seems very probable that the high priest viewed Jesus' exceptional reply as disrespectful to God's unique authority. Here, we can see how dissimilarity (rule two) and (in light of the distinctly Jewish settings and subject matter) contextual plausibility (rule six) apply. It was a claim to possess

---

[34]Trent C. Butler and Clayton Harrop, "Jewish Parties in the New Testament," in *Holman Bible Dictionary* (Nashville: Broadman & Holman, 1991), 791.

[35]Bock, "Blasphemy and the Jewish Examination," 616.

[36]Bock, "Blasphemy and the Jewish Examination," 617. See also Morna D. Hooker: "To claim for oneself a seat at the right hand of power . . . is to claim a share in the authority of God; to appropriate such authority and to bestow on oneself this unique status in the sight of God and man would almost certainly have been regarded as blasphemy." Hooker, *Son of Man in Mark* (Montreal: McGill-Queen's University Press, 1967), 173.

divine authority to judge sin. This leads to the next option, which may also contribute to the blasphemy charge in this case.

3. *Disrespecting God's chosen leaders.* Another contender for an audacious, offensive something in Jesus' reply is the implication that he possessed divine authority to judge those who saw themselves as God's representatives, including the high priest himself. Jesus was not only saying that he would be seated next to God but that the high priest himself would see it. The concept of seeing may very well be an allusion to 1 Enoch 62:3-5, which includes seeing the vindication of the Son of Man, seated on his glorious throne.[37] Here the ones who see the Son of Man are the ones who are judged in the eschaton:

> And there shall stand up in that day all the kings and the mighty,
>> And the exalted and those who hold the earth,
>> And they shall see and recognize How he sits on the throne of
>>> his glory,
>> And righteousness is judged before him,
>> And no lying word is spoken before him.
> Then shall pain come upon them as on a woman in travail,
>> [And she has pain in bringing forth]
>> When her child enters the mouth of the womb,
>> And she has pain in bringing forth.
> And one portion of them shall look on the other,
>> And they shall be terrified,
>> And they shall be downcast of countenance,
>> And pain shall seize them,
>> When they see that Son of Man Sitting on the throne of his glory.
>> (1 Enoch 62:3-5)[38]

Here the Son of Man is an eschatological, divine being who judges the sins of human leaders, and the idea of seeing the Son of Man seated appears to parallel Jesus' prediction. Not only is Jesus reducing the perceived distance between himself and God, but his reply could be heard

---

[37]Bock, "Blasphemy and the Jewish Examination," 623.

[38]R. H. Charles, trans. *The Apocrypha and Pseudepigrapha of the Old Testament* (Oxford: Clarendon Press, 1913). https://www.ccel.org/c/charles/otpseudepig/enoch/ENOCH_2.HTM.

as an insulting verbal attack on their leadership of Israel. Again, Jesus' reply to the high priest's question "Are you the Christ, the Son of the Blessed?" is, "I am, and you will see the Son of Man seated at the right hand of Power, and coming with the clouds of heaven" (Mk 14:61-62).

Some skeptics want to say, "Jesus wasn't talking about himself as the Son of Man. He was talking about someone else!" For them, Jesus is not referring to himself as the Son of Man. He is merely saying that Caiaphas will see the Son of Man. The problem with this objection is that Jesus is—in a serious legal context—answering a direct question about his own identity. There is no evidence that Jesus changed the topic mid-sentence and began referring to someone else as the Son of Man (or that Jesus broke his pattern of using "the Son of Man" to refer to himself). Casey himself, after identifying what he called the "genuine sayings" of Jesus, concludes that Jesus used the concept of the eschatological Son of Man as a self-reference when portraying himself as playing a pivotal role in the judgment: "Jesus asserted that people's attitudes to him during the historic ministry would be decisive at the final judgement. . . . Jesus used the term [Son of Man] in an idiomatic way to say this. . . . Jesus declared that people's attitude to him during the historic ministry would condition their fate at the last judgement."[39] In light of this, it would not be out of character for Jesus to speak of himself as the Son of Man while making a related eschatological claim in this scene. The idea that Jesus saw himself as the Son of Man who was God's eschatological agent is widely recognized as a highly evidenced fact of history (e.g., Mt 11:4-5; 12:28; Lk 11:20; Lk 7:22; 4Q521; Is 61:1).[40]

So, Caiaphas realized that the Son of Man here was not some third party. It was Jesus. He's the Son of Man who's coming back again. The Jewish leaders got the implication loud and clear: Jesus claimed to possess divine authority and said that he himself would ultimately

---

[39]Casey, *Solution to the "Son of Man" Problem*, 193-94.

[40]"The titles "Son of Man" and "Messiah" (= Christ) in particular arise in connection with the historical Jesus. . . . There is a consensus that Jesus had a sense of eschatological authority. He saw the dawn of a new world in his actions. Here he goes beyond the Jewish charismatics and prophets known to us before him." Gerd Theissen and Annette Merz, *The Historical Jesus: A Comprehensive Guide* (Minneapolis: Fortress, 1998), 512-13.

return on the clouds to judge them. In light of Jewish concepts of blasphemy and human exaltation, it is very probable that the high priest heard Jesus' reply as a kind of blasphemy. Regardless of whether Jesus pronounced the divine name, both his claim to sit at God's right hand and the perceived disrespect of God's chosen leaders would qualify as instances of cultural blasphemy. The offense Caiaphas felt may have been caused by a combination of both, although it would be difficult to pinpoint which held more weight in his mind. Regardless, Casey's second challenge falls flat because it fails to consider Jewish concepts of blasphemy and exaltation as relevant background material for assessing the data in this scene.

CHALLENGE THREE: THE INCOHERENCE OF A BLASPHEMY CHARGE WITH JESUS' CRUCIFIXION

Casey's third objection has to do with the criteria of coherence (rule four). He says that the blasphemy charge does not cohere with Rome's crucifixion of Jesus for the crime of sedition: "Jesus was crucified for sedition, which would be very difficult to justify from this charge of blasphemy."[41] This raises a point worth considering. It is also a point Ehrman has raised online: "Jesus wasn't accused of blasphemy before Pilate, so far as we can tell. He was charged with claiming to be the future king of Judea."[42] Indeed, many of his concerns seem to echo Casey's own concerns. But does this observation automatically mean that the blasphemy charge is incoherent?

It's true that Rome wouldn't care about a religious charge like blasphemy or any violation of Jewish law. However, Pilate would need to consider a charge against someone who claimed to be a king that Rome did not appoint. This is exactly why the Jewish leadership had to take a political charge to Rome in order to seek the death penalty. In light of this, we have to ask, "Could a blasphemy accusation in a Jewish context

---

[41]Casey, *Solution to the "Son of Man" Problem*, 244.
[42]Bart Ehrman, "Does Jesus Call Himself God in His Trial Before the Sanhedrin and the High Priest Caiaphas?," *The Bart Ehrman Blog*, August 19, 2023, https://ehrmanblog.org/does -jesus-call-himself-god-in-his-trial-before-the-sanhedrin-and-the-high-priest-caiaphus/.

be translated into a sedition charge that the Jewish leaders could take to the Roman authorities?" Yes, it certainly could. And this is the problem with this third challenge. It misses the royal aspect of Jesus' messianic claim. For many Jews, the Davidic Messiah was a warrior king who would destroy Israel's enemies.[43] It also misses the regal dimension of the idea of Jesus as a judge. For example, biblical and extrabiblical Jewish texts portray judging as synonymous with ruling and judges as synonymous with kings (e.g., Ps 2:10; Amos 2:3; 1 Kings 3:9; 2 Chron 1:10-11; Sir 45:26; Wis 1:1; 3:8; 6:4; Pss. Sol. 17:26-32; 1 Macc 9:73). That Jesus would speak of divine judgment, especially in this setting, is more than plausible. So, the sedition charge in a Roman context does not seem incoherent with the blasphemy accusation in a Jewish context. In the minds of the Jewish leaders, they could be related. And this is why the charge against Jesus was contextualized for Pilate's consideration.

We can see both similarity and dissimilarity in this scene as well. While Jesus' use of judicial language and courtroom imagery appears continuous with early Jewish tradition, his claim to judge others in the eschaton appears dissimilar from anything depicted in Jewish texts.[44] Consider the history of interpretation surrounding the first text to which Jesus alluded in his reply: Psalm 110. After 586 BC, many connected the psalm to an idealized future king.[45] During the postexilic period, some interpreters linked the text with an expectation of the Davidic dynasty's restoration after the return from exile and the rebuilding of the temple (Jer 33:14-26; Zech 3:1-10; 6:9-15; see also Hag 2:20-23). When this did not happen, many Jews saw in Psalm 110 an image of the ruling Messiah

---

[43]John J. Collins, *The Scepter and the Star: The Messiahs of the Dead Sea Scrolls and Other Ancient Literature* (New Haven, CT: Yale University Press, 2007), 68.

[44]On the use of judicial language and courtroom imagery, see Marius Reiser, *Jesus and Judgment* (Minneapolis: Fortress, 1997), 307.

[45]This appears between Ps 107–109 (the opening of book five, Ps 107–150), and the hallelujah hymns (Ps 111–113). While many in the postexilic period repurposed the former to express sorrow at what seemed to be Yahweh's rejection of the Davidic monarchy (see Ps 108–109), Gordon H. Johnston notes that "both end with future expectation: 'By God's power we will conquer; he will tramp down our enemies' (Ps. 108:13)." See Johnston, "Messianic Trajectories in the Royal Psalms," in *Jesus the Messiah: Tracing the Promises, Expectations, and Coming of Israel's King*, ed. Herbert W. Bateman IV, Darrell L. Bock, and Gordon H. Johnston (Grand Rapids, MI: Kregel, 2012), 101-2.

ushering in the eschatological kingdom and sitting at God's right hand—the ultimate eschatological king.

A Jewish text outside the Bible, 1 Enoch 37–71, may allude to Psalm 110 as well. Here the preexistent Son of Man is a figure who has both human and divine qualities (1 Enoch 46:1-14) and sits on God's own throne (1 Enoch 51:3) as a heavenly judge (see 1 Enoch 45:1-3; 55:4; 62:2-5; 69:29). This text potentially hangs in the background of Jesus' reply.[46] The Pharisees' opposition of the Sadducees may lie behind in the contrast of the "righteous"/"elect" on the one hand and "sinners"/"mighty ones" in this text.[47] If so, any allusion to this would have only increased the perceived offense among the Sadducees present. All this background suggests that Jesus' reply likely qualified his messianic claim to include not only a regal nuance but an implied claim to possess divine authority to rule and judge. Bock observes:

> Jesus' claim to possess comprehensive independent authority would serve as the basis of taking Jesus before Rome on a socio-political charge, as well as constituting a religious offense of blasphemy that would be seen as worthy of the pursuit of the death penalty. In the leadership's view, the socio-political threat to the stability of the Jewish people is an underlying reason why the claim had to be dealt with so comprehensively.[48]

Casey's view that Mark or the early church fabricated the blasphemy charge seems too hasty. Jesus' messianic claim as well as his claim to judge

---

[46]James H. Charlesworth argues, "The *Parables of Enoch* (1 En 37–71) appear to be a Jewish work that antedates Jesus." Charlesworth, "The Date and Provenience of the Parables of Enoch," in *Parables of Enoch: A Paradigm Shift*, ed. Darrell L. Bock and James H. Charlesworth, Jewish and Christian Texts 11 (New York: Bloomsbury T&T Clark, 2013), 57. Bock argues that there is "a strong likelihood that the Parables of Enoch are Jewish and most likely were composed prior to the work of Jesus of Nazareth or contemporaneous with his Galilean ministry." Darrell L. Bock, "Dating the Parables of Enoch: A Forschungsbericht," in *Parables of Enoch: A Paradigm Shift*, ed. Darrell L. Bock and James H. Charlesworth, Jewish and Christian Texts 11 (New York: Bloomsbury T&T Clark, 2013), 11. Those at Qumran held that the chosen leader was the Teacher of Righteousness. Because of this, they may have rejected the Parables of Enoch due to the importance of Enoch as the Son of Man in the text. Also, the Son of Man's role as eschatological judge might not have been attractive to a group so rooted in Torah practice and a high view of God's holiness, and they may have rejected "Two Powers" teaching in any form.

[47]R. H. Charles, *The Book of Enoch* (Eastford, CT: Martino Fine Books, 2017), 72-73.

[48]Darrell L. Bock, "Jesus as Blasphemer," in *Who Do My Opponents Say That I Am? An Investigation of the Accusations Against the Historical Jesus*, ed. Scot McKnight and Joseph B. Modica, Library of New Testament Studies 327 (New York: T&T Clark, 2008), 93.

his hearers likely carried royal undertones that could be translated into a political charge relevant to Rome. A claim of messiahship could be heard as a claim to divine sonship, which could be translated into kingship and the resulting sedition charge presented to Pilate. So, Jesus' claims are coherent with his sense of eschatological authority and his subsequent crucifixion as "King of the Jews." This passes the coherence test (rule four). Rejection and execution (rule three) and contextual plausibility (rule six) also work together to support the authenticity of the blasphemy charge. But what was the significance of Jesus' reply? Did the high priest hear this as a claim to possess divine authority in heaven as eschatological judge?

9

A Divine Claim

AUTHORITY TO JUDGE IN HEAVEN

We have arrived at the last stop on this second leg of our journey. Here we must contemplate the meaning and significance of Jesus' reply. It's one thing to conclude that his reply is authentic. It's another thing to determine what his reply meant to the council. While many studies of Jesus' self-conception focus on what his followers thought about his claims, one of the distinctives of our study is a focus on what Jesus' enemies thought about his claims. So, what was the significance of Jesus' reply in the mind of the high priest? How did he understand what Jesus said? We can get increased clarity on this by examining the Jewish idea of eschatological judgment, especially as it relates to the way Jesus used the concept of the Son of Man.

THE SIGNIFICANCE OF JESUS' TESTIMONY

First, let's go over some cultural background material. Just like most Jews believed that forgiveness ultimately came from God, they also believed that it was ultimately God who had the right to judge the sins of people. In the Old Testament, God is depicted as the eschatological judge. He is the one who distinguishes between the wicked and the righteous and metes out perfect justice (Ps 7:11; 50:2-6; 82:1-4; Ezek 7:27; Is 65). So God is the one who rules and judges the nations from his heavenly throne (Ps 9:4-9; 96:13). But could human beings be involved? We already mentioned how some people imagined certain luminaries, such as Adam, perhaps having a role in the judgment. So, what about the Son of Man—that mysterious human figure with divine authority to judge?

Considering Jewish texts before the destruction of the temple in AD 70, we find the Son of Man depicted as the eschatological judge himself in the words of Jesus and in a section of 1 Enoch (37–71) called the Parables or Similitudes.[1] In 1 Enoch, God is the judge in 1 Enoch 47:3, but otherwise the judge is identified as the Son of Man (1 Enoch 62:5, 7, 9; 63:11; 69:27; a.k.a. "the Elect One," 1 Enoch 45:3; 51:3; 61:8; 62:2). In fact, judgment day is "the Day of the Elect One" in 1 Enoch 61:5. In this scene, the Son of Man has judicial authority in heaven: God seats him on his glorious throne, where he will "judge all the works of the holy ones in heaven" (1 Enoch 61:8). Afterwards, the Son of Man judges the kings and high officials, and they appeal to him for mercy (1 Enoch 62:1-9).

If Jesus' reply had this text in the background, it would have only strengthened the implication that the respective positions of those present and Jesus would be reversed in the eschaton, when Jesus himself would become their judge. This part of 1 Enoch shows that the idea of the Son of Man as a divine human existed in Jesus' time.[2] The way the Son of Man is described in the Gospels connects to a profound and mysterious Jewish expectation of a heavenly savior who is both a savior and a judge.[3]

So, the evidence is strong that Jesus implied divine authority to judge not just anywhere but in heaven itself. To grasp the profundity of this, imagine the offense that Caiaphas would have felt to hear a man boldly

---

[1]Darrell L. Bock notes, "Within the hundreds of Jewish documents that antedate 70 CE, only in the *Parables of Enoch* and only within Jesus' teachings do we find references to the Son of Man as the eschatological Judge." Bock, "Dating the Parables of Enoch: A Forschungsbericht," in *Parables of Enoch: A Paradigm Shift*, ed. Darrell L. Bock and James H. Charlesworth, Jewish and Christian Texts 11 (New York: Bloomsbury T&T Clark, 2013), 55. This dissimilarity from Judaism further speaks to the uniqueness of Jesus' reply.

[2]Daniel Boyarin, *The Jewish Gospels* (New York: New Press, 2012), 76. Recent research by James H. Charlesworth echoes this conclusion. See Charlesworth, "Did Jesus Know the Traditions in the Parables of Enoch?," in Bock and Charlesworth, *Parables of Enoch*, 195.

[3]See John J. Collins, "The Son of Man in Ancient Judaism," in *Handbook for the Study of the Historical Jesus* (Leiden: Brill, 2010), 2:1568.

announce that he planned to move into the temple and turn the holy of holies (the symbol of God's heavenly presence) into his bedroom! Now, realize that Jesus' reply went beyond even this outlandish scenario. As Bock says, "Part of what made the remark so offensive to the leadership was its suggested locale in heaven. Jesus invoked not the symbol of God's presence but his own presence next to the very real glory of God."[4]

AN "IDEALIZED HUMAN" CLAIM

Before even getting to a historical challenge, some say that Jesus never claimed to be divine even in the literary world of Mark's Gospel. If so, why think that Jesus claimed be divine in the real world? In *A Man Attested By God*, Daniel Kirk reacts to the emphasis many biblical conservatives place on arguing for the highest Christology in the Synoptics, potentially to the exclusion of recognizing the very real human portrait of Jesus that emerges from the text. He sees the significance of Jesus' claim as something just shy of claiming to be a divine being. While Kirk says that his literary approach is "not, then, a study of the historical Jesus and how he presented himself," he also says, "It is a historical study in the sense that it attempts to provide a historically viable reading of the text from within the first-century Greek-speaking Jewish world in which they were written." Because of this, it's important to engage with his views on the kind of authority Jesus claimed to have.[5]

Kirk calls Jesus an "idealized human" who falls "between the merely human and divine," but he also challenges the uniqueness of Jesus' claimed authority by asserting that Jesus "exercises God's authority on earth as God intended for humanity at the beginning."[6] So, is Jesus an "in-betweener"? More than a man, but not quite divine? Kirk says he invented this category of an "idealized human" to talk about "non-angelic,

---

[4]Darrell L. Bock, "The Historical Jesus: An Evangelical View," in *The Historical Jesus: Five Views*, ed. James K. Beilby and Paul R. Eddy (Downers Grove, IL: IVP Academic, 2009), 275.

[5]J. R. Daniel Kirk, *A Man Attested by God: The Human Jesus of the Synoptic Gospels* (Grand Rapids, MI: Eerdmans, 2016), 9.

[6]Kirk, *Man Attested by God*, 11. Beyond the mere recognition that Jesus is a human being who acts as God's eschatological agent, Kirk seems to argue that a kind of functional divinity rather than an ontological divinity best explains the Synoptic portraits of Jesus (see 148, 262). There is no clear evidence that these contemporary categories existed in the minds of ancient people.

non-preexistent human beings, of the past, present, or anticipated future, who are depicted in textual or other artifacts as playing some unique role in representing God to the rest of the created realm, or in representing some aspect of the created realm before God." For him, Jesus is just one of the human figures who "share in ascriptions, actions, and attributes otherwise reserved for God alone."[7] But is this really the best way to explain how Jesus thought about himself and his authority?

No. It doesn't work to say that the kind of authority that Jesus claimed to have is the same as the kind of authority God gave Adam at creation (or the kind God intended all people to have). Here's why: God gave Adam authority over the earth and the animals as a representative of humanity. That's the kind of authority common to all people (Gen 1:26-28). However, humanity's general authority over the earth and the animals does not imply that one individual person has the right to have total authority over all other people and judge their sins in the eschaton.[8] Even texts that imagine Adam's mediation of divine rule or judgment always mention a very special appointment by God for what seems to be a rare, temporary honor rather than one intended for all humans. There is a problem even with Kirk's attempt to put Adam in an "idealized human" category in order to better explain how most Jews thought about humans sharing divine authority. Some Jews saw Adam as a second angel assigned to rule as king over the earth (2 Enoch 30:12). So, Kirk's creation of an "idealized human" category to understand the kind of authority Jesus claimed to have doesn't seem helpful. How likely is it that this category was in the minds of the Jewish leadership?

Think about Jesus' question in Mark 12:37 concerning the Messiah's status as David's lord: "David himself calls him Lord. So how is he his son?" This suggests that Kirk's category is inadequate for understanding Jesus' claim. It seems insufficient to categorize Jesus' reply as a claim to

---

[7]Kirk, *Man Attested by God*, 3, 176.

[8]Richard Bauckham, "Is 'High Human Christology' Sufficient? A Critical Response to J. R. Daniel Kirk's *A Man Attested by God*," *Bulletin for Biblical Research* 27, no. 4 (2017): 503-25. While Adam's rule appears restricted to animals in Philo, *On the Creation* 148, Wisdom 10:1-2 notes that God gave Adam "strength to rule all things." Still, no extant texts depict Adam as predicting he would serve as eschatological judge over other humans.

possess a merely idealized human authority when no surviving ancient texts depict any idealized human figures predicting their own role as an eschatological judge. Still, Kirk might agree that Jesus' reply suggests more than a merely human claim to authority but one that positioned him as representing God in some unique sense. But this doesn't seem to go far enough. Even on a purely literary level, Jesus' reply appears to be a claim to possess divine authority. This agrees with Adela Yarbro Collins's study of the blasphemy charge. She writes:

> [The high priest] at least, and probably other Jews, considered it "blasphemy" to claim to be a god or to have divine power. Jesus' saying in 14.62 fits this definition. In that saying, the Markan Jesus claims to be a messiah of the heavenly type, who will be exalted to the right hand of God (Ps. 110.1). Being seated at the right hand of God implies being equal to God, at least in terms of authority and power. The allusion to Dan. 7.13 reinforces the heavenly messianic claim. The "coming on the clouds" has a dual role. On the one hand, this motif, typical of divine beings, signifies the universal power that Jesus as Messiah will have. On the other, the statement that the members of the council "will see" him applies especially to his "coming on the clouds" in a public manifestation of his messianic power and glory.[9]

Indeed, Kirk's "idealized human" category doesn't seem very helpful in advancing our understanding of how Caiaphas understood Jesus' reply.

A Divine Claim

Many who doubt that Jesus claimed to be divine say that he never claims to be divine in our earliest Gospel, the Gospel of Mark. Ehrman previously taught this view but changed his mind upon further research.[10] This is significant because it shows that even some atheist scholars who reject the truth of the biblical narrative can agree that Jesus' reply in Mark 14:62 includes a divine claim. Although Ehrman doubts the authenticity of the details portrayed in our scene, he now holds that at least

---

[9] Adela Yarbro Collins, "The Charge of Blasphemy in Mark 14.64," *Journal for the Study of the New Testament* 26, no. 4 (2004): 400-401.

[10] Bart Ehrman, "Jesus as God in the Synoptics," *The Bart Ehrman Blog*, April 13, 2014, https://ehrmanblog.org/jesus-as-god-in-the-synoptics-for-members/.

in the narrative world of Mark's Gospel, this perception was shared by the council: "Jesus is apparently making some kind of divine claim for himself. . . . The council is upset with Jesus because they think he's making a divine claim."[11] Further, "There is no question that Jesus in the Gospels claims to be divine."[12] So, even for a rather skeptical atheist scholar such as Ehrman, Jesus makes a divine claim in Mark. Remember, however, his biggest problem with Jesus' reply as presented by Mark is that "if this in fact is what Jesus said, he didn't commit any blasphemy."[13] How can we respond to this objection to the plausibility of the text?

IDENTIFYING THE BLASPHEMY

We may never know whether Jesus pronounced the divine name in his reply to Caiaphas. However, this is only the first option for consideration in terms of what it is that Jesus may have said to elicit a blasphemy accusation from the high priest. In the previous chapter, our study showed that Bock's second and third options for understanding the nature of the blasphemy charge can shed light on the significance of Jesus' reply: claiming the authority to sit at God's right hand and allegedly disrespecting God's chosen leaders.

Beyond a military messianism, Jesus' claim to sit with God in heaven was likely heard as a claim to possess divine authority to judge. This was an unparalleled assertion even among human luminaries. Further, Jesus' prediction that the high priest and the council members present would see him coming on the clouds was likely understood as an attack on God's representatives precisely because he was claiming that they would one day answer to him as the Son of Man in the final judgment.[14]

---

[11]Ehrman made these comments at an event with Michael Bird. See Bart D. Ehrman and Michael F. Bird, "How Jesus Became God" (debate, New Orleans, February 12, 2016), https://youtu.be /RtkeNuCwinc, quote at timestamp 58:52.

[12]Bart Ehrman, "Does Jesus Call Himself God in His Trial Before the Sanhedrin and the High Priest Caiaphas?," *The Bart Ehrman Blog*, August 19, 2023, https://ehrmanblog.org/does -jesus-call-himself-god-in-his-trial-before-the-sanhedrin-and-the-high-priest-caiaphus/.

[13]Bart D. Ehrman, *Jesus: Apocalyptic Prophet of the New Millennium* (New York: Oxford University Press, 1999), 220.

[14]The second-person plural in Jesus' reply to the high priest, *kai opsesthe ton hyion tou anthrōpou*, "and y'all will see the Son of Man," refers to the council members present as well (Mk 14:62).

The image of coming on the clouds as the Son of Man suggests a claim to heavenly authority and divine status. So, it is likely that Jesus was heard as claiming to possess divine authority in heaven as the eschatological judge.

CONCLUSION

How probable is it that the historical Jesus claimed to possess divine authority to judge? We come to the end of the second leg of our journey. Now it is time to draw some conclusions about the data. Let's synthesize our findings and articulate a historically defensible answer to the question, "How probable is it that the historical Jesus was accurately remembered as a unique man who claimed to judge sins in heaven?" Data from Jesus' Jewish examination (Mk 14:53-65) suggest that Jewish leaders believed that Jesus' reply contained a blasphemy—a prediction that he would judge them in the eschaton as a kind of transcendent figure in heaven who possessed divine authority. While some critics, such as Casey, challenge aspects of the scene, there is no compelling evidence that suggests the core exchange between Caiaphas and Jesus is inauthentic. Even more, we uncovered Jewish concepts of blasphemy that support the authenticity of the blasphemy accusation. There is no record of anyone else claiming to judge the sins of the Jewish leaders as Jesus did.

Again, let's review our scale of historical certainty:

(–4) certainly not historical
(–3) very improbable
(–2) quite improbable
(–1) more improbable than not
(0) indeterminate (i.e., neither improbable nor probable)
(+1) more probable than not
(+2) quite probable
(+3) very probable
(+4) certainly historical (i.e., the highest possible probability)

The first leg of our quest uncovered five historical facts. Similarly, this second leg of our journey yields a second set of five facts we can hold with the following degrees of certainty:

1. **The authenticity of Jesus' rejection by Jewish leaders and crucifixion under Rome:** (+4) *certainly historical.*

- Rejection is multiply attested: for example, Synoptic tradition, including Markan clashes over the nature of Jesus' authority; Gospel of Thomas, Gospel of Peter, and Gospel of Nicodemus, Josephus.[15]
- Embarrassment: Q 7:31-35[16]
- Crucifixion is multiply attested: For example, Paul, Sayings Gospel Q, canonical Gospels, Josephus, Tacitus, Lucian of Samosata.[17]
- It's contextually plausible. This is a bedrock fact from which historians may begin to assess the core scene.[18]

2. **The authenticity of the core scene:** (+3) *very probable*

- Multiple attestation of sources: Synoptic tradition, Gospel of Thomas, Gospel of Peter, Gospel of Nicodemus
- It's contextually plausible. This also explains how the Jewish leadership rejected Jesus and what resulted in his execution.

---

[15]Josephus, *Jewish Antiquities* 18.63-64. Josephus implicates some Jewish leaders and Pilate in Jesus' execution. The former brought a charge, and the latter acted on it. This agrees with the canonical Gospels: When Jesus stood before Pilate, some Jewish leaders brought accusations against him (Mt 27:11-14; Mk 15:1-5; Lk 23:1-5; Jn 18:28-30). For a discussion on a reconstruction of *Jewish Antiquities* 18.63-64, see Robert E. Van Voorst, *Jesus Outside the New Testament: An Introduction to the Ancient Evidence* (Grand Rapids, MI: Eerdmans, 2000), 93-104. For other key clashes, see Mt 26:57-68; Lk 13:31; 22:54-71. Acts 3:12-19 suggests Jesus' rejection was a matter of public knowledge.

[16]Jesus is reported as saying that he was characterized as a "glutton and a drunkard" and "a friend of tax collectors and sinners" (Lk 7:34; Mt 11:19)—behaviors that Jewish leaders found inappropriate (see Mishnah Teharot 2:2; Babylonian Talmud Sotah 22a; Tosefta Makilta 3:7; Tosefta Demai 2:2, 11, 15; 2:20–3:10). Rudolf Schnackenburg suggests these were crass expressions in *The Gospel of Matthew*, trans. Robert R. Barr (Grand Rapids, MI: Eerdmans, 2002), 107.

[17]Paul: e.g., Gal 3:1; 5:11; 6:12-14; 1 Cor 1:17-18, 22-23; 2:1-2. While Phil 2:6-11 is likely pre-Pauline, Phil 2:8 may be a Pauline gloss. Q: see Q 14:27, "The one who does not take one's cross and follow after me cannot be my disciple." See Mt 10:38; 16:24 = Lk 14:27. Canonical Gospels: e.g., Mk 15:24, Jn 18:18. Josephus: *Jewish Antiquities* 18.63-64. Although Josephus does not mention Jesus' examination before those "leading men among us," as the canonical Gospels report (Mt 26:57-68; Mk 14:53-65; Lk 22:54-71; Jn 18:28-40), such a meeting is plausible in light of Jesus' being handed over to Pilate and crucified. That Jesus' Jewish examination is not mentioned by Josephus suggests that his focus was on Pilate's involvement in Jesus' death. Tacitus: *Annals* 15.44. Lucian: *Death of Peregrinus* 11-13. For discussion, see Van Voorst, *Jesus Outside the New Testament*, 58-64.

[18]The criterion of rejection and execution is based on this. For a discussion of the evidence for Jesus' crucifixion, see Michael R. Licona, *The Resurrection of Jesus: A New Historiographical Approach* (Downers Grove, IL: IVP Academic, 2010), 303-18.

- It coheres with Jesus' involvement in a temple controversy, his clash with the Jewish leadership over the nature of his authority, and his being handed over to Pilate by Jewish leaders.
- Preservation of Jesus' exchange with the high priest is unlikely apart from a narrative context.

3. **The authenticity of the high priest's question:** (+3) *very probable*

- Contextually plausible sources exist: for example, Jewish converts such as Nicodemus, Joseph of Arimathea, Saul of Tarsus, former priests.
- The high priest's use of *Christ* coheres with messianic expectation in the Hebrew Scriptures, Dead Sea Scrolls, the Psalms of Solomon, and 1 Enoch; use of "Son of the Blessed" coheres with the Jewish concept of God as blessed.
- "Son of the Blessed" is dissimilar to Christian titles for Jesus and Mark's style. Preservation of the question is unlikely apart from Jesus' reply.
- Contextual plausibility applies to Jewish sensitivities regarding the divine name.

4. **The authenticity of Jesus' reply:** (+3) *very probable*

- Multiple attestation of Jesus' thematic use of Son of Man, including apocalyptic Son of Man sayings
- Coherence of "Son of Man" with Jesus' manner of speech
- Multiple attestation of Jesus' use of Daniel 7
- Coherence of scriptural allusions, including midrashic-like combinations of texts
- Dissimilarity of the Danielic allusion with the New Testament
- Dissimilarity of "Power" with Mark's style and the New Testament
- Coherence of Psalm 110 with Jesus' previous use, as well as his execution as "King of the Jews"
- No evidence of any human luminary claiming to be the eschatological judge in Jewish texts suggests a novel saying that would be remembered. Preservation of the reply is unlikely apart from the question.

- Contextual plausibility applies to Jewish sensitivities regarding the divine name.

5. **The authenticity of the blasphemy charge:** (+3) *very probable*

- Garment tearing is contextually plausible, as Mishnanic procedures are less relevant to this case.
- Coherence with cultural views of blasphemy, including potential pronouncement of the divine name, claiming the authority to sit at God's right hand, and a perceived disrespect for God's chosen leaders.
- The nature of Jesus' regal claims are coherent with his execution as the "King of the Jews."
- No evidence of any human luminary claiming to be the eschatological judge in Jewish texts increases the likelihood of the offense.
- Rejection and execution also applies.

Jesus' rejection by Jewish leaders and his execution under Rome are *certainly historical*. Although I have listed the authenticity of the core scene as only *very probable*, these bedrock facts make the reality of such a meeting almost certainly historical. Further, our investigation yields second-order facts that are also highly evidenced. In terms of the details of the meeting, the exchange between the high priest and Jesus—including the blasphemy accusation—is *very probable*. Here, Jesus' prediction about sitting at God's right hand and riding the clouds indicates that he, as the Son of Man, possesses independent and comprehensive authority to judge the sins of the high priests and the present council members as a kind of transcendent being. Making himself too close to God and disrespecting God's chosen leaders would have likely been seen as a cultural form of blasphemy.

The authenticity of these facts are linked to a certain extent. They appear in the same report of a single event; the question, reply, and response are tightly connected and function together. The existence of our text shows that this exchange was deemed worthy of preservation and contemplation by those who highly respected Jesus' words.

Beyond the uniqueness of Jesus' reply when compared to human luminaries, this scene shows a category of divine authority in the claims of the historical Jesus. The best data suggests that Jesus' reply does not seem to be a claim to possess merely a human kind of authority. Rather, in light of the Jewish belief that God is the ultimate judge and in light of cultural definitions of blasphemy in the Second Temple period, the charge against Jesus fits the category of disrespecting God's unique authority—comparing himself to God by assuming a divine prerogative to judge sin.

I conclude that it is *very probable* that the historical Jesus was accurately remembered as claiming to be the Messiah, the Son of the Blessed, and predicting that the high priest and council members would see him seated at God's right hand, coming on the clouds as the eschatological Son of Man. I give this a +3 on the scale of historical certainty. In light of Jesus' cultural context, his reply was likely heard as an implicit claim to possess divine authority in heaven to judge sins—a claim that was unique even among human luminaries. This sheds further light on the nature of Jesus' claimed authority and the perceived offense that resulted in his being delivered to Pilate. Uncovering the regal dimension of Jesus' reply also helps explain the link between Jesus' claims and his crucifixion for sedition as "King of the Jews."

History tells us that Jesus was a unique man who predicted that he would judge sins in an ancient Jewish context that saw this as a blasphemous claim that came too close to usurping God's own authority. For me, this has been a helpful talking point in conversations with people who may be hesitant to accept the Bible but seem open to approaching the question from a historical lens. Many people have had exposure to lawyers cross-examining defendants when serving on a jury or watching a courtroom drama series. Perhaps because of this, some skeptics tend to perk up and lean forward with interest when I talk about our second blasphemy accusation scene as the most important legal proceeding in ancient history. Framing the conversation this way can help those who have never thought about Jesus as a figure in ancient history to consider his claims afresh.

PART FOUR

Battle of the Views

TESTING KEY EXPLANATIONS OF JESUS' CLAIMS IN THE BLASPHEMY ACCUSATION SCENES

So what if someone digs up a pot?" "What's the difference between the Bible and a fairy tale?" I continue to hear challenges like these from people like the skeptical high school senior who rejected the value of history and archaeology and the skeptical senior citizen who didn't see the difference between the Bible and fiction. Even skeptical senior scholars who are not experts in historical studies, such as Dawkins,

boldly assert similar things: "The gospels are ancient fiction."[1] In light of our analysis, however, we can be confident that Mark's portrayal of the key exchange in Jesus' Jewish examination can stand up to the toughest challenges—even the academic arguments of critical scholars such as Casey, who published respected technical monographs in the area of historical Jesus studies.

At the outset of the second leg of our journey, we were faced with what seemed to be gigantic roadblocks to taking the core exchange between Caiaphas and Jesus seriously, from Ehrman's assertion that "we don't know exactly what happened at the proceeding" to Casey's "massive argument" for the historical incoherence or implausibility of our scene.[2] Despite this, the objections that may have initially appeared to be gigantic obstacles to building a case for Jesus' divine claim are not insurmountable. After a careful historical investigation, these giants have fallen. Still, skeptics continue to repeat atheist arguments like Dawkins's insistence that "there is no good historical evidence that [Jesus] ever thought he was divine."[3] How can someone who values history choose between the various views of Jesus?

The second leg of our investigative journey was a very profitable one. Exhibit B, Jesus' Jewish examination, is admissible historical evidence. Both our first and second blasphemy accusation scenes are credible and warrant serious consideration. We are building our case for the historicity of Jesus' divine claim as historians, using this examination scene as a way to clarify some of the ambiguity present in this the healing of the paralytic.

Our historical investigation of both blasphemy accusation scenes is now complete. Now we will work as historians do to adjudicate between various hypotheses and apply standard procedures to the question of Jesus' divine claim. In part four, we will begin to weigh the evidence and test our theory along with other competing views.

---

[1]Richard Dawkins, *The God Delusion* (Boston: Houghton Mifflin, 2006), 97.
[2]Bart D. Ehrman, *Jesus: Apocalyptic Prophet of the New Millennium* (New York: Oxford University Press, 1999), 220-21.
[3]Dawkins, *God Delusion*, 92.

10

Limited Power

AUTHORITY OVER SOME OF REALITY

Let's review where we've been on our investigative journey. Think back to that castle-style home with a two-story turret library—the mental construct where we began. Our staging area highlighted key philosophical and methodological considerations for studying the historical Jesus. Despite challenges, we found that researchers can obtain at least a degree of knowledge from written sources about key sayings and events in the life of the historical Jesus. We set out on our quest to uncover the truth about the kind of authority that Jesus claimed to have with two overarching questions that directed our investigation:

1. What key events and sayings of the historical Jesus can best be demonstrated as being at least probably historical?
2. In light of Jesus' cultural context, what is the most likely significance of the sayings tied to each key event?

In part four, we move from our data-collection phase to a critical analysis of competing views. Each view is a perspective on the kind of authority Jesus claimed to possess. Which one best fits the data? Here's the plan: we'll take the ten highly evidenced data points that we uncovered from our two blasphemy accusation scenes (Mk 2:1-12; 14:53-65) and use them to evaluate two major hypotheses. Hypothesis one is that Jesus claimed to possess a kind of human authority, and hypothesis two is that Jesus claimed to possess a kind of divine authority.

First, we'll summarize and synthesize the data we uncovered so that we are clear on the facts of the case. Then we will conduct our analysis by using the approach we discussed in our staging area, called "methodological neutrality." Remember, this doesn't mean that we (or anyone else) can be entirely neutral, with no biases whatsoever. That's unrealistic for any researcher. Instead, what this means is that the one arguing for a certain hypothesis bears the burden of proof. That's the rule. That's how the game is played.

Just like historians studying any figure in ancient history, we will use standard criteria in historical studies to make inferences and evaluate hypotheses about Jesus' claim. Remember that there are five criteria. These function as checks to guide our assessment of the hypotheses.[1] We're going to ask, "Which one, if any, can best make sense of our ten historical facts?" We'll run each major hypothesis through a kind of sieve to help us see how well it passes the five key tests (these tests are different from the criteria of authenticity, or the rules of evidence we employed during our data-collection phase). Let's review those five criteria from our staging area.

1. *Plausibility:* This pertains to how much a hypothesis is implied by historical bedrock and other highly evidenced facts.

2. *Explanatory scope:* This pertains to the number of known historical facts that are accounted for by a given hypothesis. This is a key supportive element of a hypothesis.

3. *Explanatory power:* This pertains to how well the hypothesis can explain the known facts. "Is the explanation a good fit for the facts? Or does it seem forced?" This is another key supportive element of a hypothesis.

4. *Less ad hoc.* This applies when the hypothesis does not rely on poorly evidenced assumptions that go well beyond the known

---

[1]Our study adopted methodological neutrality as an approach over methodological credulity or methodological skepticism. See Michael R. Licona, *The Resurrection of Jesus: A New Historiographical Approach* (Downers Grove, IL: IVP Academic, 2010), 99; C. B. McCullagh, *Justifying Historical Descriptions* (New York: Cambridge University Press, 1984), 37-38.

facts. It helps researchers determine the least problematic view among those under consideration. Some call this one "simplicity."

5. *Illumination:* This pertains to how well a hypothesis helps us explain another historical matter or helps us clarify matters that are related to accepted facts. Think of this as a bonus. It shouldn't count negatively against a hypothesis if it doesn't apply. But if it does, it gives us another reason to accept that hypothesis as the best one.

Historians weigh competing hypotheses to determine which one is best (or least problematic). A *plausible* hypothesis with a broad *explanatory scope* is better than one that only seems *less ad hoc*. If a *plausible* hypothesis with a broad *explanatory scope* could also function as a kind of rebuttal to challenges from a competing view, that would be even better.[2] This is how we can adjudicate between the various views we've covered in our study. Think of these views as competitors in the world of ideas. Which one will outdistance the others and be recognized as the best explanation of the facts? I will award a hypothesis the label of "historical" if both of the following apply:

1. The evidence supporting the hypothesis justifies a score of *at least* +2, "quite probable," on the scale of historical certainty used in this study.[3]

2. It is shown to be superior to competing hypotheses in meeting the five criteria.

Finally, we will determine whether the hypothesis that fared best supports the thesis I proposed at the outset of our study of the historical Jesus: *There is continuity between Jesus' claims and the early Christian belief in him as a divine figure because some of Jesus' words and deeds were likely interpreted by his Jewish adversaries as unparalleled claims to possess divine authority.* Let's synthesize the data. What are the facts of the case?

---

[2]McCullagh, *Justifying Historical Descriptions*, 37-38.
[3]Again, the scale of historical certainty used in this study is (–4) certainly not historical, (–3) very improbable, (–2) quite improbable, (–1) more improbable than not, (0) indeterminate (i.e., neither improbable nor probable), (+1) more probable than not, (+2) quite probable, (+3) very probable, (+4) certainly historical (i.e., the highest possible probability).

Summary and Synthesis of Highly Evidenced Data from Mark 2:1-12; 14:53-65

Our study built independent historical cases for two ideas: (1) Jesus was accurately remembered as a unique miracle worker who claimed to possess authority on earth to forgive sin, and (2) Jesus was accurately remembered as claiming to be the eschatological Son of Man who possessed authority in heaven to judge sin. Let us review both data sets. First, a critical investigation of the healing of the paralytic (Mk 2:1-12) yielded the following highly evidenced data points, numbered 1-5:

1. The authenticity of Jesus' reputation as a miracle worker: (+4) *certainly historical*
2. The authenticity of the core scene in Mark 2:1-12: (+3) *very probable*
3. The authenticity of the forgiveness saying: (+3) *very probable*
4. The authenticity of the scribal response: (+3) *very probable*
5. The authenticity of the authority saying: (+3) *very probable*

Further, an analysis of Jesus' cultural context suggests that his forgiveness saying was likely heard as an implicit claim to somehow possess divine authority to forgive sins.

Next, a critical investigation of Jesus' Jewish examination (Mk 14:53-65) yielded the following highly evidenced data points to add to our existing list. We will continue numbering our highly evidenced data points six through ten:

6. The authenticity of Jesus' rejection by Jewish leaders and crucifixion under Rome: (+4) *certainly historical*
7. The authenticity of the core scene in Mark 14:53-65: (+3) *very probable*
8. The authenticity of the high priest's question: (+3) *very probable*
9. The authenticity of Jesus' reply: (+3) *very probable*
10. The authenticity of the blasphemy charge: (+3) *very probable*

Further, an analysis of Jesus' cultural context suggests that his reply was likely heard as an implicit claim to somehow possess divine authority in heaven to judge sins. When the data is considered together, a category of authority across key functions—forgiveness in general and eschatological judgment—begins to emerge. Those are the facts of the case. Let's turn to an analysis of competing hypotheses.

AN ANALYSIS OF COMPETING HYPOTHESES CONCERNING THE CLAIMED AUTHORITY OF JESUS TO FORGIVE AND JUDGE IN MARK 2:1-12; 14:53-65

Did the historical Jesus claim to have divine authority or not? Two major hypotheses have emerged from key works in the twenty-first century: The first hypothesis is that Jesus claimed a kind of human authority rather than divine authority. There are three representative versions of this hypothesis, promoted by scholars whose names we have mentioned in our study: Tobias Hägerland, Bart Ehrman, and Daniel Kirk. We will run each version through the same criteria to determine which version is the best contender against the alternative. The second hypothesis is that Jesus claimed a kind of divine authority. Let's consider these views using the criteria discussed in our opening chapter. This is how we can begin to adjudicate between various hypotheses. How well do these make sense of the known historical data and the implications of the data?

HYPOTHESIS ONE: JESUS CLAIMED TO POSSESS A KIND OF HUMAN AUTHORITY

Tobias Hägerland: Prophetic, human authority. Hägerland's version of hypothesis one is that Jesus claimed a kind of prophetic, human authority.[4] While he holds that Mark 2:10 portrays Jesus as the Son of Man to whom God granted authority, he accepts only Mark 2:1-5, 11-12 as historical.[5] The idea that Samuel, Daniel, and the seer in the Prayer of Nabonidus announced forgiveness is the key to Hägerland's view, which

---

[4]Tobias Hägerland, *Jesus and the Forgiveness of Sins: An Aspect of His Prophetic Mission* (Cambridge: Cambridge University Press, 2011), 137. Although Maurice Casey does not explicitly comment on the kind of authority Jesus claimed to possess, he seems to suggest a similar prophetic understanding of Jesus in Mk 2:10: "The stories of Jesus' healing ministry do not lead people to give him a special label such as 'healer' or 'exorcist'. This was rather subsumed under the general term 'prophet.'" Casey, *The Solution to the "Son of Man" Problem* (New York: Bloomsbury T&T Clark, 2007), 154. Recall that, for Casey, Jesus' authority saying meant that God gave some people the ability to heal psychosomatic infirmities (147, 165-67).

[5]Hägerland, *Jesus and the Forgiveness of Sins*, 176-78.

rejects the scribal blasphemy charge and the historicity of the scene as presented in Mark's Gospel. However, the data indicated only prophetic intercession in the texts presented as evidence for the named prophets, and the data from the Prayer of Nabonidus was inconclusive. As our study discovered, Hägerland's view relies on petitionary prayer as a metaphor for forgiveness, and there is no compelling reason to hold that Samuel, Daniel, or the seer were believed to actually forgive sin.[6]

So, there is no meaningful parallel between what these men did and the way Jesus forgave the paralytic's sins. Indeed, no human being was believed to have the authority to deviate from divinely sanctioned methods of mediating forgiveness (i.e., a sacrificial requirement in the temple). Moreover, Hägerland's theory is incompatible with concepts of blasphemy in Jesus' Jewish context. It also does not attempt to consider highly evidenced data from Jesus' Jewish examination in Mark 14, which again connect Jesus' claims to authority to a Jewish blasphemy charge. Let us weigh Hägerland's version of hypothesis one.

1. *Plausibility.* Is Hägerland's version implied by a greater number of highly evidenced facts when compared to other hypotheses? While this may appear to be implied by Jesus' reputation as a miracle worker (fact one), due to the prophetic association with miracles, Hägerland's version is not implied by data points two through ten. In regards to facts two through five, our investigation of potential mediators of forgiveness found no compelling evidence to suggest that Jewish prophets claimed to forgive sins in general. Still, this theory may potentially be implied by a single text, which we found inconclusive: the Prayer of Nabonidus. In regards to facts six through ten, no prophet ever predicted that he would sit at God's right hand as eschatological judge, although prophets predicted a coming future judgment. Even Jesus' prophetic ministry and prediction in his reply to the high priest (fact nine) does not automatically imply a merely human, prophetic claim. Further, the regal aspects of Jesus' reply (fact nine) and his execution as "King of the Jews" (fact six) do not seem to imply a merely prophetic claim. Despite its

---

[6]Hägerland, *Jesus and the Forgiveness of Sins*, 149.

potential implication by fact one and the Prayer of Nabonidus, our study found no compelling evidence suggesting that Jewish prophets pronounced forgiveness of sins. I will provisionally assign this view a rating of *tentative* (T) and potentially revise its rating after comparing it to other hypotheses.

2. *Explanatory scope.* How much of the highly evidenced data does this version account for? While it accounts for the authenticity of Jesus' reputation as a miracle worker, it accounts for only part of the core scene in Mark 2, the forgiveness saying in Mark 2:5, but does not account for the scribal response or the authority saying in Mark 2:10. It does not attempt to account for Jesus' Jewish examination or his exchange with the high priest in Mark 14. This cannot be treated lightly, as Jesus' reply in Mark 14:62 further clarifies the kind of authority he claimed to possess, and the high priest's response coheres with the scribal response in Mark 2. Both hearers understood Jesus' claims as a kind of blasphemy—claiming an authority beyond that of any human prophet. Why would Jesus be accused of blasphemy or considered as deserving of death if he merely claimed to possess prophetic authority? This version of hypothesis one is lacking in explanatory scope. Still, I will provisionally assign this a rating of *tentative* (T) at this stage.

3. *Explanatory power.* Hägerland's explanations for the data seem forced to fit his hypothesis, which must expand on the concept of forgiving sins to include petitionary prayer in order to assert that Jesus' forgiving sins was no different from what prophets did. This is the foundation of his rejection of the scribal blasphemy charge and the implication that Jesus claimed to possess divine authority. Still, this study found no meaningful parallel between prophetic claims and Jesus' encounter with the paralytic. While Hägerland's theory recognizes the forgiveness saying as historical, it does not attempt to explain Jesus' reply to the high priest or the resulting blasphemy charge in Mark 14. It cannot account for the reason Jesus was accused of blasphemy in either case. Moreover, it does not account for Jesus' execution under Rome. It is difficult to imagine how a merely prophetic claim could be translated into a political charge resulting in his crucifixion and the titulus "King of the

Jews." This version of hypothesis one appears very weak in its explanatory power. Still, I will provisionally assign it a rating of *tentative* (T) at this stage.

4. *Less ad hoc.* Does it appeal to nonevidenced or baseless facts? Hägerland's version is dependent on an unproved assertion: that Jewish prophets were believed to forgive sins in general. The only potential piece of support is an inconclusive text in the Prayer of Nabonidus. While this hypothesis also appears dependent on expanding the concept of forgiving sins to include petitionary prayer, Hägerland presents no argument from ancient concepts of forgiveness legitimizing this move. Whether his version is less ad hoc compared to the other hypotheses under investigation remains to be seen. For now, I will rate this as *tentative* (T).

5. *Illumination.* This version does not appear to assist researchers in solving issues surrounding other areas of Jesus research. Although this positive criterion may bolster a given hypothesis, it should not be used negatively. Thus, I will assign it a rating of *not met* (—).

Hägerland's version of hypothesis 1 may be implied by only one data point out of our ten highly evidenced facts. It seems weak in explanatory scope and explanatory power, and appears to contain an ad hoc component. Further, it does not provide illumination for other issues in Jesus research. The following table will be used to show how well each theory fulfills the criteria for the best explanation. The shaded area represents a less important, positive criterion that should not count negatively against this view. The first theory assessed typically earns tentative ratings for each category. These ratings will be updated as the hypotheses under consideration are assessed.

Table 10.1. Analysis of Hägerland's version

	Plausibility	Scope	Power	Less ad hoc	Illumination
Hägerland	T	T	T	T	—

Bart Ehrman: Priestly, human authority. Ehrman's view under consideration is similar to the conclusions of earlier studies by Sanders, Casey, Borg, and Crossan. Still, reading his popular works is a very common way that people hear about this perspective on Jesus' claims. In light of this, we will consider Ehrman's version of the first hypothesis as expressed in *How Jesus Became God*. In this book, he writes that Jesus viewed himself as a prophet and that the historical Jesus claimed only a kind of priestly, merely human authority (not divine authority) when forgiving the paralytic in Mark 2.[7]

To be fair, Ehrman's views have evolved since then—at least when it comes to a literary discussion of the text.[8] For example, he wrote in 2018, "In the Synoptic Gospels of Matthew, Mark, and Luke, Jesus never says he is God."[9] However, in a blog post dated August 19, 2023, he states, "There is no question that Jesus in the Gospels claims to be divine," while noting, "The fact that the Gospels claim that Jesus called himself a divine being doesn't mean the historical Jesus himself did. For that you need to engage in historical (not literary) analysis."[10] This is an important observation. Despite his change of mind on a literary level, Ehrman still says, "I am firmly convinced that Jesus never talked about himself as God."[11] Still, *How Jesus Became God* was a *New York Times* bestseller, and people continue to read it. So, we will engage in historical analysis using Ehrman's thought during this era.

This version of hypothesis one is based on the idea that Jewish priests explicitly pronounced forgiveness during sacrifices at the temple.[12] There are at least two problems with this: First, there is no meaningful parallel,

---

[7]Bart D. Ehrman, *How Jesus Became God: The Exaltation of a Jewish Preacher from Galilee* (New York: HarperOne, 2015), 124. For Ehrman, Jesus claimed "a priestly prerogative, but not a divine one" (*How Jesus Became God*, 126-27). Without commenting on the kind of authority Jesus claimed to possess, Casey supports a merely human view of Jesus as well: "The general level meaning of the Son of Man saying does not imply that Jesus was an ordinary person just like any other . . . [but it] does however imply that Jesus was a human being, not God" (*Solution to the "Son of Man" Problem*, 167).

[8]Bart Ehrman, "Jesus as God in the Synoptics," *The Bart Ehrman Blog*, April 13, 2014, https://ehrmanblog.org/jesus-as-god-in-the-synoptics-for-members/.

[9]Bart Ehrman, "Did Jesus Call Himself God?," *The Bart Ehrman Blog*, October 26, 2018, https://ehrmanblog.org/did-jesus-call-himself-god/.

[10]Bart Ehrman, "Does Jesus Call Himself God in His Trial Before the Sanhedrin and the High Priest Caiaphas?," *The Bart Ehrman Blog*, August 19, 2023, https://ehrmanblog.org/does-jesus-call-himself-god-in-his-trial-before-the-sanhedrin-and-the-high-priest-caiaphus/.

[11]Alex O'Connor, "Did Jesus Even Claim to Be God? Bart Ehrman Says No . . . ," June 19, 2023, YouTube, 1:31:12, www.youtube.com/watch?v=2STiabRV8TE, at timestamp 13:40.

[12]Ehrman, *How Jesus Became God*, 127.

as Jesus' forgiveness saying occurred outside the temple—without prayer, mention of God, or a sacrifice. Second, no extant text records a Jewish priest making a pronouncement of forgiveness as Jesus did in Mark 2:5. In fact, no human being was believed to possess the authority to deviate from divinely sanctioned methods of mediating forgiveness. This version is also based on the assumption that Jesus used a "divine passive," rather than speaking in the active, as Ehrman suggests God might have spoken. However, our study noted both that Mark includes passives that seem to allow Jesus as the subject and that Jesus' forgiveness saying follows God's own use of the passive when declaring forgiveness in the Hebrew Scriptures and other Jewish texts. Further, the context of Jesus' sayings—a healing incident—seems incoherent with a priestly function, as priests did not heal people but rather sought to keep the temple areas free of the infirm. Moreover, the text also seems to indicate that Jesus' remark was not perceived as merely prophetic by those who heard it.

In regard to the data gleaned from Mark 14, Ehrman grants that a meeting like the Jewish examination must have taken place before the authorities handed Jesus over to Pilate. Although he recognizes that (in the narrative world of Mark's Gospel) the high priest and the council would have heard Jesus' reply in Mark 14:62 as some kind of a divine claim, he rejects the authenticity of Mark's portrayal of the scene.[13] Ehrman raises the question of Mark's source(s), suggesting that no witnesses sympathetic to the Jesus movement were present at the examination.[14] This, however, ignores potential witnesses present (e.g., false witnesses, guards, servants, or anyone else present) and those who may have had access to records of the examination (e.g., Saul of Tarsus, Joseph of Arimathea). There is no reason that unsympathetic witnesses could not have recounted the details of the examination, and there is good reason to think they did, as the ongoing public debate with Jesus' followers surely included debates regarding his guilt or innocence. While historians may not be able to identify pre-Markan source(s) for Jesus' Jewish examination with certainty, our

---

[13]Bart D. Ehrman, *The New Testament: A Historical Introduction to the Early Christian Writings*, 7th ed. (New York: Oxford University Press, 2020), 115.

[14]Bart D. Ehrman, *Jesus: Apocalyptic Prophet of the New Millennium* (New York: Oxford University Press, 1999), 220-21.

study has identified highly evidenced data present in the Markan tradition. Let us weigh Ehrman's version of hypothesis one.

1. Plausibility. Is Ehrman's theory implied by a greater number of highly evidenced facts when compared to other theories? It does not seem to be implied by facts one, two, four through eight, and ten. This could be appear to be an implication of fact three, Jesus' forgiveness saying, due to the association of priests with atonement rites. While fact nine, Jesus' reply to the high priest, might suggest a priestly *dimension* to his claim, it does not suggest a merely human claim. Indeed, Ehrman's theory is not implied by any other highly evidenced data points, including the authority saying in Mark 2 and the blasphemy charges in both Markan scenes. This version lacks plausibility, as only the first data point might imply it, and our investigation found no compelling evidence suggesting that Jewish priests ever pronounced forgiveness. I will assign this version a rating of *failed* (F).

2. Explanatory scope. How much of the highly evidenced data does Ehrman's version account for? While it attempts to account for Jesus' forgiveness and authority sayings in Mark 2, it does not account for the blasphemy charge. It is also difficult to connect to the healing itself. While it acknowledges a meeting between Jesus and the Jewish leadership, it does not attempt to account for the exchange between Jesus and the high priest, including the blasphemy charge, in Mark 14. Again, historians cannot treat this lightly. Jesus' exchange with the high priest further clarified the kind of authority he claimed to possess. The blasphemy charges in Mark 2 and Mark 14 appear related to claiming an authority beyond that of any human priest. So, this hypothesis lacks explanatory scope. Why would Jesus be accused of blasphemy or considered as deserving of death if he merely claimed to possess a merely human, priestly authority? This does not seem to account for the sign posted by the Romans on Jesus' cross (a.k.a. the *titulus*), which identified the charge against at Jesus at his crucifixion: "King of the Jews." In light of all of this, I will rate it as *failed* (F).

3. Explanatory power. Do Ehrman's explanations for the data seem forced to fit his hypothesis? It appears so, as there is no meaningful

parallel between the way in which Jesus purported to forgive sins and
any kind of merely human, priestly activity. While a priestly dimension
to Jesus' claims may be plausible, this does not automatically suggest that
all we have is Jesus making a strictly human, priestly claim with no possibility of anything more.

For example, consider the observations of two scholars: Nicholas
Perrin and Crispin Fletcher-Louis. Perrin sees Jesus as presented in the
Gospel of Mark as a priestly Messiah and relates the blasphemy charge
in Mark 2 to Jesus' assuming a high priestly prerogative.[15] Still, he notes
that in Mark, demons identify Jesus not as a regular human priest but as
the eschatological high priest who would conquer the forces of evil.[16]
Fletcher-Louis holds that "Jesus thought he was Israel's long-awaited eschatological high priest," noting a high priestly dimension to the Danielic
Son of Man. However, Fletcher-Louis also sees Jesus as claiming to be
more than a man. He sees a juxtaposition of Jesus' claim to be the long-
awaited "true, high priestly Son of Man" who is a divine warrior with the
merely human high priest, Caiaphas.[17]

Ehrman's hypothesis rejects the authenticity of highly evidenced data
from Jesus' Jewish examination, where any priestly dimension to
Jesus' claims may be clarified. It also ignores the regal dimension of Jesus'
claims to authority at this meeting, which coheres with the *titulus* at Jesus'
crucifixion. Ehrman's attempt to account for Jesus' crucifixion as king of
the Jews seems ad hoc, as I will note below. This version lacks explanatory
power. I will rate this as *failed* (F).

4. Less ad hoc. Does it appeal to nonevidenced or baseless facts? Yes.
Ehrman's version is dependent on at least two unproven assertions:

---

[15]Nicholas Perrin, "Jesus as Priest in the Gospels," *Southern Baptist Journal of Theology* 22, no. 2
(2018): 87. "As far as the Jewish leaders are concerned at that moment, Jesus' blasphemy consists
in his having disrupted the chain of authority set into place by God and operationalized by the
high priest" (84).

[16]He holds that demons in Mk 1:24 identify Jesus as the Holy One of God—"a title ordinarily
reserved for Israel's high priest. . . . The demon is identifying Jesus not with the regnant priest
but the eschatological high priest who would one day—so the faithful hoped—destroy the de-
monic forces" (Perrin, "Jesus as Priest," 83). Note that Jesus is also identified as Christ in Lk 4:41.

[17]Crispin Fletcher-Louis, "Jesus as the High Priestly Messiah: Part 2," *Journal for the Study of the
Historical Jesus* 5, no. 1 (January 2007): 57, 74, 59.

(1) Jewish priests pronounced forgiveness of sins, and (2) someone who possesses divine authority would pronounce the forgiveness of sins in the active voice. There is no surviving ancient text suggesting the former, and there are Markan texts demonstrating the error of the latter. Why would Rome crucify Jesus as "King of the Jews" if he claimed only a merely human, priestly authority? Ehrman suggests that Judas might have privately told the Jewish authorities that Jesus taught his disciples that he was the king of the Jews.[18] As there is no evidence of such a possibility, I will rate this as *failed* (F).

5. *Illumination.* This version does not seem to help historians solve issues surrounding other areas of Jesus research. However, it may raise the question of whether Jesus' claims could potentially have a kind of priestly *dimension*. While this may contribute to the discussion, insisting on a very strong separation between a priestly claim and a divine claim may be too limiting. For example, studies by Perrin and Fletcher-Louis suggest that a divine claim may not exclude the possibility of a priestly dimension as well. I will assign Ehrman's version a rating of *not met* (—).

Although Ehrman's version of hypothesis one might initially appear to be implied by a single data point (fact three) out of our ten historical facts, careful investigation suggests otherwise. While Hägerland's theory may be supported by an inconclusive text, the Prayer of Nabonidus, there is no text that might possibly support Ehrman's theory. So, Ehrman's view trails Hägerland's view in plausibility. Still, both are very weak in explanatory power and scope. So, both will share a *failed* rating for these categories. They also appear similarly ad hoc and will share a *failed* rating for this category as well.

In terms of Hägerland's view, we initially assessed the criteria as "tentative" because, before comparing it to Ehrman's view, it seemed to potentially hold some degree of viability. We assessed both views independently. However, upon further investigation and comparison with Ehrman's view, its problems became evident. The re-evaluation

---

[18]Ehrman, *How Jesus Became God*, 112.

from "tentative" to "failed" reflects that Hägerland's view, like Ehrman's, did not adequately meet certain criteria.

Although Ehrman's theory may suggest investigating the possibility of a priestly *dimension* to (fact nine) Jesus' reply to the high priest, it lacks explanatory scope and explanatory power. Further, it denies the historicity of Jesus' exchange with the high priest (facts eight through ten) and does not provide illumination for other issues in Jesus research.

The following table shows how well Ehrman's version fulfills the criteria for the best explanation.

Table 10.2. Analysis of Ehrman's version of hypothesis one and competitor

	Plausibility	Scope	Power	Less ad hoc	Illumination
Hägerland	P	F	F	F	—
Ehrman	F	F	F	F	—

Our table currently shows Hägerland's version of hypothesis one in first place but only because Ehrman's hypothesis failed to pass any of the tests. Let's see how a unique version of hypothesis one fares in our competition. Can it do better than Hägerland's version?

Daniel Kirk: Idealized human authority. Kirk holds that in Mark's Gospel, Jesus claims to possess a kind of *idealized* human authority.[19] On his view, Jesus' claims are fully consistent with prophets and human luminaries. That is, Jesus "enacts" God's own authority on earth to forgive sins and "exercises God's authority on earth as God intended for humanity at the beginning." Although he does not present this as a true hypothesis about the claims of the historical Jesus, Kirk's literary analysis is relevant to our study because it proports to provide a historically viable reading of the text.[20] Some people may read his work and reason to themselves, "If Jesus never made divine claims in the biblical narrative, then he didn't make divine claims in the real world, either."

---

[19] Although Kirk's work is not presented as a study of the historical Jesus, it claims to offer a historically viable reading of the text and in part argues against preexistence Christology in Mark and ontological divinity in the Synoptics. See J. R. Daniel Kirk, *A Man Attested by God: The Human Jesus of the Synoptic Gospels* (Grand Rapids, MI: Eerdmans, 2016), 9.

[20] Kirk, *Man Attested by God*, 11, 12, 206, 9.

But what about this? Kirk's insistence on placing Jesus' claims in the same category as Jewish prophets or human luminaries appears rather dubious. In fact, there is no compelling evidence of any such person claiming to forgive sins in general (recall that our study found the data from the Prayer of Nabonidus inconclusive), and there is no evidence of any Jewish person predicting their future role as eschatological judge. In his work, Kirk mentions Jesus' claim to forgive sins in Mark 2 but does not connect this to Jesus' reply to the high priest in Mark 14. Overlooking this is a problem because Jesus' Jewish examination sheds light on his previous claim. Kirk mentions Mark 14 only when he argues that because Jesus distinguishes himself from "Power," that means that Jesus does not claim to be God himself.[21] This fails to recognize the unprecedented nature of the combined scope of Jesus' claims—something that may not be readily apparent when considering each scene in isolation.

What does connecting our conclusions from both Mark 2 and Mark 14 show about the novelty and significance of Jesus' claim? Here is a key observation that many miss: Jesus' claim to possess authority *on earth* to forgive sin and his claim to possess authority *in heaven* to judge sin implies a unique claim to comprehensive divine authority. That is, he is claiming to possess authority over *all things*, not merely to share God's authority in a limited capacity, as certain prophets did on earth or as certain luminaries may have done in heaven. For example, in regard to Moses' being depicted as sharing in God's rule in a Jewish text called Ezekiel the Tragedian (third to second century BC), historical Jesus scholar Richard Bauckham observes: "God rules the whole cosmos, and Moses rules on God's behalf *on earth*. Moses has 'a share' in something larger. In the case of Jesus, on the other hand, he really does sit on the cosmic throne; he participates in the whole of God's cosmic rule. It is this rule over *all things* that is unique to God."[22]

---

[21]Kirk, *Man Attested by God*, 329-30. This seems to be Kirk's main concern. Although Casey holds that Jesus was not God, he rejects the idea that the kind of authority Jesus claimed to possess was meant for all of humanity (see *Solution to the "Son of Man" Problem*, 166-67). Casey does not explicitly propose a hypothesis regarding the kind of authority Jesus claimed to possess.

[22]Richard Bauckham, "Is 'High Human Christology' Sufficient? A Critical Response to J. R. Daniel Kirk's *A Man Attested by God*," *Bulletin for Biblical Research* 27, no. 4 (2017): 509. He defines

Kirk says that Jesus claimed to *enact, exercise,* or *share* divine authority—but only in the same way that other idealized humans did.[23] For him, the kind of authority Jesus claims to *possess* is something less than divine authority.[24] Kirk also holds that the Jesus' "claim to be the son of man finds a surprising path, privately disclosed to Jesus' followers, of suffering and death prior to resurrection glory. In this authority Jesus exorcises, heals, and rules the created order," and that "Jesus claims, as son of man, to exercise authority on the earth in healing and forgiveness, in royal authority over the stipulations of the law, and in exorcism. Such wide-ranging authority Jesus claims because he is the Human One, or in colloquial parlance, the Man."[25] While Kirk seems to recognize Jesus' claims to authority span a broad range of key divine functions, he stops short of saying that Jesus claimed to possess divine authority. However, it is important to note that the language of sharing does not always have to be limiting. For example, historical Jesus experts such as Bock can speak of Jesus "sharing in divine ruling authority" while also recognizing "Jesus' comprehensive claim of vindication and authority."[26] Bock also notes that Jesus' "coming with the clouds seems to be another suggestion that Jesus as the Son of Man is a person who possesses more than human authority or honor."[27]

Remember the illustration of a judge-appointed bailiff we used to describe the authority of Jesus' disciples to pronounce forgiveness of sins? This may also be one illustration that approximates the way Kirk

---

"the unique identity of God (for this purpose) very precisely: sole Creator of *all things* and sole Ruler of *all things,* to whom is due the worship of which only the sole Creator and Ruler of *all things* is worthy. . . . I have identified the primary source of 'early high Christology' as the belief that Jesus was enthroned on the cosmic throne from which God rules all things. Later, his participation in the creative work of God was added" (512).

[23]Kirk seems to position his hypothesis as a larger umbrella under which prophets and other luminaries may fall: "What Fletcher-Louis depicts as angelomorphic humans might well be one particular manifestation of my larger category of idealized human figures" (*Man Attested by God,* 35).

[24]For Kirk, "Jesus embodied God's authority, [and] exercises the rule and dominion of God" (Kirk, *Man Attested by God,* 573).

[25]Kirk, *Man Attested by God,* 574-76.

[26]Darrell L. Bock, "Blasphemy and the Jewish Examination of Jesus," in *Key Events in the Life of the Historical Jesus: A Collaborative Exploration of Context and Coherence,* ed. Darrell L. Bock and Robert L. Webb (Grand Rapids, MI: Eerdmans, 2010), 842.

[27]Darrell L. Bock, *Proclamation from Prophecy and Pattern: Lucan Old Testament Christology,* Journal for the Study of the New Testament Supplement Series 12 (Sheffield: JSOT Press, 1997), 136.

characterizes Jesus' claim. Again, although the bailiff might, in some sense, *share* in ruling authority while maintaining order during a trial or supervising a jury, the bailiff does not purport to *possess* the judge's authority while *enacting* or *exercising* the judge's authority in what is a very limited capacity. Rather, the bailiff can perform the duties required by the judge only in the courts of a given county. Again, the bailiff's authority is not as comprehensive as the judge's authority, and the bailiff can in fact overstep their authority by making unauthorized statements. If the illustration of a bailiff's authority can adequately characterize Kirk's view of the kind of authority Jesus claimed to possess, then Kirk's view seems to occupy a middle ground between the two major hypotheses under investigation. Still, what individual Jewish figure ever claimed to have authority in heaven and on earth? The outstanding novelty of Jesus' radical claims was not lost on his adversaries.

While Kirk rejects the idea that Jesus claimed to *possess* divine authority, his view coheres with the idea that Jesus (even as a human being in the narrative world of Mark's Gospel) claimed to *at least* enact, exercise, or share divine authority—claims that were *at least* on par with idealized human luminaries. In regard to Jesus' reply to the high priest, this appears to fit at least one cultural conception of blasphemy: comparing oneself to God, disrespecting God's appointed leaders, or perhaps both. Still, Kirk does not assert that Jesus claimed to possess authority that was *at least* on par with idealized human luminaries. Instead, his view is that Jesus merely claimed to possess authority that was *no more* than on par with idealized human luminaries. This is why Kirk's theory is categorized as a version of hypothesis one (although it seems to represent a kind of mediating or transitional view between hypotheses one and two).

Still, Kirk's version fails to synthesize Jesus' claims from Mark 2 and Mark 14. It also misses the difference between a claim to *exercise* or *share* authority in a limited way and a claim to *possess* comprehensive divine authority—including key functions such as forgiveness and judgment. Kirk's focus on demonstrating that Jesus could *share* authority with God without being divine fails to recognize the possibility that Jesus, even as a human being, nevertheless claimed to possess divine authority. It also fails to recognize the outstandingly novel and comprehensive nature of Jesus' claimed authority, especially in Mark 14. Let us weigh Kirk's version of hypothesis one.

1. *Plausibility.* Is Kirk's version implied by a greater number of highly evidenced facts when compared to other hypotheses? It may be implied by facts two through five and seven through ten:

- Fact one: Performing miracles was not necessarily associated with enacting divine authority, and no other miracle workers were accused of blasphemy for their claims. Still, this is not inconsistent with the theory.
- Fact two: the core scene in Mark 2:1-12
- Fact three: Jesus' forgiveness saying
- Fact four: the scribal blasphemy charge
- Fact five: Jesus' authority saying may imply a claim to at least *enact*, *exercise*, or *share* divine authority to forgive sins in general.
- Fact six: While Jesus' rejection and execution does not appear to imply Kirk's theory, it is not incoherent with it.
- Fact seven: the authenticity of the core scene in Mark 14:53-65
- Fact eight: the high priest's question
- Fact nine: Jesus' reply
- Fact ten: The resulting blasphemy charge may imply a claim to share divine authority to judge in the eschaton.

I will rate this as *passed* (P).

2. *Explanatory scope.* How much of the highly evidenced data does this version account for? Kirk's theory may potentially account for all of the highly evidenced data (facts one through ten) uncovered by our study. While it may not be inaccurate to say that Jesus, as a human being, implied a claim to *enact*, *exercise*, or *share* divine authority, it may not be fully adequate to explain the significance of all of the data. Still, I will rate this as *passed* (P).

3. *Explanatory power.* Some of Kirk's explanations for the data seem forced to fit his hypothesis. While he asserts a parallel between Jesus' claims and the claims of prophets and luminaries, this study found no

meaningful parallel between prophetic claims and Jesus' claim to forgive the paralytic. Why would Jesus be accused of blasphemy in Mark 2 if Kirk is right to connect Jesus' claim to forgive sins with the authority of prophets? Similarly, there is no evidence supporting any parallels between the claims of human luminaries and Jesus' reply to the high priest. In regard to this exchange, Kirk asserts that "a Jewish person who asserts that an idealized human figure is enthroned at God's right hand, based on Daniel 7, might be accused of blasphemy."[28] However, highly evidenced data suggests Jesus claimed the authority to judge God's representatives in the eschaton himself—a novel assertion even among human luminaries. Thus, Kirk's version is strongly lacking in its explanatory power. I will rate this as *failed* (F).

4. *Less ad hoc.* This theory appears to be based on two nonevidenced assertions: first, the idea that Jesus' claim to forgive sins is consistent with the claims of prophets, and second, that Jesus' reply to the high priest is consistent with the claims of human luminaries. However, there is no clear evidence that prophets claimed to forgive sins, and there is no known ancient text that depicts a Jewish luminary predicting their own role as eschatological judge. It seems difficult to place Jesus' own claims in the category of idealized human where there is not even one example of "idealized humans" making the claims that Jesus made as reflected in Mark 2:5, 10; 14:62. I will rate this as *failed* (F).

5. *Illumination.* Like the previous versions of hypothesis one, this version does not seem to assist researchers in solving issues surrounding other areas of Jesus research. However, it may raise the question of whether Jesus' reply to the high priest would have been a sufficient cause for the blasphemy charge—even if the implication was no more than a claim to possess authority on par with human luminaries. This may well be the case, but it does not necessarily illuminate a separate issue from the current study. I will assign Kirk's version a rating of "not met" (—).

While this hypothesis appears plausible and passed the explanatory scope section of the assessment, it nevertheless lacks explanatory power

---

[28]Kirk, *Man Attested by God*, 29. He cites Simon J. Gathercole, *The Preexistent Son: Recovering the Christologies of Matthew, Mark, and Luke* (Grand Rapids, MI: Eerdmans, 2006), 59-61.

and contains ad hoc components. It is at least noteworthy, however, that Kirk's version fares the best out of the three versions of hypothesis one, potentially even providing some level of illumination for the blasphemy charge in Mark 14. Table 10.3 shows how well this version fulfills the criteria for the best explanation.

Table 10.3. Analysis of Kirk's version of hypothesis one and competitors

	Plausibility	Scope	Power	Less ad hoc	Illumination
Hägerland	P	F	F	F	—
Ehrman	F	F	F	F	—
Kirk	P	P	F	F	—

While Kirk's version seems to represent a kind of mediating or transitional view between hypotheses one and two, it appears stronger than the other two versions of the hypothesis that Jesus claimed to possess a kind of human authority. So, Kirk's version takes the lead and Hägerland's version loses its place in the top spot. This means that Kirk's view is the best version of hypothesis one and is the version that has the strongest chance of competing against hypothesis two.

CONCLUSION

At my dissertation defense, one of my committee members asked me whether anything surprised me as I worked through these competing views. What immediately came to mind was the way that Kirk's version of hypothesis one surpassed the other two versions. Initially, I didn't think it would fare any better than Hägerland's version. While Kirk's view may include observations that are not entirely inaccurate, his characterization of Jesus' claims appears inadequate to fully explain the data. I was also surprised that Ehrman's version failed every single one of the criteria. But what was even more surprising is what happened when I ran the alternative hypothesis two through the same sieve. I honestly did not expect the results. Hypothesis two is the view that Jesus claimed to possess a kind of divine authority, and it is to this view that we now turn our attention. How well does it stack up against the competition?

Total Power

AUTHORITY OVER ALL OF REALITY

Times have changed since my teenage experience with the high school senior skeptic who first challenged my faith. Many young people today first hear objections to belief in Jesus through short-form video content on social media apps such as TikTok, Instagram, or YouTube. In this vertical format, where creators have less than five seconds to grab a viewer's attention before the viewer scrolls away to view the following video, it's common to see "social skeptics" immediately beginning with emotional, attention-grabbing assertions that never engage with the historical facts. This is the new public square where people often hear, "Jesus never said he was God," "He didn't consider himself God," and "Jesus never said, 'I am God.'"

These are challenges often heard from atheists, agnostics, Jehovah's Witnesses, and Muslims. But saying "I am God" isn't the only way that Jesus could have claimed to be divine. In our study, we uncovered highly evidenced data that helped us assess views of critical scholars who believe that Jesus never claimed to be divine. We called his hypothesis one, reviewed three versions of it, and found Kirk's view the strongest of them. Now we'll assess the competing hypothesis—the idea that the historical Jesus did in fact claim to be divine. We call this hypothesis two. How well does it stand up against the competition?

THE FACTS OF THE CASE

Let us review the facts. Jesus' cultural context suggests that his forgiveness saying was heard as an implicit claim to possess divine authority to forgive sins and that his reply to the high priest was heard as an implicit claim to possess divine authority in heaven to judge sins. Our critical examination of the healing of the paralytic and Jesus' Jewish examination yielded ten highly evidenced data points:

1. The authenticity of Jesus' reputation as a miracle worker: (+4) *certainly historical*
2. The authenticity of the core scene in Mark 2:1-12: (+3) *very probable*
3. The authenticity of the forgiveness saying: (+3) *very probable*
4. The authenticity of the scribal response: (+3) *very probable*
5. The authenticity of the authority saying: (+3) *very probable*
6. The authenticity of Jesus' rejection by Jewish leaders and crucifixion under Rome: (+4) *certainly historical*
7. The authenticity of the core scene in Mark 14:53-65: (+3) *very probable*
8. The authenticity of the high priest's question: (+3) *very probable*
9. The authenticity of Jesus' reply: (+3) *very probable*
10. The authenticity of the blasphemy charge: (+3) *very probable*

Again, Kirk's view is the best version of hypothesis one—the suggestion that Jesus claimed to possess a kind of human authority rather than divine authority. His version is the strongest competitor to hypothesis two. This brings us to our next assessment. How well can this second hypothesis explain the facts of the case?

HYPOTHESIS TWO: JESUS CLAIMED TO POSSESS A KIND OF DIVINE AUTHORITY

Hypothesis two is the idea that Jesus claimed to possess divine authority—not just human authority. The historical evidence for this view emerges from our investigative journey. Our highly evidenced data points (ten historical facts) support the idea that Jesus claimed to possess both authority on earth to forgive sins and authority in heaven to judge sins.

Again, we need to synthesize both of our blasphemy accusation scenes, exhibits A and B, in order to more clearly understand Jesus' claims.

The first part of our journey focused on a critical examination of the healing of the paralytic in Mark 2 (exhibit A). In light of our findings, we concluded that it is *very probable* (+3) that the historical Jesus was accurately remembered as a unique miracle worker who claimed to forgive sins. This conclusion was anchored in our first set of five historical facts. Here, Jesus' forgiveness saying was likely heard in light of the Jewish ideas that God alone could forgive sins in general and a general definition of blasphemy as disrespecting God's unique authority by usurping a divine prerogative. The resulting blasphemy charge was a reaction to the implication that Jesus was a special kind of human being who possessed authority on earth to do something believed to be an exclusively divine action—autonomously forgiving sins in general.

The second part of our journey focused on a critical examination of Jesus' Jewish examination in Mark 14 (exhibit B). In light of our findings, we concluded that it is *very probable* (+3) that Jesus was accurately remembered as claiming to be the Messiah, the Son of the Blessed, and predicting that the high priest and council members would see him seated at God's right hand and coming on the clouds as the eschatological Son of Man. This conclusion was anchored in our second set of five historical facts. Here, Jesus' reply was likely heard in light of the Jewish ideas that God alone is the ultimate judge and cultural definitions of blasphemy that included disrespecting God's unique authority by comparing oneself to God or assuming a divine prerogative. The resulting blasphemy charge was likely a reaction to the implication that Jesus was a special kind of human being who possessed authority in heaven to judge the sins even of God's own representatives—a claim that was unique even among human luminaries.

Together, both of these conclusions further strengthen the hypothesis that Jesus claimed to possess a kind of divine authority. First, divine forgiveness and divine judgment seem to be two sides of the same coin in Jewish thought. For example, a second-century BC text found among the Dead Sea Scrolls called Jubilees describes God as an impartial judge who cannot be bribed (5:15-16; 21:4; 33:18) and the one who forgives sin (5:17). This further supports the divine nature of Jesus' claims to authority. Second, Jesus' claims to authority in Mark 14 further clarify his claims to authority in Mark 2. Bringing together Jesus' claims to possess authority in heaven and authority on earth is reminiscent of the trope "heaven and earth"—the dominant picture of the world used in the Old Testament.[1] It is important to note that "heaven and earth" is a Jewish merism (a merism juxtaposes opposite extremes to express a unified concept) for all of reality. For example, in the Old Testament Apocrypha, Judith 9:12 makes a reference to God as the Lord of "heaven and earth" as well as the king of all creation. This contrasts God's unlimited authority over the entire created order with the limited authority of human kings over specific geographic areas. The Gospel According to Matthew expresses unique cosmic authority in this way and reports Jesus claiming to possess it: "All authority in heaven and on earth has been given to me" (Mt 28:18).[2] This is coherent with Jesus' manner of speech. Not only does it refer to the totality of the cosmos, but it also contrasts Jesus' authority on earth with his authority in heaven.[3] This coheres with the idea that Jesus claimed to possess divine authority. Let us run hypothesis two through the same sieve we used to assess the various versions of hypothesis one.

1. *Plausibility.* Is this implied by a greater number of highly evidenced facts when compared to other hypotheses? Like Kirk's version of hypothesis one, this may be implied by facts two through five and seven through ten.

- Fact one: Performing miracles was not necessarily associated with possessing divine authority and no other miracle workers were accused of blasphemy for their claims. Still, this is not inconsistent with the hypothesis.

---

[1]Jonathan T. Pennington, "Heaven and Earth in the Gospel of Matthew" (PhD diss., University of St Andrews, 2005), 146.

[2]Luke 24:49 may indirectly allude to Jesus' exaltation, as Peter's speech in Acts 2:33-35 presents the coming of the Holy Spirit as evidence of Jesus' enthronement and connects it to Ps 110:1—the very text to which Jesus himself alludes in Mk 14:62.

[3]Jonathan T. Pennington, *Heaven and Earth in the Gospel of Matthew*, 2nd ed. (Grand Rapids, MI: Baker Academic, 2009), 203-6.

- Fact two: the core scene in Mark 2:1-12
- Fact three: Jesus' forgiveness saying
- Fact four: the scribal blasphemy charge
- Fact five: Jesus' authority saying may imply a claim to possess divine authority to forgive sins in general.
- Fact six: While Jesus' rejection and execution does not appear to imply this hypothesis, it is not incoherent with it.
- Fact seven: the authenticity of the core scene in Mark 14:53-65
- Fact eight: the high priest's question
- Fact nine: Jesus' reply
- Fact ten: The resulting blasphemy charge may imply a claim to possess divine authority to judge in the eschaton.

I will rate this as *passed* (P).

2. *Explanatory scope.* Like Kirk's view, our hypothesis appears to account for all of the highly evidenced facts (facts one through ten). This hypothesis may amend Kirk's version of hypothesis one by recognizing that Jesus, as a human being, *at least* implied a claim to *enact*, *exercise*, or *share* divine authority—but while Jesus' claim implies no less than this, it implies more. In contrast to Kirk's view, our hypothesis that Jesus claimed to *possess* divine authority seems to be a more adequate way to account for the data from both blasphemy accusation scenes: authority on earth to forgive sins (Mk 2) and authority in heaven to judge sins (Mk 14) seem to constitute a unique claim to possess comprehensive divine authority. Since our hypothesis does not seem to trail any versions of hypothesis one, I will rate it as *passed* (P).

3. *Explanatory power.* The quality of hypothesis two's explanations appear superior to each version of hypothesis one. Unlike Hägerland's version, hypothesis two recognizes key differences between the claims of prophets and Jesus' forgiveness saying and does not rely on an unjustified expansion of the concept of forgiveness to include petitionary prayer. It also accounts for the resulting scribal blasphemy charge as well as the blasphemy charge at Jesus' Jewish examination. Unlike Ehrman's version, hypothesis two recognizes key differences between the pronouncements

of priests and the way in which Jesus purported to forgive sins. It also explains Jesus' rejection and execution as "King of the Jews" by recognizing the regal dimension of Jesus' claims rather than appealing to an unevidenced conversation between Judas and the Jewish leadership. Unlike Kirk's version, it recognizes key differences between the limited claims of prophets and human luminaries to *share, enact,* or *exercise* divine authority and Jesus' comprehensive claim to *possess* divine authority in heaven and on earth. Again, highly evidenced data suggests Jesus claimed to possess authority to both forgive sins in general and judge God's representatives in the eschaton—both outstandingly novel assertions without parallel even among prophets, priests, and other human luminaries. Our hypothesis easily fits all of the highly evidenced data points (facts one through ten) without strain, and I will rate it as *passed* (P).

4. *Less ad hoc.* Hypothesis two does not appear to be based on nonevidenced assertions. Rather, it is based on synthesizing our ten historical facts. In contrast, all three versions of hypothesis one seem dependent on two unproven assertions each. So, our hypothesis appears *less ad hoc* than these, and I will rate it as *passed* (P).

5. *Illumination.* This hypothesis may well assist historians in solving issues surrounding other areas of Jesus research such as how Jesus came to be regarded as a divine figure in a Jewish context. Was this early belief linked to something Jesus said about himself? This was the impetus for our study, and it seems that this hypothesis can contribute to the evidence supporting continuity between the early belief in Jesus as a divine figure and Jesus' remembered words and deeds. Synthesizing data from both blasphemy accusation scenes and paying close attention to Jesus' claimed authority in heaven and on earth may support the authenticity of other highly evidenced authority sayings as well. Indeed, the category of divine authority may apply to key sayings such as the following: "*All things* have been handed over to me by my Father, and no one knows the Son except the Father, and no one knows the Father except the Son and anyone to whom the Son chooses to reveal him" (Mt 11:27). It may also help us evaluate authority sayings outside the Synoptics such as, "The Father loves the Son and has given *all things* [literally "all flesh"] into his

hand" (Jn 3:35), and "since you [God] have given him [Jesus] *authority over all flesh*, to give eternal life to all whom you have given him" (Jn 17:2). This a close parallel to *"All authority in heaven and on earth* has been given to me" (Mt 28:18).

Further, this hypothesis can also suggest continuity with the comprehensive authority ascribed to Jesus in texts outside the Gospels such as Revelation 17:14. This apocalyptic text depicts Jesus as "Lord of lords and King of kings." In Ephesians 1:20-21, Paul declares that God "raised him [Jesus] from the dead and seated him at his right hand in the heavenly places, *far above all rule and authority and power and dominion*, and above every name that is named, not only in this age but also in the one to come."

This hypothesis can also contribute to an understanding of how the Jewish leadership translated a religious charge into a political charge relevant to Rome's legal system. It recognizes the regal nuance of Jesus' reply to the high priest alongside an implied claim to possess divine authority to rule and judge. This further illuminates a crucial link between Jesus' sayings and his death, including the reason for the charge on the *titulus* posted on Jesus' cross: "King of the Jews" (Mk 15:26; Lk 23:38; Mt 27:37). I will rate this as *passed* (P).

So, this hypothesis appears very strong. In fact, it passed every single criteria. Beyond this, the bonus criteria of illumination seems to apply as well. Table 11.1 shows how well hypothesis two fulfills the criteria for the best explanation in contrast to the versions of hypothesis one we analyzed in the previous chapter.

Table 11.1. Analysis of hypothesis two and competitors

	Plausibility	Scope	Power	Less ad hoc	Illumination
Hägerland	P	F	F	F	—
Ehrman	F	F	F	F	—
Kirk	P	P	F	F	P
Hypothesis 2	P	P	P	P	P

The preferred hypothesis is clear. Table 11.1 shows that hypothesis two comes in first place. It fulfills all four of the main criteria and passes the additional criteria of illumination as well. It is not only superior to all three versions of hypothesis one, but it outdistances them all. How well this hypothesis fared was unexpected. Hypothesis two best explains all ten historical facts, while each version of hypothesis one appears to include ad hoc assertions and struggles to explain the highly evidenced data.

So, how do the versions of hypothesis one compare to one another? Again, Kirk's version took the top spot, although it seems to represent a middle ground between hypotheses one and two. Hägerland's version could pass one only category at best: plausibility. It trails Kirk's version but is still more plausible than Ehrman's version, which could not pass even a single one of our adopted criteria. I will therefore place Kirk's version in second place, Hägerland's view in third place, and Ehrman's view in fourth place. One thing we can learn from evaluating these competing views is that the more a hypothesis recognizes that Jesus claimed an authority greater than the authority of priests or prophets, the better sense it makes of our ten historical facts.

In the end, hypothesis two rises to the top of the pack and earns the label of "historical." The evidence supporting it warrants a score of *very probable* (+3) on the scale of historical certainty. It has shown itself to be superior to competing hypotheses in meeting the five criteria. This is significant because hypothesis two supports the thesis I proposed at the outset of this work: *There is continuity between Jesus' claims and the early Christian belief in him as a divine figure because some of Jesus' words and deeds were likely interpreted by his Jewish adversaries as unparalleled claims to possess divine authority.*

Conclusion of Our Study

We examined two major hypotheses using methodological neutrality. After a critical analysis of hypothesis one, we found Hägerland's and Ehrman's versions weak, while Kirk's middle-of-the-road version trailed hypothesis two by a significant margin. Hypothesis two fulfilled all five criteria, and it is the best explanation of our ten highly evidenced facts. This justifies placing Jesus' divine claim on our spectrum of historical certainty as *very probable* (+3). In historical studies, this is a very favorable verdict, and it is not easily awarded.

But why might some reject the idea that the historical Jesus claimed to possess divine authority (hypothesis two)? They may object to our ten highly evidenced data points, make ad hoc appeals to apparently unevidenced assertions, or ignore the outstandingly novel, comprehensive nature of Jesus' claims to authority. It will not do, however, to simply reject the data we've uncovered or our conclusions. The skeptic's challenge would be to engage with this study and provide a more likely explanation—an alternative hypothesis that can at least fare as well as hypothesis two when subjected to standard criteria used in historical investigations.

Compared to representative versions of hypothesis one, we saw hypothesis two emerge as the best explanation of the ten historical facts. In light of highly evidenced data gleaned from both blasphemy accusation scenes, it appears *very probable* that Jesus claimed to possess a kind of divine authority rather than a kind of merely human authority similar to Jewish priests, prophets, or even human luminaries. That Jesus claimed to possess divine authority should be recognized as a highly evidenced fact of history. He didn't just make human claims. The historical Jesus claimed to be divine.

PRACTICAL APPLICATION

While social skeptics insist that Jesus never said he was God, our study shows that the historical Jesus made implicit divine claims. The evidence supports the authenticity of his claims to have authority on earth to forgive sins (Mk 2) and authority in heaven to judge sins (Mk 14). Indeed, it seems rather hasty and perhaps even disingenuous to dismiss these divine claims as the creation of Mark (or the church)—especially in light of the ten historical facts we uncovered by our analysis of each scene. In light of our critical evaluation of the hypotheses, how can we answer the question "Did Jesus really say he was God?" and share the implications of this with those who see Christianity differently? That is what our final chapter is all about.

CONCLUSION

How Jesus Said
He Was God

Christ is either Lord of all, or He is not Lord at all.

HUDSON TAYLOR

Remember the Bible grabber? The vivid image of this woman holding my Bible and confidently declaring, "According to this, Jesus never claimed to be God," is still clear in my mind. You may have already met someone like her or someone like one of the senior skeptics I've encountered over the years. For you, maybe it's a coworker, a neighbor, a friend, or family member. Perhaps you know someone like the 43 percent of American evangelicals who agreed with the statement, "Jesus was a great teacher, but he was not God." While we've assessed skeptical challenges to Jesus' deity and his divine claim, it's important to recognize that some who may not be coming from a skeptical place may still wonder, "Did Jesus really say he was God?"

For example, a Bible college student wrote after seeing my presentation on Jesus' divine claim, "I remember asking this exact question when I was 9 or 10 years old of 'Did Jesus really say he was God?' and talking to my Mom about it."[1] For some, these questions can lead to a spiritual crisis. Remember the Christian man who discovered Ehrman's views denying the historicity of Jesus' claims? He was the Redditor who posted, "This is destroying my faith. . . . There has to be a defense against this. . . . This is making me doubt big time."[2] The ideas espoused by scholars such as Hägerland, Casey, Kirk, and others like them influence popular conversations in the public square, on social media, and even in the church. How can the results of our study help us respond to common challenges to Jesus' divine claim?

In this chapter, I will briefly summarize our study and the historical case for the authenticity of Jesus' divine claim. Then, I will discuss our conclusions in light of common objections Christians encounter in conversations about Jesus and share some personal reflections. By the end, you will be able to explain the truth and significance of Jesus' divine claim—even in conversations with people who doubt the historical reliability of the Bible.

THE HISTORICAL CASE FOR JESUS' DIVINE CLAIM: REVIEW OF OUR STUDY

Our study demonstrated that recognizing highly evidenced data reflected in the Synoptics and putting those pieces together supports the historicity of Jesus' divine claim—much like putting together key pieces of a puzzle allows us to see the claims of the historical Jesus more fully.

In part one, we discussed how historians discover past events and use rules of evidence to uncover data about Jesus. Despite challenges to the traditional criteria of authenticity, we found that historical data can lead to knowledge about Jesus and that texts based on the memories of those

---

[1] Comment by @ariannathomas9373 on Apologetics Guy – Dr. Mikel Del Rosario, "Did Jesus Say He Was God? How the Historical Jesus Claimed to Be Divine | Apologetics Presentation," August 14, 2023, YouTube, 37:46, https://youtu.be/yEqBm58Z13k?si=B3JOp-2CPmo-4LCN.

[2] CorbinTheChristian, "According to Bart Ehrman, Jesus Never Claimed to Be God?," Reddit, *R/Christianity*, September 7, 2023, www.reddit.com/r/Christianity/comments/16cprgr/according_to_bart_ehrman_jesus_never_claimed_to/.

who had experiences of Jesus can help us construct an adequate representation of sayings and events in Jesus' life.

In part two, we examined our first blasphemy accusation scene (exhibit A, the healing of the paralytic in Mk 2:1-12) to discover the kind of authority Jesus claimed to have, using his reputation as a miracle worker and exorcist as a foundational fact. I concluded that it is *very probable* (+3) that the historical Jesus was accurately remembered as a unique miracle worker who claimed to possess authority on earth to forgive sins. Here Jesus made an implicit claim to possess divine authority.

In part three, we examined our second blasphemy accusation scene (exhibit B, Jesus' Jewish examination in Mk 14:53-65) to discover the kind of authority Jesus claimed to have at his Jewish examination, using his arrest and interrogation by Jewish authorities as a historical starting place. I concluded that it is *very probable* (+3) that the historical Jesus was accurately remembered as claiming to be the Messiah, the Son of the Blessed, and predicting that the high priest and council members would see him seated at God's right hand, coming on the clouds as the eschatological Son of Man. Jesus' reply was likely heard as an implicit claim to somehow possess divine authority in heaven to judge sins—a claim that was unique even among human luminaries.

In part four, we analyzed two major hypotheses concerning the type of authority that Jesus claimed to possess by using five criteria for weighing hypotheses about the sayings of a person or the cause of a past event. The evidence best supported the historicity of Jesus' claim to possess a kind of divine authority. Combining highly evidenced data from both scenes allowed us to present a strong historical case for the authenticity of Jesus' divine claim. Additionally, we observed that the early church saw the truth of Jesus' divine claim evidenced by his resurrection.

Throughout this book, we've carefully built a historical case for the authenticity of Jesus' divine claim. In order to better engage with the toughest challenges from people who don't see the Bible as an authority, we worked as historians to uncover ten historical facts from the Markan blasphemy accusation scenes. Then, we made inferences to the best explanation based on our analysis of these texts. The first scene (exhibit A) was the healing of the paralytic in Mark 2:1-12. Here, we learned that Jesus was a unique miracle worker because he claimed to have authority on earth to forgive sins—that's a divine claim. The second scene (exhibit B) was Jesus' Jewish examination in Mark 14:53-65. Here, we learned that Jesus made another unique claim—to have authority in heaven to judge sin. This is a second divine claim. I advanced two independent arguments for the authenticity of Jesus' divine claim based on these two scenes and found that synthesizing the data strengthened the historical case. Authority in heaven and on earth is a merism for all of reality. Indeed, forgiveness and judgment seem to be two sides of the same coin. If all sin is ultimately an offense against the Creator God (whose jurisdiction is the created order), then only God can forgive in an ultimate sense, and only he has the right to judge in an ultimate sense. We analyzed four views in two categories that have emerged in scholarly discussions during the twenty-first century. Hypothesis one was that Jesus claimed to possess a kind of human authority. We examined three versions of this:

1. Jesus claimed a kind of prophetic human authority (Hägerland)
2. Jesus claimed a kind of priestly human authority (Ehrman)
3. Jesus claimed a kind of idealized human authority (Kirk)

Hypothesis two was that Jesus claimed to possess a kind of divine authority. The view that Jesus claimed to have a merely human kind of authority (hypothesis one) doesn't explain the historical data nearly as well as the view that Jesus claimed to possess divine authority (hypothesis two). The latter fulfilled all five criteria and emerged as the best explanation for all ten historical facts. So, we concluded that the evidence supports the thesis of this book: *There is continuity between Jesus' claims and the early Christian belief in him as a divine figure because some of Jesus' words and deeds were likely interpreted by his Jewish adversaries as unparalleled claims to possess divine authority.*

LITERARY AND HISTORICAL CHALLENGES

Skeptics often question Jesus' deity or the historicity of his divine claims by combining literary challenges with historical ones. These objections tend to pit the Gospels against each other and assume the absence of a divine claim even on a literary level in Mark. For example: "Since Jesus did not make divine claims in the narrative world of Mark's Gospel, the historical Jesus probably did not make divine claims." In other words, if Jesus didn't say he was God in Mark, then he probably didn't say he was God in the real world. This is the rationale that lurks behind atheist challenges to the authenticity of Jesus' divine claims in John, such as, "If the historical Jesus really said, 'Before Abraham was, I am' and 'I and the Father are one,' why don't we see any hint of a divine claim anywhere in Mark's Gospel?'" But these kinds of literary objections begin with the false assumption that Jesus does not make any divine claims in Mark. However, the Markan blasphemy accusation scenes demonstrate that—even on a literary level (in the narrative world of the text)—Jesus made divine claims to legitimately forgive and judge sins.

Jesus' divine claims in the Gospel of John are not without precedent in earlier, highly evidenced Synoptic sayings. Recall John's report that some Jews sought to kill Jesus because "he was even calling God his own Father, making himself equal with God" (Jn 5:18). Then think about Jesus' divine claim in John 10:30, "I and the Father are one." This was met with hostility by Jesus' Jewish adversaries, who prepared to stone him to death, saying, "It is not for a good work that we are going to stone you but for blasphemy, because you, being a man, make yourself God" (Jn 10:33). Although skeptics reject the authenticity of Jesus' sayings in John as later theological developments, our study shows that Jesus' divine claims do not exclusively appear in John but are present in Mark as well. Similarly, blasphemy accusations do not appear exclusively in John either. The blasphemy accusation scenes we examined in this study show that in both John and Mark, Jesus' Jewish adversaries believed that he made divine claims and committed a kind of blasphemy.

WHAT SKEPTICS OFTEN MISS

Those who challenge the existence of divine claims in Mark often fail to recognize how implicit claims work in the Gospels. We must understand each blasphemy accusation scene as a whole in order to understand the significance of Jesus' words and deeds. That's why our historical conclusions were drawn only after carefully analyzing Jesus' implicit claims within each narrative and in the context of his Jewish culture.

Michael Kruger is the president and Samuel C. Patterson Professor of New Testament and Early Christianity at the Charlotte campus of Reformed Theological Seminary. He is also a noted alumnus of University of North Carolina at Chapel Hill, where Ehrman teaches. I like how Kruger responded to Ehrman's book *How Jesus Became God* by highlighting the importance of Jesus' implicit claims:

> We can agree that John's Gospel makes such claims to divinity even more direct—as the last Gospel it is not surprising that it offers a more sustained theological reflection on the person of Jesus. But, we should not confuse the directness of a claim with the existence of a claim. The historical evidence suggests the Synoptic Jesus and the Johannine Jesus both claimed to be the God of Israel.[3]

One of our historical rules of evidence was called *contextual plausibility* (rule six). This applies when a saying or event corresponds with Jesus' cultural context. We saw how Jesus' forgiveness saying in Mark 2 was likely heard as an implicit claim to somehow possess divine authority to forgive sins and that his reply to the high priest in Mark 14 was likely heard as an implicit claim to somehow possess divine authority in heaven to judge sins. The idea of *contextual plausibility* can be applied on the literary level as well.

Think about the literary assumption behind a common Muslim objection to the deity of Jesus: "Where does Jesus say, 'I am God'?" Skeptics who ask this question assume that saying "I am God" is the only way

---

[3]Michael Kruger, "Did Jesus Claim to Be God? A Response to Bart Ehrman (Part 3)," *Canon Fodder*, June 11, 2014, https://michaeljkruger.com/did-jesus-claim-to-be-god-a-response-to-bart-ehrman-part-3/.

Jesus could have made a divine claim. But why must Jesus' divine claims be limited to only direct statements? No, as Kruger recognized, this challenge confuses the directness of a claim with the existence of a claim. If I were to say, "I'm married," that would be an explicit claim. But if I said, "My wife and I just celebrated our twenty-fifth wedding anniversary," that would include an implicit claim to be married. The simple act of wearing my wedding ring every single day is another way to implicitly claim to be married—even without words. Talking about our silver anniversary dinner while wearing my wedding ring is one example of the way statements and actions can work together to reinforce implicit claims.

In Mark's Gospel, Jesus' statements and actions work together to reveal his implicit claims of comprehensive authority—often connected to divine prerogatives (such as divine forgiveness and judgment) and pointing to the coming of God's kingdom. Jesus speaks as God does and does the things that God does. Indeed, the idea that Jesus claimed to possess divine authority (hypothesis two) fits very well in Mark's Gospel. Beyond Jesus' claim to have divine authority to forgive and judge sin, consider these five additional examples:

1. Jesus is portrayed as having authority over sacred things: In Mark 2:28, Jesus claims to be the Lord of the Sabbath—a sacred Jewish institution enshrined in one of God's Ten Commandments delivered to Moses (Ex 20:8-11). In Mark 3:1-6 Jesus heals a man on the Sabbath, and his adversaries plot against him after his seeming violation of Sabbath prohibitions (Ex 20:10-11: "On it you shall not do any work. . . . The LORD blessed the Sabbath day and made it holy."). In Mark 11:15-19, he drives out those doing business in the Jerusalem temple—another claim of authority over sacred things that resulted in further plots against his life. At the Last Supper in Mark 14:22-24, Jesus even reconfigures the symbolism of a sacred Passover meal to refer to himself. The Passover was a profound institution of God in connection with the exodus: "it is the LORD's Passover. . . . This day shall be for you a memorial

day, and you shall keep it as a feast for the LORD; throughout your generations, as a statute forever, you shall keep it as a feast" (Ex 12:11, 14). Again, the Old Testament background is key to understanding how this coheres with Jesus' divine authority.

2. Jesus is portrayed as having authority over nature: In Mark 4:38-41, he commands the wind and calms the storm. Interestingly, in Psalm 107:28-29 we read that the Lord (the God of Israel) commands the winds and calms the storm.[4] The Old Testament supplies the relevant cultural and literary background to appreciate how this scene coheres with Jesus' divine authority.

3. Jesus is portrayed as having authority over demons: In Mark 5:1-20, he exorcises a legion of demons from a man, and in Mark 3:22-27, he previously spoke of binding up Satan himself—another novel claim that coheres with Jesus' divine authority.[5]

4. Jesus is portrayed as having authority over disease: In Mark 5:25-34, he heals a woman with a bleeding hemorrhage who merely touches him—without even praying. Again, Jesus is not merely a petitioner of numinous power. He doesn't ask God to heal. Rather, he is a bearer of numinous power himself. This and the mention of his power and his knowledge of her faith also cohere with Jesus' divine authority.

5. Jesus is portrayed as having authority even over death: In Mark 5:35-43, Jesus raises Jairus's daughter from the dead—without praying—by his own authority. This contrasts with the way that the prophet Elijah prayed and asked God to raise a widow's son from the dead in 1 Kings 17:21-22.[6] This also coheres with Jesus' divine authority.

So, the blasphemy accusation scenes fit the way that Mark's Gospel portrays Jesus. It's important to recognize and appreciate how Jesus' authority is not limited to one or two areas but extends over a range of key

---

[4]Michael R. Licona, "Did Jesus Claim to Be God?," July 8, 2017, YouTube, 47:18, www.youtube .com/watch?v=gT2TN6kA5kY.

[5]Licona, "Did Jesus Claim to Be God?"

[6]Licona, "Did Jesus Claim to Be God?"

areas: Jesus has authority over sacred things, over nature, over demons, disease, and death. Who else has that kind of authority—in all these different areas? These Markan texts give us a glimpse of what possessing authority in heaven and on earth looks like.

While Kirk focuses on a literary analysis of Jesus' claims, his conclusions have historical implications. Many people who read his work can walk away thinking, "If Jesus never claimed to be God in the text, then he didn't claim to be God in the real world either." However, if the historical Jesus made divine claims, as our study demonstrates from just two scenes in Mark, critics should take more seriously the implications of Jesus' words and deeds recorded in John. Those who continue to insist, "In John, Jesus is God, but in Mark, he's not God," miss the profundity of Jesus' implicit divine claims not only in his words but in his actions. Recall that even an atheist scholar such as Ehrman, who rejects the historicity of Jesus' divine claim, now agrees that in the literary world of Mark's Gospel, "the high priest . . . would have understood that Jesus was claiming to be divine in some sense" and in fact, "There is no question that Jesus in the Gospels claims to be divine."[7] Indeed, the divide between the portraits of Jesus in Mark and John is not as wide as many skeptics insist. What this means is that John's Gospel reflects and magnifies what was already presented in Mark: Jesus' divine authority. In both the earliest Gospel and the latest Gospel, Jesus is presented as somehow being part of the divine identity.

How to Answer "Did Jesus Really Say He Was God?"

Did Jesus really say he was God? Yes, but not the way most people today might have expected him to say it. He claims to be divine implicitly through a combination of his words and actions. The historical data from the Markan blasphemy accusation scenes show that Jesus' enemies believed that he claimed to have divine authority on earth to forgive sins

---

[7]Bart D. Ehrman, *The New Testament: A Historical Introduction to the Early Christian Writings*, 7th ed. (New York: Oxford University Press, 2020), 115; Ehrman, "Does Jesus Call Himself God in His Trial Before the Sanhedrin and the High Priest Caiaphas?," *The Bart Ehrman Blog*, August 19, 2023, https://ehrmanblog.org/does-jesus-call-himself-god-in-his-trial-before-the-sanhedrin-and-the-high-priest-caiaphus/.

and divine authority in heaven to judge sins—this points to his authority over all of reality. This sets him above angels or any human ruler who was believed to be divine in some sense (e.g., Alexander the Great, Caesar Augustus) because none of these figures were believed to possess authority over all of reality. If Jesus' divine claims are true, then there is good reason to believe that he's more than a man; he's God Almighty.

TRUTH AND SIGNIFICANCE

In 2023, Anna Sorokin started a podcast while under house arrest in her New York apartment. She launched her show as part of an effort to revitalize her public image and distance herself from her reputation as an infamous con artist known as Anna Delvey. Previously, Sorokin used this alias to claim to be the daughter of a diplomat or an oil tycoon. After convincing many people that she was a wealthy German heiress with a $67 million trust fund, she took out large loans and ran up debts while living an extravagant, lavish lifestyle. In 2019, she was convicted of larceny and theft for scamming banks, hotels, and New Yorkers out of about $275,000.[8] This was popularized in 2022 when an adaptation of her story called *Inventing Anna* was released on Netflix.

Sorokin's case raised the question of identity: Was she really who she claimed to be? The evidence demonstrated that the accusations against her were true because she was not in fact who she claimed to be. Similarly, Jesus' case also raises the question of identity: Was he really who he claimed to be? Our study found that Jesus' adversaries likely heard his words as divine claims. But were the blasphemy accusations against him true? The truth or falsity of Jesus' divine claim is important because Jesus would be guilty of any alleged blasphemy only if he was not divine, as he claimed to be. Uncovering the truth about this is significant because, for Jesus' followers, it was his divine claim that filled the resurrection with theological meaning. How did the early church connect Jesus' resurrection to his deity?

---

[8]John Carucci, "Under House Arrest, Fake Heiress Anna 'Delvey' Sorokin Launches Podcast to Rehab Public Image," AP News, June 9, 2023, https://apnews.com/article/anna-delvey-sorokin -podcast-interview-2a694e71f19f30c0b7e8a37816db8e2b.

THE FIRST APOLOGETIC FOR JESUS AS LORD AND CHRIST

The earliest form of the church's preaching can be seen in the apostle Peter's speech on the day of Pentecost (Acts 2:14-36)—the very first apologetic argument for Jesus as Lord and Christ. Pentecost was a Jewish pilgrimage feast that drew people from various locations to Jerusalem (Acts 2:9-11). On this day, an international gathering of Jews is bewildered when they hear disciples talking about God's mighty works in each of their own foreign languages. "And they were amazed and astonished, saying, "Are not all these who are speaking Galileans? And how is it that we hear, each of us in his own native language?" (Acts 2:7-8). While some are curious, others say the disciples are drunk (Acts 2:13). Because of this, Peter explains what is happening: this miraculous, multilingual proclamation is the result of Jesus' outpouring of the Holy Spirit.

For Peter, this is further evidence that God vindicated Jesus' divine claim by raising him from the dead.[9] He cites three key Old Testament texts to explain the theological significance of the crowd hearing the disciples preach in each of their languages. First, Peter cites the prophet Joel, who predicted an outpouring of the Holy Spirit before the day of the Lord (Joel 2:28-32): "And it shall come to pass that everyone who calls upon the name of the Lord shall be saved" (Acts 2:21; see Joel 2:32). Here, it's important to appreciate that the word *Lord* indicates the divine name in Hebrew. Joel's appeal was to cry out to Israel's God, Yahweh, for salvation. Peter's argument puts an unexpected twist on this, arguing that the Lord is Jesus the Messiah (Acts 2:36). Bock notes that as the sermon progresses, "Peter will give Jesus a place alongside Yahweh as carrying out the plan [of salvation] and will make clear that the name one is to call on belongs to Jesus (2:38; 4:10-12)."[10]

Second, Peter turns to the Psalms and argues that King David's prophecies ultimately foretold both the Messiah's resurrection (Ps 16:8-11) and ascension to the right hand of God (Ps 110:1). For Peter,

---

[9]Luke mentions that Peter was an eyewitness to Jesus' empty tomb (Lk 24:12), and Paul quotes an early creed—which predates the Gospels—listing Peter as eyewitness to the risen Jesus (1 Cor 15:5).
[10]Darrell L. Bock, *Acts* (Grand Rapids, MI: Baker Academic, 2007), 118.

"My flesh also dwells secure. For you will not abandon my soul to Sheol, or let your holy one see corruption" (Ps 16:9-10) points beyond God's protection of the king of Israel to Jesus' vindication via resurrection (Acts 2:26-27). Indeed, "my flesh" points to Jesus' bodily resurrection, as Jesus' flesh did not see corruption—unlike King David, whose undisturbed grave shows that he could not be the ultimate fulfillment of the confidence in divine protection reflected in Psalm 16.[11] Peter's speech culminates in a quotation of Psalm 110:1 (Acts 2:34-35). This is the same text to which Jesus alluded at his Jewish examination: "The Lord said to my Lord, 'Sit at my right hand, until I make your enemies your footstool.'" This final quotation is a crucial link between Jesus' own divine claim and the early Christian belief in him as a divine figure. Peter uses both psalms to argue that David predicted the Messiah's resurrection and ascension:

> Brothers, I may say to you with confidence about the patriarch David that he both died and was buried, and his tomb is with us to this day. Being therefore a prophet, and knowing that God had sworn with an oath to him that he would set one of his descendants on his throne, he foresaw and spoke about the resurrection of the Christ, that he was not abandoned to Hades, nor did his flesh see corruption. This Jesus God raised up, and of that we all are witnesses. Being therefore exalted at the right hand of God, and having received from the Father the promise of the Holy Spirit, he has poured out this that you yourselves are seeing and hearing. For David did not ascend into the heavens. (Acts 2:29-34)

Peter argues that while no Davidic king ever literally ascended to God's right hand, Jesus did. So, what was metaphorical in this coronation psalm saw a literal fulfillment in Jesus. This speech is a key witness to the early church's basic Christology: Jesus' divine identity was vindicated by God via the resurrection and ascension and further evidenced by the disciples' miraculous, multilingual speech empowered by the Holy Spirit.

---

[11]"To realize fully the expression of confidence the psalm expresses about God's continual presence, the one referred to must be raised, and this cannot be about a still-buried David, whose grave is undisturbed." Bock, *Acts*, 127.

JESUS, GOD THE FATHER, AND JEWISH MONOTHEISM

For the early church, it was God's vindication of Jesus' divine claim that allowed them to conceptually include Jesus in God's authority over all things, see him as sharing in God's exaltation over angels, refer to him using the divine name, and see him within the divine identity.[12] Cambridge New Testament Professor Andrew Chester notes the significance of this in Jesus' cultural context: "To affirm all this of Christ, within the context of strict Jewish monotheism, is also to affirm that he belongs unambiguously within the divine identity. There is an absolute boundary between the one God and all created reality: Christ belongs on one side of this boundary, while angels and all other 'intermediary' figures belong equally clearly on the other."[13] The early church gave Jesus the kind of devotion beyond what was given to human rulers, angels, or intermediary figures on the creature side of the Creator-creature divide. Bird notes, "Jesus was worshipped, not as a subordinate angel, but alongside God the Father, and in conscious continuity with the worship of the one God of Israel's monotheistic tradition."[14] Indeed, Saul of Tarsus (before he followed Jesus and became known as the apostle Paul) began to persecute Christians because of the perception that the church was a messianic cult that worshiped Jesus alongside the God of Israel.[15] However, his personal experience of the risen Jesus on the Damascus road (Acts 9:1-9) transformed him from a persecutor of the Jesus movement to one of its greatest proponents.

One reason that Jesus did not go around saying "I am God" is that he did not want to be misunderstood as either claiming to be a rival deity in competition with God the Father or claiming to be identical to God the Father. No, he suggested both a unity and a distinction between himself and God the Father. Some people who insist that Jesus never

---

[12]Andrew Chester, "High Christology: Whence, When and Why?," *Early Christianity* 2, no. 1 (2011): 30.
[13]Chester, "High Christology," 30.
[14]Michael F. Bird, *Jesus Among the Gods: Early Christology in the Greco-Roman World* (Waco, TX: Baylor University Press, 2022), 246.
[15]Larry W. Hurtado, *Lord Jesus Christ: Devotion to Jesus in Earliest Christianity* (Grand Rapids, MI: Eerdmans, 2005), 175-76.

claimed to be God wrongly assume that if Jesus didn't claim to be God the Father, then he didn't claim to be God. Many of Jesus' contemporaries did not see it this way.

Jews who accepted Jesus' divine claims believed they could legitimately incorporate Jesus into the identity of the God of Israel without compromising Jewish monotheism. Consider three texts from epistles that critical scholars call "the undisputed letters" written by the apostle Paul: Romans 9:5; 1 Corinthians 8:6; Philippians 2:9-11.[16] Paul could call Jesus "the Christ, who is God over all" (Rom 9:5) while holding to Jesus' unity and distinction from God the Father.[17] To communicate this, he most often used *Lord* to refer to Jesus and *God* to refer to the Father. For example, here is how he modifies the sacred Jewish Shema to include Jesus in the identity of Yahweh: "Yet for us there is one God, the Father, from whom are all things and for whom we exist, and one Lord, Jesus Christ, through whom are all things and through whom we exist" (1 Cor 8:6). This is especially profound, as the original monotheistic creed in Deuteronomy connected God and Lord to a single Creator. Further, Paul uses both terms to express the deity of both God the Father and Jesus without compromising the monotheistic creed. This is why Jewish converts could outright worship Jesus as God in a Jewish context.

Paul also quotes an ancient hymn in Philippians 2:9-11 that portrays Jesus as receiving the kind of universal worship that Yahweh will receive. The hymn includes these lines: "At the name of Jesus every knee should bow, in heaven and on earth and under the earth, and every tongue confess that Jesus Christ is Lord, to the glory of God the Father" (Phil 2:10-11). These words strikingly echo Yahweh's words in Isaiah 45:22-23, "I am God, and there is no other. . . . To me every knee

---

[16]Ehrman, *New Testament*, 290n34.

[17]Similarly, Paul also refers to Jesus as "our great God and Savior Jesus Christ" (Titus 2:13), although critical scholars dispute Paul's authorship of this. On Rom 9:5, see *The NET Bible First Edition Notes* (Richardson, TX: Biblical Studies Press, 2006), Rom 9:5. See also Bruce M. Metzger, "The Punctuation of Rom. 9:5," in *Christ and the Spirit in the New Testament*, ed. Barnabas Lindars and Stephen S. Smalley (Cambridge: Cambridge University Press, 1973), 95-112; Murray J. Harris, *Jesus as God: The New Testament use of Theos in Reference to Jesus* (Grand Rapids, MI: Baker, 1992), 144-72.

shall bow, every tongue shall confess to God."[18] The hymnic lyrics are especially profound in light of the fact that Isaiah 45 is one of the strongest monotheistic texts in the entire Old Testament. Here we see a unity and a distinction of Jesus and God the Father. These are just some examples of how Jesus' followers understood his divine claim in a Jewish context, connected to the resurrection, and spoke of him as being on the creator side of the Creator-creature divide.

These texts highlight elements of continuity with the Nicene Creed (AD 325/381), which many Christians historically have used to proclaim belief in Jesus from the fourth century to our present day.

> We believe in one Lord, Jesus Christ
> the only Son of God
> eternally begotten of the Father
> God from God, Light from Light
> true God from true God
> begotten, not made,
> of one Being with the Father;
> through him all things were made.

While a resurrection on its own would not have resulted in this kind of devotion, Jesus' divine claim filled the resurrection with profound theological meaning. This is why I stated at the outset of our study that recovering the historicity of Jesus' divine claim is crucial to appreciating the significance of the resurrection. For the earliest Christians, the resurrection preaching was only worth believing if it was actually true.

THE IMPORTANCE OF THE RESURRECTION

"Just because someone claims to be God, that doesn't make it true." This is a response I once received from a skeptical middle-aged woman in California. Was Jesus telling the truth? The truth of Jesus' divine claim hinges on the truth of Jesus' resurrection. In fact, so does the validity of the apostles' gospel preaching (and the Christian faith itself).

---

[18]English translation of the Septuagint from the Orthodox Study Bible (Ancient Faith ed.). The ESV translates the MT, "Every tongue shall swear allegiance."

Paul's clearest definition of the gospel relies on an ancient creed that began by proclaiming the resurrection itself and the resurrection appearances, and he quotes it this way: "Christ died for our sins in accordance with the Scriptures, that he was buried, that he was raised on the third day in accordance with the Scriptures and that he appeared to Cephas, then to the twelve" (1 Cor 15:3-5). Ehrman agrees that "Paul is almost certainly quoting an earlier creed."[19] Besides the appearances to Jesus' followers, this creed also mentions Jesus' appearance to James (1 Cor 15:7). It's notable that James, Jesus' brother, was a skeptic who did not previously believe that Jesus was Lord or Messiah (Mk 3:2-21). Still, he later led the church in Jerusalem (Gal 2:9) and was eventually martyred by stoning.[20]

Moreover, Paul—himself a former church persecutor—adds that the risen Jesus appeared to him as well (1 Cor 15:8-10). This likely occurred about two years after Jesus' crucifixion.[21] Paul's Damascus road experience resulted in his preaching about the truth of Jesus' identity and resurrection right away (Gal 1:15-17). For Paul, the resurrection was the litmus test of the validity of the Christian faith: "If Christ has not been raised, then our preaching is in vain and your faith is in vain" (1 Cor 15:14). Paul's dramatic conversion tells us that the resurrection preaching did not emerge through legendary development over many decades but existed very soon after Jesus' crucifixion. Here's why: Paul had to already know about the resurrection preaching in order to disagree with it and persecute those who believed it (Gal 1:23). Further, he also had to know about the resurrection preaching to believe that he was seeing the risen Jesus. If this preaching was around before Paul's conversion, then the content of the ancient gospel creed quoted in 1 Corinthians 15 likely goes back to before this time. The late British New Testament scholar James D. G. Dunn taught as Lightfoot Professor of Divinity at the University of Durham. He dates the creed to within less than a year of the crucifixion (before any New Testament book was written): "This tradition, we can

---

[19]Bart D. Ehrman, *How Jesus Became God: The Exaltation of a Jewish Preacher from Galilee* (New York: HarperOne, 2015), 217.

[20]Josephus, *Jewish Antiquities* 20.9.

[21]Ehrman, *How Jesus Became God*, 213-14.

be entirely confident, was formulated as tradition within months of Jesus' death."[22] The early belief in Jesus as a divine figure is related not only to Jesus' divine claim but to the belief in his resurrection—the validation of Jesus' divine claim.

NEXT STEPS: WHERE DO WE GO NOW?

See how other highly evidenced data from events in Jesus' life reveal his divine identity. Consider the following resources for more details on this and the evidence for Jesus' resurrection.

Introductory

- Bock, Darrell L. *Who Is Jesus? Linking the Historical Jesus with the Christ of Faith.* New York: Howard, 2012.

- Habermas, Gary R., and Michael Licona. *The Case for the Resurrection of Jesus.* Grand Rapids, MI: Kregel, 2004.

Advanced

- Bird, Michael F. *Jesus Among the Gods: Early Christology in the Greco-Roman World.* Waco, TX: Baylor University Press, 2022.

- Bock, Darrell L., and Robert L. Webb, eds. *Key Events in the Life of the Historical Jesus: A Collaborative Exploration of Context and Coherence.* Grand Rapids, MI: Eerdmans, 2010.

- Habermas, Gary. *On the Resurrection.* Vol. 1, *Evidences.* Nashville: B&H Academic, 2024.

- Licona, Michael R. *The Resurrection of Jesus: A New Historiographical Approach.* Downers Grove, IL: IVP Academic, 2010.

Listen to authors like these on episodes of my podcast, *The Apologetics Guy Show,* available on YouTube and popular audio platforms (e.g., Apple Podcasts and Spotify), https://apologeticsguy.com.

PERSONAL REFLECTIONS AND A CHALLENGE TO THE READER

The research that stands behind this book did not merely end with academics for me. Our findings are not dead facts locked away in the first

---

[22]James D. G. Dunn, *Jesus Remembered*, Christianity in the Making 1 (Grand Rapids, MI: Eerdmans, 2003), 855.

century. As I concluded my study, I reflected on Jesus afresh. And I developed a renewed appreciation of the profundity of his divine identity and the personal relevance of his divine authority. Recognizing that Jesus' authority in heaven and on earth means that he has authority over all of reality should lead us all to contemplate the areas of our lives where we have yet to yield to his authority—his authority to assess the morality of our thoughts, words, and deeds. As nineteenth-century Protestant missionary Hudson Taylor writes, "Christ is either Lord *of* all, or He is not Lord *at* all."[23] It's humbling to ponder the areas of our lives where we fall short, where we do things we shouldn't do and fail to do things that we should, so often failing to love our neighbors as ourselves. "Lord, have mercy."

But the good news is that Jesus has divine authority not only to judge sin as the eschatological Son of Man but also to forgive sin, just like he forgave the paralytic. There is a historical basis for Jesus' authority to forgive sins that can strengthen our confidence in Jesus' pivotal connection to obtaining divine forgiveness (Acts 2:38; 1 John 1:7-9). After Peter gave the first apologetics sermon arguing for Jesus as Lord and Messiah, about three thousand people repented and were baptized in the name of Jesus Christ for the forgiveness of their sins (Acts 2:37-41). This is a reminder that the end goal of our apologetics should not merely be to persuade people of Jesus' divine claim or even his deity but to invite them to call on his name. In the end, yielding to his lordship and entering into a life-changing relationship with God is what brings lasting human flourishing and fulfillment. No matter where you are in your spiritual journey, the historical evidence for Jesus' divine claim invites us all to answer for ourselves the question that Jesus once posed to the apostle Peter: "Who do you say that I am?" (Mk 8:29).

Preparing to engage people who see the Bible differently means seeking to understand their concerns and being sensitive to their hesitancy to accept the historicity of Gospel events. This is one reason we approached our study of Jesus as historians. Behind the Bible grabber's

---

[23]Howard Taylor, *Biography of James Hudson Taylor* (London: Hodder & Stoughton, 1985), 439-40, emphasis added.

assertions that fateful Sunday afternoon was the underlying question, "Why should anyone believe that Jesus is God if he never said he was God?" Our investigation exposed the problems with this faulty premise and revealed a continuity between Jesus' own claims and the early Christian belief in him as a divine figure.

The church has always believed that God acted in history through Jesus Christ. It's my hope that this book has given you more confidence to navigate conversations about Jesus with people who do not see the Bible as an authority but might be open to the answers of history. Our journey has provided a framework that can help you engage with people like the Bible grabber, a variety of senior skeptics, church attendees, Christian kids, and anyone who asks, "Did Jesus really say he was God?" They've already heard from the skeptics. Now, they need to hear the rest of the story. Let's help them make sense of his historical claims. And may they develop an openness to the idea that Jesus is more than a man—he's God Almighty.

Glossary

INTRODUCTION

Christ of faith: Jesus the Messiah in Christian doctrine, including the reality of his divinity, his role in salvation, and various christological concepts.

historical Jesus / Jesus of history: Jesus as reconstructed through critical historical methods, including textual analysis and archaeological evidence, distinguished from the Christ of faith. This reconstruction is part of an ongoing scholarly discussion.

historical Jesus studies: A scholarly investigation of Jesus as historical figure using critical analysis of ancient sources. This field aims to understand Jesus as a first-century Jew through interdisciplinary approaches from history and archaeology, often applying criteria of authenticity to uncover historical facts about him from the New Testament.

quests for the historical Jesus: Scholarly efforts to reconstruct Jesus' life and teachings via critical historical methods, categorized by eras of research that reflect evolving approaches to the Bible:

- **First Quest** (late eighteenth to early twentieth centuries): From Hermann Samuel Reimarus to Adolf Schweitzer, scholars distinguished the historical Jesus from the Christ of faith, with many questioning the reality of miracles and the reliability of the Bible's portrait of Jesus.
- **No Quest** (early twentieth century to 1950s): Scholars such as Rudolf Bultmann were skeptical about uncovering substantial historical facts about Jesus from the Bible, while form criticism laid the groundwork for the criteria of authenticity.

- **Second Quest** (1950s to 1970s): Ernst Käsemann's reaction to the "No Quest" period revived interest in historical Jesus research, leading to the development of the criteria of authenticity to identify memories of Jesus in the Gospels.
- **Third Quest** (1980s to present): Scholars such as E. P. Sanders sought to understand Jesus as a first-century Jew, using interdisciplinary approaches that emphasize historical context and critical analysis of sources.

Synoptics: Derived from the Greek word *synoptic*, meaning "seen together," the Gospels of Matthew, Mark, and Luke share similar content and wording, distinguishing them from the Gospel of John.

CHAPTER 1

correspondence theory: The view that true statements must reflect objective reality, supporting the idea that historical accounts can accurately represent past events.

deconstruction: A postmodern approach that questions traditional assumptions about truth, revealing multiple meanings and contradictions within texts.

hermeneutics: The theory and methodology of interpretation that employs the historical-grammatical approach to understand texts by considering their historical and cultural contexts. This method is essential for accurate interpretation, bridging the gap between ancient audiences and contemporary readers.

historiography: The study of how history is written, focusing on methods to recover knowledge about past events and analyzing historians' perspectives and the construction of historical narratives.

history: A historian's narrative account of past events based on the historian's interpretation of the surviving traces of past events (adapted from Webb's definition).[1]

---

[1]Darrell L. Bock and Robert L. Webb, eds., *Key Events in the Life of the Historical Jesus: A Collaborative Exploration of Context and Coherence* (Grand Rapids, MI: Eerdmans, 2010), 16.

horizon: In hermeneutics, *horizon* refers to how a person's understanding is shaped by their historical and cultural context, highlighting both the limitations and possibilities of interpretation.

minimal facts: In historical Jesus studies, the minimal facts approach, developed by Gary Habermas, identifies a core set of well-evidenced facts about Jesus accepted by nearly all scholars, including skeptics, to establish a foundation of historical data acknowledged across diverse perspectives.

postmodernism: A philosophical movement that rejects modernity, characterized by skepticism toward grand narratives and objective truth. It emphasizes how perspective and power shape historical narratives.

CHAPTER 3

Dead Sea Scrolls: A collection of ancient Jewish manuscripts discovered near the Dead Sea (1947–1956), dating from the third century BC to the first century AD. These texts include biblical manuscripts, sectarian writings, and other works that provide crucial insights into Second Temple Judaism and the context of early Christianity.

CHAPTER 7

New Testament criticism: A scholarly approach to analyzing New Testament texts using critical methods to understand their origins, development, and historical meaning by examining manuscripts, sources, and literary structures.

CHAPTER 8

Mishnah: The first major written collection of Jewish oral traditions, compiled around AD 200, forming the core of the Talmud and providing further context for understanding Jewish law and practice in the time of Jesus.

CHAPTER 11

merism: A rhetorical device that juxtaposes opposite extremes to express a unified concept. In biblical literature, it's often used to convey completeness or universality (e.g., Rev 22:13, "I am the Alpha and the Omega, the first and the last, the beginning and the end").

Shema: A central Jewish prayer and declaration of Jewish monotheism, beginning with "Hear, O Israel: The Lord our God, the Lord is one," recorded in Deuteronomy 6:4-9.

Bibliography

Akenside, Mark. *The Pleasures Of Imagination: A New Edition.* London: Old Bailey, 1806. https://ia803207.us.archive.org/27/items/pleasuresofimagi00aken/pleasures ofimagi00aken.pdf.

Allison, Dale C., Jr. "It Don't Come Easy: A History of Disillusionment." In *Jesus, Criteria, and the Demise of Authenticity*, edited by Chris Keith and Anthony Le Donne, 186-99. London: T&T Clark, 2012.

———. *Resurrecting Jesus: The Earliest Christian Tradition and Its Interpreters.* New York: T&T Clark, 2005.

"Ancient Bones May Be of Priest Who Handed Jesus to Romans." *Los Angeles Times*, August 14, 1992. www.latimes.com/archives/la-xpm-1992-08-14-mn-5366-story.html.

Anderson, Hugh. *The Gospel of Mark.* Grand Rapids, MI: Eerdmans, 1981.

Apologetics Guy – Dr. Mikel Del Rosario. "Did Jesus Say He Was God? How the Historical Jesus Claimed to Be Divine | Apologetics Presentation." August 14, 2023. YouTube, 37:46. https://youtu.be/yEqBm58Z13k?si=B3JOp-2CPmo-4LCN.

"Author Traces Christianity's Path from 'Forbidden Religion' to a 'Triumph.'" *Fresh Air*. National Public Radio, March 20, 2018. www.npr.org/2018/03/20/595161200/author -traces-christianitys-path-from-forbidden-religion-to-a-triumph.

"Baptistery Wall Painting: Christ Healing the Paralytic." Yale University Art Gallery, accessed September 1, 2023. https://artgallery.yale.edu/collections/objects/34498.

Barnett, Paul. *Finding the Historical Christ.* After Jesus 3. Grand Rapids, MI: Eerdmans, 2009.

Bauckham, Richard. "The Caiaphas Family." *Journal for the Study of the Historical Jesus* 10 (2012): 3-31.

———. "Is 'High Human Christology' Sufficient? A Critical Response to J. R. Daniel Kirk's *A Man Attested by God.*" *Bulletin for Biblical Research* 27, no. 4 (2017): 503-25.

Bernier, Jonathan. *The Quest for the Historical Jesus After the Demise of Authenticity: Toward a Critical Realist Philosophy of History in Jesus Studies.* Library of New Testament Studies 540. New York: T&T Clark, 2016.

Bible & Culture Collective. *The Postmodern Bible.* New Haven, CT: Yale University Press, 1997.

Bird, Michael F. *Jesus Among the Gods: Early Christology in the Greco-Roman World*. Waco, TX: Baylor University Press, 2022.

Blackburn, Barry. *Theios Anēr and the Markan Miracle Traditions: A Critique of the Theios Anēr Concept as an Interpretative Background of the Miracle Traditions Used by Mark*. Tübingen: Mohr Siebeck, 1991.

Blinzler, Josef. *Der Prozess Jesu*. 4th ed. Regensburg: Friedrich Pustet, 1969.

Bock, Darrell L. *Acts*. Grand Rapids, MI: Baker Academic, 2007.

———. *Blasphemy and Exaltation in Judaism: The Charge Against Jesus in Mark 14:53-65*. Grand Rapids, MI: Baker Academic, 2000.

———. "Blasphemy and the Jewish Examination of Jesus." In *Key Events in the Life of the Historical Jesus: A Collaborative Exploration of Context and Coherence*, edited by Darrell L. Bock and Robert L. Webb, 589-668. Grand Rapids, MI: Eerdmans, 2009.

———. "Dating the Parables of Enoch: A Forschungsbericht." In *Parables of Enoch: A Paradigm Shift*, edited by Darrell L. Bock and James H. Charlesworth, 58-113. Jewish and Christian Texts 11. New York: Bloomsbury T&T Clark, 2013.

———. "The Historical Jesus: An Evangelical View." In *The Historical Jesus: Five Views*, edited by James K. Beilby and Paul R. Eddy, 249-81. Downers Grove, IL: IVP Academic, 2009.

———. "Jesus as Blasphemer." In *Who Do My Opponents Say That I Am? An Investigation of the Accusations Against the Historical Jesus*, edited by Scot McKnight and Joseph B. Modica, 67-94. Library of New Testament Studies 327. New York: T&T Clark, 2008.

———. "Jewish Expressions in Mark 14.61-62 and the Authenticity of the Jewish Examination of Jesus." *Journal for the Study of the Historical Jesus* 1, no. 2 (2003): 148.

———. *Luke 1:1–9:50*. Grand Rapids, MI: Baker Academic, 1994.

———. *Luke 9:51–24:53*. Grand Rapids, MI: Baker Academic, 1996.

———. *Mark*. Cambridge: Cambridge University Press, 2015.

———. *Proclamation from Prophecy and Pattern: Lucan Old Testament Christology*. Journal for the Study of the New Testament Supplement Series 12. Sheffield: JSOT Press, 1997.

———. "The Son of Man in Luke 5:24." *Bulletin for Biblical Research* 1 (1991): 109-21.

———. *Studying the Historical Jesus: A Guide to Sources and Methods*. Grand Rapids, MI: Baker Academic, 2002.

———. *Who Is Jesus? Linking the Historical Jesus with the Christ of Faith*. New York: Howard, 2012.

———. "The Words of Jesus: Live, Jive, or Memorex?" In *Jesus Under Fire: Modern Scholarship Reinvents the Historical Jesus*, edited by Michael J. Wilkins and J. P. Moreland, 73-99. Grand Rapids: Zondervan Academic, 1995.

Bock, Darrell L., and James H. Charlesworth, eds. *Parables of Enoch: A Paradigm Shift*. Jewish and Christian Texts 11. New York: Bloomsbury T&T Clark, 2013.

Bock, Darrell L., and Benjamin I. Simpson. *Jesus According to Scripture: Restoring the Portrait from the Gospels*. 2nd ed. Grand Rapids, MI: Baker Academic, 2017.

Bock, Darrell L., and Robert L. Webb, eds. *Key Events in the Life of the Historical Jesus: A Collaborative Exploration of Context and Coherence*. Grand Rapids, MI: Eerdmans, 2010.

Borg, Marcus J. *Jesus, a New Vision: Spirit, Culture, and the Life of Discipleship*. San Francisco: HarperCollins, 1987.

Borg, Marcus J., and John Dominic Crossan. *The Last Week: What the Gospels Really Teach About Jesus's Final Days in Jerusalem*. San Francisco: HarperOne, 2007.

Boyarin, Daniel. *The Jewish Gospels*. New York: New Press, 2012.

Brown, Dan. *The Da Vinci Code*. New York: Vintage, 2003.

Brown, Raymond E. *The Death of the Messiah, from Gethsemane to the Grave: A Commentary on the Passion Narratives in the Four Gospels*. Vol. 2. Anchor Bible Reference Library. New Haven, CT: Doubleday, 1994.

——, trans. "The Gospel of Peter." Early Christian Writings. Accessed April 7, 2021. www.earlychristianwritings.com/text/gospelpeter-brown.html.

Bultmann, Rudolf. *Jesus and the Word*. Translated by L. P. Smith and E. H. Lantero. London: Collins, 1958.

Butler, Trent C., and Clayton Harrop, eds. "Jewish Parties in the New Testament." In *Holman Bible Dictionary*, 791. Nashville: Broadman & Holman, 1991.

Carson, D. A., and G. K. Beale, eds. *Commentary on the New Testament Use of the Old Testament*. Grand Rapids, MI: Baker Academic, 2007.

Carucci, John. "Under House Arrest, Fake Heiress Anna 'Delvey' Sorokin Launches Podcast to Rehab Public Image." AP News, June 9, 2023. https://apnews.com/article/anna-delvey-sorokin-podcast-interview-2a694e71f19f30c0b7e8a37816db8e2b.

Casey, Maurice. *Jesus of Nazareth: An Independent Historian's Account of His Life and Teaching*. New York: T&T Clark, 2010.

——. *The Solution to the "Son of Man" Problem*. New York: Bloomsbury T&T Clark, 2007.

Charles, R. H. *The Book of Enoch*. Eastford, CT: Martino Fine Books, 2017.

Charlesworth, James H. "The Date and Provenience of the Parables of Enoch." In *Parables of Enoch: A Paradigm Shift*, edited by Darrell L. Bock and James H. Charlesworth, 37-57. Jewish and Christian Texts 11. New York: Bloomsbury T&T Clark, 2013.

——. "Did Jesus Know the Traditions in the Parables of Enoch?" In *Parables of Enoch: A Paradigm Shift*, edited by Darrell L. Bock, 173-217. Jewish and Christian Texts 11. New York: Bloomsbury T&T Clark, 2013.

——. *Jesus Within Judaism: New Light from Exciting Archaeological Discoveries*. Anchor Bible Reference Library. New York: Doubleday, 1988.

Chester, Andrew. "High Christology: Whence, When and Why?" *Early Christianity* 2, no. 1 (2011): 22-50.

Collins, John J. *The Scepter and the Star: The Messiahs of the Dead Sea Scrolls and Other Ancient Literature*. New Haven, CT: Yale University Press, 2007.

——. "The Son of Man in Ancient Judaism." In *Handbook for the Study of the Historical Jesus*, 2:1545-68. Leiden: Brill, 2010.

———. "The Son of Man in First-Century Judaism." *New Testament Studies* 38, no. 3 (July 1992): 448-66.

CorbinTheChristian. "According to Bart Ehrman, Jesus Never Claimed to Be God?" Reddit. *R/Christianity*, September 7, 2023. www.reddit.com/r/Christianity /comments/16cprgr/according_to_bart_ehrman_jesus_never_claimed_to/.

Cotter, Wendy. *Miracles in Greco-Roman Antiquity: A Sourcebook for the Study of New Testament Miracle Stories*. London: Routledge, 1999.

Cranfield, C. E. B. *The Gospel According to St Mark: An Introduction and Commentary*. New York: Cambridge University Press, 1959.

Crossan, John Dominic. *The Historical Jesus: The Life of a Mediterranean Jewish Peasant*. San Francisco: HarperSanFrancisco, 1991.

———. *Jesus: A Revolutionary Biography*. New York: HarperOne, 2009.

Danby, Henry. "The Bearing of the Rabbinical Criminal Code on the Jewish Trial Narratives in the Gospels." *Journal of Theological Studies* 21, no. 81 (October 1919): 51-76.

Daube, David. *The New Testament and Rabbinic Judaism*. London: Athlone, 1956.

Dawkins, Richard. *The God Delusion*. Boston: Houghton Mifflin, 2006.

"The Dead Sea Scrolls." Israel Museum, Jerusalem. Accessed July 26, 2024. www.imj.org .il/en/wings/shrine-book/dead-sea-scrolls.

Denton, D. L., Jr. *Historiography and Hermeneutics in Jesus Studies: An Examination of the Work of John Dominic Crossan and Ben F. Meyer*. London: T&T Clark, 2004.

Dodd, C. H. *History and the Gospel*. London: Nisbet, 1938.

———. *The Parables of the Kingdom*. London: Nisbet, 1935.

Dunn, James D. G. *Jesus Remembered*. Christianity in the Making 1. Grand Rapids, MI: Eerdmans, 2003.

———. *The Parting of the Ways: Between Christianity and Judaism and Their Significance for the Character of Christianity*. 2nd ed. London: SCM Press, 2011.

Edwards, James. "The Authority of Jesus in the Gospel of Mark." *Journal of the Evangelical Theological Society* 37, no. 2 (1994): 217-33.

Ehrman, Bart. "Are the Gospels Historically Reliable? The Problem of Contradictions." June 27, 2020. YouTube, 59:18. www.youtube.com/watch?v=AymnA526j9U.

———. "Did Jesus Call Himself God?" *The Bart Ehrman Blog*, October 26, 2018. https:// ehrmanblog.org/did-jesus-call-himself-god/.

———. "Did Jesus Exist?" *HuffPost*, March 20, 2012. www.huffpost.com/entry/did -jesus-exist_b_1349544.

———. "Does Jesus Call Himself God in His Trial Before the Sanhedrin and the High Priest Caiaphas?" *The Bart Ehrman Blog*, August 19, 2023. https://ehrmanblog.org/does -jesus-call-himself-god-in-his-trial-before-the-sanhedrin-and-the-high-priest-caiaphus/.

———. *How Jesus Became God: The Exaltation of a Jewish Preacher from Galilee*. New York: HarperOne, 2015.

———. *Jesus: Apocalyptic Prophet of the New Millennium*. New York: Oxford University Press, 1999.

———. "Jesus as God in the Synoptics." *The Bart Ehrman Blog*, April 13, 2014. https:// ehrmanblog.org/jesus-as-god-in-the-synoptics-for-members/.

———. *Jesus Before the Gospels: How the Earliest Christians Remembered, Changed, and Invented Their Stories of the Savior*. New York: HarperOne, 2016.

———. "My Resentment at Moody Bible Institute." *The Bart Ehrman Blog*. May 21, 2015. https://ehrmanblog.org/my-resentment-at-moody-bible-institute/.

———. "My Resistance to Change at Princeton Seminary." *The Bart Ehrman Blog*, May 8, 2017. https://ehrmanblog.org/my-resistance-to-change-at-princeton-seminary/.

———. *The New Testament: A Historical Introduction to the Early Christian Writings*. 7th ed. New York: Oxford University Press, 2020.

———. "On Being an Agnostic Atheist." *The Bart Ehrman Blog*, May 23, 2021. https:// ehrmanblog.org/on-being-an-agnostic-or-atheist.

Ehrman, Bart D., and Michael F. Bird. "How Jesus Became God." Debate, New Orleans, February 12, 2016. https://youtu.be/RtkeNuCwinc.

Esparza, Daniel. "The First Painting of Any of Jesus' Miracles Dates from the 3rd Century." Aleteia, October 12, 2019. https://aleteia.org/2019/10/12/the-first-painting-of-any-of -jesus-miracles-dates-from-the-3rd-century/.

Evans, C. A. "Caiaphas Ossuary." In *Dictionary of New Testament Background: A Compendium of Contemporary Biblical Scholarship*, edited by Craig A. Evans and Stanley E. Porter Jr., 522-25. Downers Grove, IL: IVP Academic, 2000.

———. *Jesus and His Contemporaries: Comparative Studies*. Arbeiten zur Geschichte des antiken Judentums und des Urchristentums 25. Leiden: Brill, 1995.

Evans, Richard J. *In Defense of History*. New York: Norton, 1999.

Eve, Eric. *The Jewish Context of Jesus' Miracles*. London: A&C Black, 2002.

Federal Rules of Evidence, "ARTICLE VIII. HEARSAY › Rule 803. Exceptions to the Rule Against Hearsay," www.law.cornell.edu/rules/fre/rule_803.

Fletcher-Louis, Crispin. "Jesus as the High Priestly Messiah: Part 2." *Journal for the Study of the Historical Jesus* 5, no. 1 (January 2007): 57-79.

Flew, Antony, and Roy Abraham Varghese. *There Is a God: How the World's Most Notorious Atheist Changed His Mind*. New York: HarperOne, 2008.

Fraenkel, M., ed. *Inscriptiones Graecae Aeginae, Pityonesi, Cecryphaliae, Argolidis*. Berlin, 1902.

Fredriksen, Paula. *Jesus of Nazareth: King of the Jews*. New York: Vintage, 1999.

Funk, Robert W. *The Acts of Jesus: The Search for the Authentic Deeds of Jesus*. San Francisco: HarperSanFrancisco, 1997.

Funk, Robert W., Roy W. Hoover, and the Jesus Seminar. *The Five Gospels: What Did Jesus Really Say? The Search for the Authentic Words of Jesus*. San Francisco: HarperOne, 1996.

Funk, Robert Walter, and the Jesus Seminar. *The Acts of Jesus: What Did Jesus Really Do?* San Francisco: HarperSanFrancisco, 1998.

Gathercole, Simon J. *The Preexistent Son: Recovering the Christologies of Matthew, Mark, and Luke*. Grand Rapids, MI: Eerdmans, 2006.

"Geza Vermes." *The Economist*, May 18, 2013. www.economist.com/obituary/2013/05/18/geza-vermes.

Goodman, Martin. "Mishnah." *Oxford Research Classical Dictionary*, July 6, 2015. https://doi.org/10.1093/acrefore/9780199381135.013.4222.

Greenhut, Zvi. "Burial Cave of the Caiaphas Family." *Biblical Archaeology Review* 18, no. 5 (September/October 1992): 29-36, 76.

Grindheim, Sigurd. *God's Equal: What Can We Know About Jesus' Self-Understanding?* London: A&C Black, 2011.

Gundry, Robert H. *Mark: A Commentary on His Apology for the Cross*. Grand Rapids, MI: Eerdmans, 1993.

Habermas, Gary R. "The Minimal Facts Approach to the Resurrection of Jesus: The Role of Methodology as a Crucial Component in Establishing Historicity." *Southeastern Theological Review* 3, no. 1 (2012): 15-26.

———. *On the Resurrection*. Vol. 1, *Evidences*. Nashville: B&H Academic, 2024.

———. "Resurrection Research from 1975 to the Present: What Are Critical Scholars Saying?" *Journal for the Study of the Historical Jesus* 3, no. 2 (June 2005): 135-53.

Habermas, Gary R., and Michael R. Licona. *The Case for the Resurrection of Jesus*. Grand Rapids, MI: Kregel, 2004.

Hägerland, Tobias. *Jesus and the Forgiveness of Sins: An Aspect of His Prophetic Mission*. Cambridge: Cambridge University Press, 2011.

———. "Prophetic Forgiveness in Josephus and Mark." *Svensk Exegetisk Årsbok* 79 (2014): 125-39.

Harris, Murray J. *Jesus as God: The New Testament use of Theos in Reference to Jesus*. Grand Rapids, MI: Baker, 1992.

Hiehle, Johnathan Alan, and Kelly Whitcomb. "Enoch, First Book Of." In *The Lexham Bible Dictionary*, edited by John Barry. Bellingham, WA: Lexham, 2016.

Hirsch, E. D. *Validity in Interpretation*. New Haven, CT: Yale University Press, 1967.

Hooker, Morna D. *Son of Man in Mark*. Montreal: McGill-Queen's University Press, 1967.

Horbury, William. "The Messianic Associations of the Son of Man." *Journal of Theological Studies* 36, no. 1 (April 1985): 34-55.

Hurtado, Larry W. "Christ." In *Dictionary of Jesus and the Gospels*, edited by Joel B. Green, Scot McKnight, and I. Howard Marshall, 106-17. Downers Grove, IL: InterVarsity Press, 1992.

———. *Lord Jesus Christ: Devotion to Jesus in Earliest Christianity*. Grand Rapids, MI: Eerdmans, 2005.

Hurtado, Larry W., and Paul L. Owen, eds. *"Who Is This Son of Man?" The Latest Scholarship on a Puzzling Expression of the Historical Jesus*. London: T&T Clark, 2012.

James, M. R., trans. "Gospel of Nicodemus." Early Christian Writings, accessed April 2, 2021. www.earlychristianwritings.com/text/gospelnicodemus.html.

Johansson, Daniel. "Jesus and God in the Gospel of Mark: Unity and Distinction." PhD diss., University of Edinburgh, 2012.

Johnston, Gordon H. "Messianic Trajectories in the Royal Psalms." In *Jesus the Messiah: Tracing the Promises, Expectations, and Coming of Israel's King*, edited by Herbert W. Bateman IV, Darrell L. Bock, and Gordon H. Johnston, 75-105. Grand Rapids, MI: Kregel, 2012.

Jones, Robert. "Aristeas, Letter Of." In *The Lexham Bible Dictionary*, edited by John Barry. Bellingham, WA: Lexham, 2016.

Justin Martyr. "Dialogue with Trypho." Translated by Marcus Dods and George Reith. New Advent. Accessed June 21, 2021. www.newadvent.org/fathers/01286.htm.

Kahl, Werner. *New Testament Miracle Stories in Their Religious-Historical Setting: A Religionsgeschichtliche Comparison from a Structural Perspective*. Forschungen zur Religion und Literatur des Alten und Neuen Testaments 163. Göttingen: Vandenhoeck & Ruprecht, 1994.

Keith, Chris, and Anthony Le Donne, eds. *Jesus, Criteria, and the Demise of Authenticity*. London: T&T Clark, 2012.

Kirk, J. R. Daniel. *A Man Attested by God: The Human Jesus of the Synoptic Gospels*. Grand Rapids, MI: Eerdmans, 2016.

Kitson Clark, G. *The Critical Historian: Guide for Research Students Working on Historical Subjects*. History and Historiography. New York: Garland, 1985.

Klauck, Hans-Josef. *The Religious Context of Early Christianity: A Guide to Graeco-Roman Religions*. Translated by Brian McNeal. Studies of the New Testament and Its World. Edinburgh: T&T Clark, 2000.

Knibb, Michael A. *The Qumran Community*. Cambridge: Cambridge University Press, 1987.

Kopman, Robert. *30 Minute Seder: The Haggadah That Blends Brevity with Tradition*. Scottsdale, AZ: 30 Minute Seder, 2007.

Kruger, Michael. "Did Jesus Claim to Be God? A Response to Bart Ehrman (Part 3)." *Canon Fodder*, June 11, 2014. https://michaeljkruger.com/did-jesus-claim-to-be-god-a-response-to-bart-ehrman-part-3/.

Le Donne, Anthony. "The Criterion of Coherence: Its Development, Inevitability, and Historiographical Limitation." In *Jesus, Criteria, and the Demise of Authenticity*, edited by Chris Keith, 94-114. London: T&T Clark, 2012.

Lewis, C. S. *Surprised by Joy: The Shape of My Early Life*. San Francisco: HarperOne, 2017.

Licona, Michael R. "Did Jesus Claim to Be God?" July 8, 2017. YouTube, 47:18. www.youtube.com/watch?v=gT2TN6kA5kY.

———. "Is the Sky Falling in the World of Historical Jesus Research?" *Bulletin for Biblical Research* 26, no. 3 (2016): 353-68.

―――. "Jesus's Resurrection, Realism, and the Role of the Criteria of Authenticity." In *Jesus, Skepticism and the Problem of History*, edited by Darrell L. Bock and J. Ed Komoszewski, 258-304. Grand Rapids, MI: Zondervan, 2019.

―――. *The Resurrection of Jesus: A New Historiographical Approach*. Downers Grove, IL: IVP Academic, 2010.

Lyons, William. "On the Life and Death of Joseph of Arimathea." *Journal for the Study of the Historical Jesus* 2, no. 1 (January 2004): 29-53.

MacIntyre, Alasdair. *Whose Justice? Which Rationality?* Notre Dame, IN: University of Notre Dame Press, 1988.

Maier, Paul L. *The New Complete Works of Josephus*. Rev. ed. Translated by William Whiston. Grand Rapids, MI: Kregel Academic & Professional, 1999.

Marshall, I. Howard. *The Gospel of Luke*. Grand Rapids, MI: Eerdmans, 1978.

McCullagh, C. B. *Justifying Historical Descriptions*. New York: Cambridge University Press, 1984.

―――. *The Truth of History*. New York: Routledge, 1997.

McDowell, Sean. *The Fate of the Apostles: Examining the Martyrdom Accounts of the Closest Followers of Jesus*. Burlington, VT: Routledge, 2016.

McKnight, Scot. *Jesus and His Death: Historiography, the Historical Jesus, and Atonement Theory*. Waco, TX: Baylor University Press, 2005.

"The Megiddo Mosaic." Biblical Archaeology Society, November 13, 2024. www.biblicalarchaeology.org/exhibits-events/the-megiddo-mosaic/.

"The Megiddo Mosaic: A Community Coming Together to the Table." Museum of the Bible, September 26, 2024. www.museumofthebible.org/magazine/exhibitions/the-megiddo-mosaic-a-community-coming-together-to-the-table.

Meier, J. P. *A Marginal Jew: Rethinking the Historical Jesus*. Vol. 2, *Mentor, Message, and Miracles*. New York: Doubleday, 1994.

―――. *A Marginal Jew: Rethinking the Historical Jesus*. Vol. 1, *The Roots of the Problem and the Person*. New York: Doubleday, 1991.

Metzger, Bruce M. "The Punctuation of Rom. 9:5." In *Christ and the Spirit in the New Testament*, edited by Barnabas Lindars and Stephen S. Smalley, 95-112. Cambridge: Cambridge University Press, 1973.

Meyer, Ben F. *Critical Realism and the New Testament*. Allison Park, PA: Wipf & Stock, 1989.

Milgrom, Jacob. *Leviticus 1–16: A New Translation with Introduction and Commentary*. New Haven, CT: Yale University Press, 1998.

The NET Bible First Edition Notes. Richardson, TX: Biblical Studies Press, 2006.

Noriega, Richa. "Look It's a Miracle! Crippled Beggar Chases, Tries to Stab Coast Guard Man on EDSA Bus Stop." *Manila Bulletin*, June 3, 2021. https://mb.com.ph/2021/6/3/look-its-a-miracle-crippled-beggar-chases-tries-to-stab-coast-guard-man-on-edsa-bus-stop.

O'Brien v. Seattle. No. 52 Wn.2d 543. The Supreme Court of Washington, Department One. July 3, 1958.

O'Connor, Alex. "Did Jesus Even Claim to Be God? Bart Ehrman Says No . . ." June 19, 2023. YouTube, 1:31:12. www.youtube.com/watch?v=2STiabRV8TE.

Pascut, Beniamin. *Redescribing Jesus' Divinity Through a Social Science Theory: An Interdisciplinary Analysis of Forgiveness and Divine Identity in Ancient Judaism and Mark 2:1-12*. Wissenschaftliche Untersuchungen zum Neuen Testament 2/438. Tübingen: Mohr Siebeck, 2017.

Pelling, Christopher. *Plutarch and History: Eighteen Studies*. Swansea: Classical Press of Wales, 2011.

Pennington, Jonathan T. "Heaven and Earth in the Gospel of Matthew." PhD diss., University of St Andrews, 2005.

———. *Heaven and Earth in the Gospel of Matthew*. 2nd ed. Grand Rapids, MI: Baker Academic, 2009.

Perrin, Nicholas. "Jesus as Priest in the Gospels." *Southern Baptist Journal of Theology* 22, no. 2 (2018): 81-99.

"Plastic." *Merriam Webster Dictionary*. Accessed October 22, 2018. www.merriam-webster .com/dictionary/plastic.

Porter, Stanley E. "How Do We Know What We Think We Know? Methodological Reflections on Jesus Research." In *Jesus Research: New Methodologies and Perceptions—The Second Princeton-Prague Symposium on Jesus Research, Princeton 2007*, edited by James H. Charlesworth, Brian Rhea, and Petr Pokorny, 82-102. Grand Rapids, MI: Eerdmans, 2014.

———. *Idioms of the Greek New Testament*. 2nd ed. London: Bloomsbury T&T Clark, 1992.

Reiser, Marius. *Jesus and Judgment*. Minneapolis: Fortress, 1997.

Ryan, Jordan. "No Model Minority, Part I: Invisible Asian Americans in the Midst of Apocalypse (RECLAIM)." Asian American Christian Collaborative, January 5, 2021. https://web.archive.org/web/20210106130123/https://www.asianamericanchristian collaborative.com/article/no-model-minority-invisible-asian-americans-apocalypse.

Sanders, E. P. *The Historical Figure of Jesus*. New York: Penguin, 1996.

———. *Jesus and Judaism*. Philadelphia: Fortress, 1985.

———. *Jewish Law from Jesus to the Mishnah: Five Studies*. New edition. Philadelphia: Trinity Press International, 1990.

———. *Judaism: Practice and Belief, 63 BCE–66 CE*. London: SCM Press, 1992.

Schnackenburg, Rudolf. *The Gospel of Matthew*. Translated by Robert R. Barr. Grand Rapids, MI: Eerdmans, 2002.

Shear, Adam. "William Whiston's Judeo-Christianity." In *Philosemitism in History*, edited by Jonathan Karp and Adam Sutcliffe, 92-110. Cambridge: Cambridge University Press, 2011.

Snodgrass, Klyne R. "The Temple Incident." In *Key Events in the Life of the Historical Jesus: A Collaborative Exploration of Context and Coherence*, edited by Darrell L. Bock and Robert L. Webb, 429-80. Grand Rapids, MI: Eerdmans, 2009.

State of Theology, The. "Data Explorer." Accessed July 31, 2024. https://thestateoftheology .com/data-explorer/.

State of Theology, The. "Statement 7." Accessed November 3, 2022. https://thestateof theology.com/data-explorer/.

Stein, Robert H. *A Basic Guide to Interpreting the Bible: Playing by the Rules*. 2nd ed. Grand Rapids, MI: Baker Academic, 2011.

Strack, Hermann Leberecht, and Paul Billerbeck. *Kommentar zum Neuen Testament aus Talmud und Midrasch*. Vol. 2. Munich: Beck, 1922–1961.

Swinburne, Richard. *The Existence of God*. 2nd ed. Oxford: Clarendon, 2004.

Tacitus. *The Complete Works of Tacitus*. Translated by Alfred John Church, William Jackson Brodribb, and Sara Bryant. New York: Perseus, Random House, 1942.

Taylor, Howard. *Biography of James Hudson Taylor*. London: Hodder & Stoughton, 1985.

Theissen, Gerd. "Historical Skepticism and Criteria in Jesus Research." In *Handbook for the Study of the Historical Jesus*, edited by Tom Holmen and Stanley E. Porter, 549-88. Leiden: Brill Academic, 2011.

Theissen, Gerd, and Annette Merz. *The Historical Jesus: A Comprehensive Guide*. Minneapolis: Fortress, 1998.

Theissen, Gerd, and Dagmar Winter. *The Quest for the Plausible Jesus: The Question of Criteria*. Louisville, KY: Westminster John Knox, 2002.

———. *Saving the Quest*. Translated by M. Eugene Boring. Louisville, KY: Westminster John Knox, 2002.

Twelftree, Graham H. *Jesus the Miracle Worker: A Historical and Theological Study*. Downers Grove, IL: InterVarsity Press, 1999.

Tyrrell, George. *Christianity at the Cross-Roads*. New York: Longmans, Green, 1913.

Tzaferis, Vassilios. "Inscribed 'To God Jesus Christ.'" Biblical Archaeology Society Library, accessed December 16, 2024. https://library.biblicalarchaeology.org/article /inscribed-to-god-jesus-christ/.

UNESCO World Heritage Centre. "QUMRAN: Caves and Monastery of the Dead Sea Scrolls." Accessed July 26, 2024. https://whc.unesco.org/en/tentativelists/5707/.

Van Voorst, Robert E. *Jesus Outside the New Testament: An Introduction to the Ancient Evidence*. Grand Rapids, MI: Eerdmans, 2000.

Várhelyi, Zsuzsanna. "'To Forgive Is Divine': Gods as Models of Forgiveness in Late Republican and Early Imperial Rome." In *Ancient Forgiveness: Classical, Judaic, and Christian*, edited by Charles L. Griswold and David Konstan, 115-36. Cambridge: Cambridge University Press, 2011.

Vermes, Geza. *The Complete Dead Sea Scrolls in English*. New York: Penguin, 2004.

Wallace, Daniel B. *Greek Grammar Beyond the Basics: An Exegetical Syntax of the New Testament with Scripture, Subject, and Greek Word Indexes.* Grand Rapids, MI: Zondervan, 1997.

"Wall Painting of Christ Healing the Paralytic." New York University Institute for the Study of the Ancient World, accessed January 25, 2025. https://isaw.nyu.edu/exhibi tions/edge-of-empires/highlights/christ-healing-paralytic.

Wansbrough, Henry. *Jesus and the Oral Gospel Tradition.* New York: T&T Clark, 2004.

Washington Courts. "Bailiff Orientation—Interaction with Jurors." Accessed June 17, 2021. www.courts.wa.gov/training/global_printversion/bailiff_printversion .htm#bailresp.

Wilken, Robert L. "Jaroslav Pelikan and the Road to Orthodoxy." *Concordia Theological Quarterly* 74, nos. 1-2 (January 2010): 92-103.

Wilkins, Michael J. "Peter's Declaration Concerning Jesus' Identity in Caesarea Philippi." In *Key Events in the Life of the Historical Jesus: A Collaborative Exploration of Context and Coherence*, edited by Darrell L. Bock and Robert L. Webb, 293-382. Grand Rapids, MI: Eerdmans, 2009.

Wise, Michael O., Martin G. Abegg, and Edward M. Cook Jr. *The Dead Sea Scrolls: A New Translation by Michael O. Wise, Martin G. Abegg, Jr., Edward M. Cook.* San Francisco: HarperOne, 1997.

Woolf, Daniel. "Historiography." In *New Dictionary of the History of Ideas*, edited by Maryanne Cline Horowitz, 1: xxxv-lxxxviii. New York: Thomson Gale, 2004.

Wrede, William. "Zur Heilung Des Gelähmten (Mc 2, I Ff.)." *Zeitschrift für die neutesta- mentliche Wissenschaft und die Kunde der älteren Kirche* 5 (1904): 354-58.

Wright, N. T. *Jesus and the Victory of God.* London: SPCK, 1996.

———. *The New Testament and the People of God.* Minneapolis: Fortress, 1992.

———. *The Resurrection of the Son of God.* Minneapolis: Fortress, 2003.

Yarbro Collins, Adela. "The Charge of Blasphemy in Mark 14.64." *Journal for the Study of the New Testament* 26, no. 4 (2004): 379-401.

General Index

Scripture Index